DATE DUE			

PRINTED IN U.S.A.

new exhibition design

neue ausstellungs gestaltung 1900-2000

new
neue
exhibition
ausstellungs
design
gestaltung
1900-2000

Herausgegeben von
Edited by
Anna Müller
Frauke Möhlmann

In Zusammenarbeit mit
In cooperation with
edi – Exhibition Design Institute
Fachhochschule Düsseldorf

Uwe J. Reinhardt
Philipp Teufel
Kai-Uwe Hemken

avedition

Inhalt
Content

1.1 Sammeln, Sortieren, Publizieren:
Eine Ausstellung von Anisa Azouz,
Kyra Porada und Laura Weidenfeller
Sammeln, Sortieren, Publizieren:
An exhibition by Anisa Azouz,
Kyra Porada and Laura Weidenfeller
© Anna Müller / Frauke Möhlmann

Anna Müller, Frauke Möhlmann
Uwe J. Reinhardt, Philipp Teufel

Das Prinzip des Sammelns und Ausstellens hat sich seit langer Zeit in vielen Bereichen unseres alltäglichen Lebens etabliert und nimmt großen Raum in der Konfiguration der Lebensverhältnisse ein. Überall werden gestalterische wie inhaltliche Ideen und Konzepte aus dem 20. Jahrhundert aufgegriffen und neu interpretiert respektive auch »nur« wieder aufgenommen. Die Grenzen verschwimmen in alle Richtungen, so findet man heute in klassischen Kunstausstellungen Medieninszenierungen, museale Aspekte auf Produktmessen und künstlerische Verfahren in wissenschaftlichen Ausstellungen. Das Format der Ausstellung hat Konjunktur. Zahlreiche Museumsbauten von Stars der Architekturszene eröffnen, inklusive der Anziehungskraft spektakulärer Wechselausstellungen, die nicht selten Besucherrekorde erzielen. Die strategische Hand der Institution Museum wird theoretisch in nahezu jeder Kleinstadt, gelungen ausgespielt, zum Ort des lebenslangen Lernens sowie zum Standortfaktor für ökonomische Wünsche. Im gesamten expositorischen Kosmos dürfen wir jedoch einen prinzipiellen Leitgedanken nicht aus unserem Fokus verlieren. »Ausstellen ist nicht hinstellen, Ausstellen ist gestalten«, wie Gottfried Korff, der große Theoretiker der Ausstellung, so treffend formulieren konnte.

Bild der Moderne: »Gestaltung höherer Ordnung«

Wenn man einen Gang durch die Titel der wichtigsten Ausstellungen des 20. Jahrhunderts unternimmt, dann wundert man sich beispielsweise über Begrifflichkeiten und konzeptionelle Programme. Es geht um Orientierung und Alltag; kunstgeschichtliche Kategorien werden nur allzu selten angespielt. Es geht um Formatierung und Prägung, um Zerrissenheit und Konflikte, um Spurensicherungen und ethnografische Programme, um Erfahrungsfelder und Aufklärung, um Kennzeichen und Bewegung. Meilensteine werden durch Expositionen markiert, Stationen der Moderne besetzt und Veränderungen sowie Prägungen analysiert. Ausstellungen erscheinen als Kommunikationsmaschinen und versuchen, Bilanz zu ziehen. Oftmals wird beispielsweise der Begriff »Zeit« im Titel thematisiert. Sentimentale Konzepte werden erfunden beziehungsweise wieder aufgenommen. Die Wunderkammer, die Chemie des Lebens, wird entworfen. Man sucht nach Übersicht, nach Verstehen und Grundlagen, nach dem großen Ganzen im Gesamtkunstwerk oder wenigstens im Versuch der Repräsentation von Bildern als Zeichen. Objekte werden in die Visionen einbezogen, Maschinen- und Industriewerke dienen als Referenz – auratisch oder wie auch

The principle of collecting and exhibiting has long since established itself in many areas of our daily life and greatly influences the configuration of our living conditions. Everywhere 20th century ideas and concepts on design and the presentation of information are being rediscovered and either reinterpreted or »simply« reused. The boundaries are blurring in all directions; today we find media presentations in classic art exhibitions, museum concepts at product fairs and artistic methods in scientific shows. Exhibitions are in great demand as a format. Numerous museum buildings by stars of the architecture scene are opening, and there is also the appeal of spectacular temporary shows, which do not infrequently generate record visitor numbers. Theoretically the strategic device of the institution of the museum thus becomes, when successfully deployed, a place of lifelong learning and a location factor for economic wishes even in virtually every small city. Yet however large the vast expositional cosmos has become, we must not lose sight of a principal guiding idea, for »exhibiting is not simply placing, exhibiting is designing«, as Gottfried Korff, the great exhibition theorist, so fittingly put it.

Image of Modernism: »Designing a higher order«

Looking through the titles of the most important exhibitions of the 20th century, one often finds oneself wondering, for instance, at some of the terms and conceptual programs used. They tend to focus on orientation and everyday life, while categories of art history are only rarely intimated. They address formatting and embossing, fragmentation and conflicts, forensics and ethnographical programs, fields of experience and education, icons and movements. Milestones are marked by expositions, stages in Modernism occupied, and changes and influences analyzed. Exhibitions appear as communication machines and seek to take stock. The concept of »time«, for example, often appears in the title as a theme. Sentimental notions are invented or revisited. The chamber of wonders, the chemistry of life, is created. We search for an overview, for understanding and fundamentals, for the big picture in the total artwork or at least in the attempt at representing images as symbols. Objects are drawn into the visions, machine and industrial plants serve as references, be they auratic or not. Spaces are used as mission or vision, an image of Modernity, indeed an image of the future is outlined ideologically and poetically – education and enlightenment in »designing a higher order«, developing the senses and experience through dynamic labyrinths, turning viewers into witnesses and serving up the dream of a better world. The history of the

SAMMELN, SORTIEREN, PUBLIZIEREN

Die Buchreihe »New Exhibition Design« zeigt die gestalterisch und inhaltlich besten Projekte ausgewählter Architekten und Designer weltweit. Anhand von Beispielen werden außergewöhnliche, technologisch und sozial innovative Ausstellungen in Text und Bild vorgestellt.

1.1

1.2 Sammeln, Sortieren, Publizieren:
Eine Ausstellung von Anisa Azouz,
Kyra Porada und Laura Weidenfeller
Sammeln, Sortieren, Publizieren:
An exhibition by Anisa Azouz,
Kyra Porada and Laura Weidenfeller
© Anna Muller / Frauke Mohlmann

immer. Räume werden zur Mission oder Vision genutzt, ein Bild der Moderne, ja ein Bild der Zukunft wird ideologisch und poetisch skizziert. Es handelt sich um Bildung und Aufklärung in der »Gestaltung höherer Ordnung«, Entfaltung der Sinne und Erfahrungsfelder dynamischer Labyrinthe, Streifzüge der Zeugenschaft und den Traum einer besseren Welt.

Die Geschichte der Ausstellung ist bisher nicht wirklich gut beschrieben, obwohl es viele Storys und das eine oder andere unscharfe dokumentarische Bild gibt. Oft kolportieren Gestalter und Museologen Geschichten von alten, großen Ausstellungen und berichten, aus zweiter Hand, von stilbildenden oder gar sensationellen Beispielen. Das macht einen genaueren Blick in die Geschichte der Ausstellung spannend und eröffnet uns sowohl neue Interpretationen wie auch Erkenntnisse über inhaltliche, formale und szenische Wirkungen.

Aufklärerische Programme und szenografische Integrale

Die Ausstellungen der 1920er und 1930er Jahre, entworfen etwa von Gestaltern wie Friedrich Kiesler oder Lilly Reich, waren neuartige Inszenierungen – durch den ganzen Raum geführt, umgreifend eingerichtet. Es waren bereits wegweisende Versuche, den Raum in Zeitabfolgen und Gleichzeitigkeiten aufzulösen. Friedrich Kiesler erfand ein »Telemuseum«, eine Art drahtlose Übertragung von Bildergalerien, ein »Museum ohne Wände«. Auch grafische Medien wurden experimentell und neuartig in den Arbeiten der Avantgarde der Zwanziger Jahre eingesetzt, wie wir das eindrucksvoll von El Lissitzky und Herbert Beyer vorgeführt bekamen.

Die Rückkehr der grafischen Expertise, des Grafischen an sich, in Ausstellungen und Museen könnte als eine Art reaktionäre Gegenbewegung oder sogar moderne Neuinterpretation gelesen werden – das Vinyl der Museumsgestalter. Der begehbare Film sozusagen, das integrale, begehbare Bild. Letztlich ist diese Idee nicht allzu fern vom Holodeck aus dem Raumschiff Enterprise. Schon damals bestand der visionäre Grundgedanke darin, den Besucher als Akteur in die Gestaltung einzubeziehen.

Nach dem Zweiten Weltkrieg entwickelten die Museen ihre aufklärerischen Programme und nutzten das Format Ausstellung für ein lesendes und dazu schauendes Verstehen: Schaulust gegen Leselast. Nach einer »Literarisierung« in den 1970er Jahren stolperte das Medium in inszenierte Schauräume – multimediale Verzauberung und szenografische Integrale in Form von Text, Glas und Szene. Bewegliche »Show Cases« wurden zum Modell. Paul Virilio sprach schon 1993 von »elektronischen Vitrinen«,

exhibition has not been particularly well documented to date, although there are lots of stories and the one or other blurred documentary photograph. Often designers and museologists peddle stories of old, major shows and relate, second hand, trailblazing and sensational examples. This makes a closer look into exhibition history fascinating and paves the way to both new interpretations and insights into contentrelated, formal and scenic effects.

Educational programs and scenographic integrals

The exhibitions of the 1920s and 1930s, designed for instance by such figures as Friedrich Kiesler or Lilly Reich, were novel stagings – encompassing the entire space and furnished all round. These early examples were already groundbreaking attempts to break up the space into temporal sequences and simultaneities. Friedrich Kiesler invented a »telemuseum«, a kind of wireless transmission of picture galleries, a »museum without walls«. Graphic media were likewise employed in novel, experimental ways in the avant-garde works of the 1920s, as impressively demonstrated by El Lissitzky and Herbert Beyer.

The return of graphic expertise, of prints, in exhibitions and museums could be seen as a kind of reactionary countermovement or even a modern reinterpretation – the museum designers' version of vinyl. The accessible film, so to speak, the integral, accessible image. Ultimately this idea can be considered not all too far removed from the holodeck on Starship Enterprise. Even back then the visionary basic idea was to involve the visitor in the design as an actor.

After the Second World War the museums developed their educational programs and used the exhibition format to enable understanding by means of both text and images: looking is easier than reading. Following a »literarization« in the 1970s, the medium stumbled into staged display spaces – multimedia enchantment and scenographic integrals in the form of text, glass and scene. Moving showcases became the model. As early as 1993 Paul Virilio talked about »electronic display cases«, which opened up the visual field of the digital space. Furthermore, at the end of the century Expo 2000 in Hanover and Expo02 in Switzerland represented the cultural turn for this medium, which in turn ushered in the start of a new way of accessing the museum and the exhibition.

1.2

die das Sehfeld in den digitalen Raum öffneten. Den Cultural Turn für dieses Medium stellen überdies am Ende des Jahrhunderts die Expo 2000 in Hannover beziehungsweise die Expo02 in der Schweiz dar, die wiederum den Beginn eines veränderten Zugangs zum Museum und der Ausstellung implementierten.

Die inhaltlich motivierte, komplexe konzeptionelle Form der Ausstellung wird mehr und mehr zugunsten einer rein szenischen, von Atmosphäre und Emotion dominierten, Form der Kommunikation von und über Kunst und deren Objektivierungen verdrängt. Es dominiert der Event beziehungsweise das »Reden über« das Objekt der Kunst. Eine Autonomie des Formats Ausstellung erscheint, kulturwissenschaftlich betrachtet, ein Mythos zu sein. Der Funktionszusammenhang ist nicht abgeschlossen, sondern eingebunden in gesellschaftliche und ökonomische Prozesse. Normative Erwartungen prägen die Kommunikationsformen Ausstellung, Publikation und Rezeption. Es handelt sich hierbei um Prozesse der Kommunikation sowie um Funktionen jenseits der Erscheinung von Präsentation. Ästhetische Erfahrung vermittelt sich offenbar gegenwärtig weitgehend über gestalterische Einrichtungen. Ist Ausstellungsgestaltung dann als eine Strategie ästhetischen Handelns zu verstehen?

The complex conceptual form of the exhibition, motivated by its content, is replaced more and more by a purely scenic form of communication, dominated by atmosphere and emotion, of and about art and its objectivization. The event or »talking about« the object of art dominates. In view of cultural studies, the autonomy of the exhibition format appears to be a myth. The functional context is not complete, but integrated in social and economic processes. Normative expectations shape the forms of communication of the exhibition, publication and reception. These are processes of communication and functions beyond the appearance of presentation. At present aesthetic experience is seemingly largely communicated via formal set-ups. Should exhibition design thus be understood as a strategy of aesthetic action?

Bricolage und Szenografie – Einrichten und Formatieren

Die Praxis des Ausstellungmachens, Einrichtens und Formatierens wird mehr und mehr zur Hauptaufgabe des Kunstbetriebs; kuratorische Tätigkeiten überlagern explizit die künstlerische Tätigkeit. Deshalb wird Ausstellungsgestaltung in ein unmittelbares Beziehungsgeflecht hinsichtlich Kunstproduktion und Kunstrezeption zu stellen sein. Letztlich können diese Erkenntnisse für die Trendforschung und die Konzeption von Ausstellungen nutzbar gemacht werden. Im ersten Schritt des Projekts werden wir klären, welche Epoche empirisch-vergleichend untersucht werden soll. Außerdem erscheint auch ein Vergleich mit historischen oder kulturgeschichtlichen Ausstellungen möglich.

Der Blick auf das 20. Jahrhundert zeigt eine riesige Collage, eine ganze Landschaft von Themen und Feldern, von Formen und Formaten. Gestaltung in Form von Ausstellung, als Mittel, die Welt zu erläutern, zu verstehen, einzuordnen, zu sortieren und wieder neu anzuordnen – in eine Art von räumlich eingerichtetem Wissensarchiv. Manche Ausstellung hat die Welt verändert oder große Folgen ausgelöst, zwischen Vision und Ideologie, zwischen Aufklärung und politischem Programm. Eine rechte Übersicht oder gar Chronik ist kaum zu leisten. Oft werden Ausstellungen als Muster zitiert, als besonders markiert, und doch gibt es über viele, immer wieder als Belege aufgeführte, Expositionen nur wenig verlässliche Analysen, oft nicht einmal gute Fotografien. Einzelne Ausstellungen sind sogar zu Legenden geworden, die die Kuratoren und Gestalter, Szenografen und Architekten wieder und wieder kolportieren.

Deshalb hat edi, das Exhibition Design Institute der Fachhochschule Düsseldorf, ein Projekt auf die Beine gestellt, das sich in den nächsten Jahren folgendem Thema widmen wird: »Exposition/Disposition. Die Kunstausstellung in der Moderne. Forschungsprojekt zur Geschichte, Theorie und Ästhetik der Kunstausstellung in der Moderne (18.–21. Jahrhundert).«

Dieses Projekt untersucht die Geschichte und Form der Ausstellung im Kontext von gestalterischen Prozessen und Formen. Der Blick wendet sich auf gestalterische Konfigurationen des Ausstellens im Rahmen ästhetischer, gesellschaftlich-diskursiver Prozesse und deren Akteure und Protagonisten. Der ausstellende Werkprozess wird dabei sowohl als Wissenskonstrukt als auch hinsichtlich ästhetisch-gestalterischer Formatierung verstanden. Dabei werden methodisch das noch junge Forschungsfeld der Designtheorie und deren Forschungen reflektiert.

Bricolage and scenography – set-up and formatting

The practice of making exhibitions, setting up and formatting is increasingly becoming the main task of the art business; curatorial activities are explicitly displacing artistic activity. As such, exhibition design will have to be put in a direct web of relations in terms of art production and reception. After all, insights can be useful for trend research and exhibition conception. In the first phase of the project we will clarify which epoch is to be empirically and comparatively examined. Moreover, a comparison with historical or cultural-historical exhibitions, for example, seems possible.

A look back at the 20th century shows a giant collage, an entire landscape of themes and fields, forms and formats. Design in the form of an exhibition as a means to explain, understand, categorize, sort and rearrange the world in a kind of spatially set-up knowledge archive. Some exhibitions changed the world or had major consequences, between vision and ideology, between education and political agenda. A real overview or even chronicle is barely affordable. Exhibitions are often cited as patterns, as particularly marked and yet given the many expositions repeatedly named as evidence there are only rather unreliable analyses, and often not even decent photographs. A few exhibitions have even become legends, repeatedly referenced by curators and designers, scenographers and architects.

This is why edi, the Exhibition Design Institute at Düsseldorf University of Applied Sciences, has initiated a project that will address the following topic over the next few years: »Exposition/Disposition. The art exhibition in the Modern Age. A research project on the history, theory and aesthetics of the art exhibition in the Modern Age (18th–21st centuries).«

This project examines the history and form of the exhibition in the context of creative processes and forms. It focuses on design configurations of exhibiting within the framework of aesthetic socio-discursive processes and their agents and protagonists. Here the exhibiting work process is understood both as a knowledge construct and in terms of aesthetic-creative formatting. It methodically reflects the still young research field of design theory and its research projects.

1.4

Gesellschaftliche Verhältnisse, Funktionen handelnder Gestalter-Persönlichkeiten sowie ihre eindeutigen Kommunikationstypen werden analysiert. Die Frage nach der Autonomie der künstlerischen Ausstellung wird dabei thematisiert und auf die Verhältnisse des Zustandekommens von Ausstellungen bezogen, auf das »Designen« von räumlich-narrativen Strukturen. Analysiert wird das Spannungsverhältnis Künstler/Werk/Kurator und Ausstellung. Das Format der Ausstellung wird nach Ästhetik, konzeptionellen Prozessen und gesellschaftlichen Kontextualisierungen umfassend betrachtet. Die Ausstellung wird in diesem Sinne als gestalterischer Prozess aufgefasst.

Die Analyse kann folglich zeigen, welche Objektivierung und Raumkonfiguration Displays ergeben beziehungsweise, wie gestalterische Präsentationen und Inszenierungen eine ästhetische Verfasstheit von Sinndimensionen schaffen und optische Settings dysfunktionale Erfahrungs- und Erkenntnissphären ergeben. Gestaltung wird dabei, im Sinne gesellschaftlicher Relevanz, als Gravitationsfeld und Impulsgeber für Ausstellungen gesehen.

Gravitationsfeld Gesellschaft und Umgang mit Sachen

Wir stellen die Frage, inwieweit historisch ein Funktionswandel stattgefunden hat und wie dies perspektivisch auf das Kommunikationsformat der Ausstellung wirken kann. Das Feld der Betrachtung sind Erscheinungsformen der Ausstellungen im Atelier, der Galerie, im Museum und in anderen soziokulturellen Orten der Exposition. Inwieweit Objektverhältnisse oder der »Umgang mit Sachen« (siehe Dingforschung) betrachtet werden muss, kann zu diesem Zeitpunkt noch nicht abschließend bestimmt werden. Herausgearbeitet werden soll ein systemisches »Psychogramm« der Handlungspersönlichkeiten und Akteure der Ausstellung: Macht- und Interessenverhältnis sowie Wahrnehmungsverhältnis von Künstler, Kunsthändler, Kurator, Pädagoge, Gestalter – und eben Betrachter.

Zum genauen Verständnis von Funktionen und Strukturen sollen diese Akteure der Ausstellung beziehungsweise der Ausstellungsgestaltung genauer betrachtet werden. Dabei analysieren wir deren Funktionen und Rollen, aber auch die historischen Entwicklungslinien einzelner Gestalterschulen und deren stilbildende Wirkung. Definiert wird, wie Stile und handwerkliche Entscheidungen, Design-Prinzipien und -Methoden in der Präsentation von Ausstellungen jeweils unterschiedliche Konfigurationen setzen sowie Form und Wirkung der Ausstellung prägen.

It will analyze social relations, the functions of active designer personalities and their unequivocal types of communication. The question of the autonomy of the artistic exhibition is thematized and related to the circumstances of exhibition realization, to the designing of spatial-narrative structures. It will analyze the dynamic relationship between artist/work/curator and exhibition. The format of the exhibition will be comprehensively considered in terms of aesthetics, conceptual processes and social contextualizations. In this sense the exhibition is understood as a creative process. Consequently the analysis can show which objectivization and spatial configurations displays produce, or how creative presentations and orchestrations create an aesthetic configuration of sensory dimensions and visual settings produce dysfunctional spheres of experience and knowledge. Here design is seen, in the sense of social relevance, as a gravitational field and source of inspiration for exhibitions.

Society as gravitational field and dealing with things

We ask the question as to how far, historically, a functional change has taken place and how this can affect, in terms of perspective, the communication format of the exhibition. We consider how exhibitions manifest themselves in the studio, the gallery, the museum or other sociocultural exposition venues. The extent to which we need to consider object relations or »dealing with things« (see object research) cannot be conclusively stated at this point. The aim is to draw up a systemic »psychogram« of the people and actors involved in the exhibition: the relations of power, interest and perception of artists, art dealers, curators, educators, designers – and observers.

To gain a precise understanding of functions and structures we aim to take a closer look at these agents of the exhibition or exhibition design. We will analyze their functions and roles, as well as the historical development trajectories of individual design schools and their formative effects. We will define how styles and artisanal decisions, design principles and methods each set different configurations in the presentation of exhibitions and influence the form and impact of the show.

Das Verhältnis beziehungsweise Gravitationsfeld von Künstler/Kurator/Werk zur Ausstellung wird um die Wirkungsmächtigkeit des Gestalters und die sich daraus ergebenden ästhetischen Konstrukte erweitert. Welche gesellschaftlichen Entwicklungen führen zu welchen Veränderungen von Wahrnehmung und Vermittlung, zu welchen gestalterischen Manifestationen und wie reagiert man darauf mit dem ganzen Kanon der Vermittlungsformen? Ausstellungsgestaltung wäre als ein nicht herrschaftsfreier Raum zu beschreiben.

Das Projekt soll insgesamt die Herausbildung einer Theorie der Ausstellungsgestaltung befördern und erste empirisch fundierte kritische Reflexionen anbieten. Methodisch wollen wir den Fokus allerdings auf kulturwissenschaftliche Zugänge und semiotische Analyseverfahren am empirischen Beispiel setzen. Forschungsgegenstand ist das Amalgam, das Verhältnis von »Personage« und Ausstellungsdesign und dessen Veränderung. Als Forschungsgegenstand betrachten wir das Medium Ausstellung beziehungsweise dreidimensionale Kommunikation. Erforscht werden Narrativität, Transformation und Medialität historischer und zeitgenössischer szenografischer Interventionen. Der Fokus richtet sich auf die Historie von Ausstellungen und deren Gestaltung/Design, vor allem in einem soziokulturellen Kontext.

Zur Grundlegung einer Ästhetik und Theorie der Kunstausstellung liefert das Projekt Aussagen zu ästhetischen (hier: gestalterischen) Verhältnissen, Prozessen und Wirkungsweisen. Ziel ist es, möglichst eindeutige Parameter für eine Typologie der Ausstellung sinnfällig zu beschreiben, empirisch-exemplarisch zu analysieren und belastbar für kunstwissenschaftliche und museologische Studien nutzbar zu machen. Zu prüfen gilt, wie historische Ausstellungen rückwirkend aus der Quellenlage analysiert werden können. Die Heterogenität der Ausstellung zwingt förmlich zu einer vergleichenden Betrachtung von Faktoren der Formatierung in den entsprechenden Räumen, wobei auch digitale Räume einbezogen werden können: Gestaltung, Szenografie, Raumorganisation, architektonische Rahmenbedingungen, Oberflächen und Materialität, Bildverhältnisse und Abbildungsmaßstäbe, Grafik und Typografie, Farbgebung, Lichtstimmung und Atmosphäre, Publikation, Katalog und Plakat. Hierdurch können Entwicklungen historisch beschrieben und analysiert werden. In einer Art Analyse-Matrix wird es möglich sein, wichtige Faktoren der Gestaltung von Ausstellungen zu beschreiben und deren Wechselwirkung vergleichend zu deuten.

The relationship or gravitational field of the artist/curator/work to the exhibition is expanded to include the degree of impact of the designer and the resulting aesthetic constructs. Which social developments lead to which changes in perception and mediation, to which creative manifestations, and how should we respond to them with the entire canon of mediative forms? We could describe exhibition design as a not non-hierarchical space.

Overall the project aims to promote the formation of a theory of exhibition design and provide initial, empirically founded critical reflections. Methodically however we wish to focus on the perspective of cultural studies and semiotic methods of analysis using empirical examples. The research subject is the entire ensemble, namely the relationship between »personage« and exhibition design and how it has changed. As a research subject we will consider the medium of the exhibition or three-dimensional communication. We will study the narrative, transformation and mediality of historical and contemporary scenographic interventions. The focus is on the history of exhibitions and their design, particularly in a sociocultural context.

Regarding the foundation of an aesthetic and theory of the art exhibition, the project provides statements on aesthetic (here: formal) relations, processes and modes of effect. The goal is to plainly describe the clearest possible parameters for a typology of the exhibition, to analyze them empirically by specimen examples, and to make them a reliable tool for studies on aesthetics and museology. We seek to examine how historical exhibitions can be retrospectively analyzed from the original situation. The heterogeneity of the exhibition literally compels us to take a comparative view of factors of exhibition formatting in the relevant spaces, although digital spaces can also be included: design, scenography, spatial organization, architectural framework conditions, surfaces and materiality, image proportions and reproduction scales, graphics and typography, color, lighting mood and atmosphere, publication, catalog and poster. In this way, we can historically describe and analyze developments. In a kind of analysis matrix, it will be possible to describe key factors in exhibition design and to comparatively interpret how they interact.

1.6 Sammeln, Sortieren, Publizieren:
Eine Ausstellung von Anisa Azouz,
Kyra Porada und Laura Weidenfeller
Sammeln, Sortieren, Publizieren:
An exhibition by Anisa Azouz,
Kyra Porada and Laura Weidenfeller
© Anna Muller / Frauke Mohlmann

HARALD
SZEEMANN:
»MEIN ARCHIV
IST MEIN
GEDÄCHTNIS«

1.6

Denkmaschine Ausstellung – zu diesem Buch

Für die Zeit von 1900 bis 2000 versucht dieser Band nun, einen ersten Zwischenstand zu einem weiter entstehenden Archiv anzubieten, freilich noch sehr vage und keinesfalls vollständig. Das hier entstehende Archiv will eine »lebendige Denkmaschine« entwerfen, die uns als Basis für die Publikationsreihe »New Exhibition Design – Neue Ausstellungsgestaltung« dient. Die Reihe dokumentiert und reflektiert das flüchtige Medium Ausstellung und gibt ihm eine Plattform für eine weiterführende wissenschaftliche und gestalterische Auseinandersetzung.

Wir stellen uns hierbei unter anderem folgende Fragen: Wo hat das Medium Ausstellung seinen Ursprung? Welche Ausstellungen sind von historischer Bedeutung? Wie wurde im 20. Jahrhundert ausgestellt? Was waren die Themen und wie wurden sie erzählt? Was waren die roten Fäden, die Dramaturgien und Szenografien der Beispiele? Wie haben Architekten und Designer Bilder und Räume gesetzt und geformt, wie haben Kulturwissenschaftler und Museumsmacher gedacht und analysiert? Welche Darstellungsformen wurden gefunden? Die Geschichte der Ausstellung und des Museums hat in den letzten Jahren viele Würdigungen in einzelnen Publikationen und Tagungen gefunden, eine Systematik scheint dennoch fast unmöglich zu sein.

Diesen Band sehen wir nun als eine Sammlung, einen ersten Versuch, wichtige Entwicklungen des Mediums Ausstellung im 20. Jahrhundert festzuhalten und anhand bedeutender Projekte zu dokumentieren. Harald Szeemanns »Mein Archiv ist mein Gedächtnis« mag ein Mantra dazu abgeben. »Neue Ausstellungsgestaltung 1900–2000« zeigt zukunftsweisende Ausstellungen des 20. Jahrhunderts in einem überblicksartigen Bogen. Das Buch blickt zurück und zeigt hundert exemplarische Ausstellungen aus Europa und den USA. Es beinhaltet Kurzportraits und vertiefende Expertenbeiträge, beleuchtet Tendenzen und zeigt Gestaltungsideen aus hundert Jahren des Ausstellens. Dazu kommen kleine, jedoch wertvolle Exkurse in die Geschichte. Dabei handelt es sich um helfende Anker zur fokussierten Analyse und deutlichen Einschätzung des Kontexts als psychologischem Thema, den Fragen danach, welche gesellschaftlichen und geschichtlichen Entwicklungen zu welchen Veränderungen von Wahrnehmung und Vermittlung führen. Hierzu haben wir mit unserem Kollegen Prof. Dr. Kai-Uwe Hemken, Kunsthochschule Kassel, einen Kunsthistoriker und Ausstellungstheoretiker besonderer Umsicht und hoher Reflexionskraft gewinnen können.

Exhibition as thinking machine – on this book

For the period from 1900 until 2000 this publication aims to offer an initial status report, albeit a very vague one and by no means complete, on a continually growing archive. The archive being created here seeks to design a »living thinking machine«, serving as our basis for the series of publications »New Exhibition Design«. The series documents and reflects on the fleeting medium of the exhibition and offers it a platform for continued scientific and artistic study.

In this context we ask ourselves, among others, the following questions: What is the origin of the medium of the exhibition? Which exhibitions are historically significant? What form did exhibitions take in the 20th century? What were the themes and how were they conveyed? What were the red threads, the dramatic concepts and scenographies of the examples? How did architects and designers conceive of and shape images and spaces? How did cultural scholars and museum organizers think and analyze? Which forms of representation were found? The history of the exhibition and the museum has seen numerous acknowledgements in various publications and conferences in recent years, yet nonetheless a systematic approach seems almost impossible.

We see this publication as a collection, a first attempt to highlight key developments in the medium of the exhibition in the 20th century and document them by way of significant projects. Harald Szeemann's »My archive is my memory« can be seen as a fitting mantra. »New Exhibition Design 1900–2000« compiles the new exhibition design of the 20th century into something of an overview. The book takes a look back, showing a hundred examples of exhibitions from Europe and the USA. It contains brief portraits and in-depth expert essays, illuminates trends and points to new design ideas from one hundred years of exhibiting. It moreover features brief, yet worthwhile historical excursuses. These constitute helpful anchors for focused analysis and a clear assessment of the context as a psychological topic, and for questions as to which social and historical developments lead to which changes in perception and mediation. Here we are able to benefit from the expertise of our colleague Prof. Dr. Kai-Uwe Hemken, Kunsthochschule Kassel, a particularly discriminating and reflective art historian and exhibition theorist.

1.7 Sammeln, Sortieren, Publizieren:
Eine Ausstellung von Anisa Azouz,
Kyra Porada und Laura Weidenfeller
Sammeln, Sortieren, Publizieren:
An exhibition by Anisa Azouz,
Kyra Porada and Laura Weidenfeller
© Anna Müller / Frauke Mohlmann

Der Band bietet einen kleinen Überblick hinsichtlich der Entwicklung von Ausstellungsgestaltung im letzten Jahrhundert. Hierbei ist die analytische Beschäftigung mit historischen und typologischen Beispielen ebenso wichtig wie die Suche nach experimentellen Formen des Ausstellens, die das Format nachhaltig weiterentwickelt haben. Mehr als drei Jahre haben wir am edi – Exhibition Design Institute in Düsseldorf intensiv zur Geschichte der Ausstellung gesammelt und geforscht. Die Zwischenergebnisse wurden immer wieder mit verschiedenen Experten diskutiert und reflektiert.

Oft war die Suche nach Informationen und Fotografien so mühsam, dass ein komplettes Bild kaum zu geben ist. Eine Konzentration auf deutsche/europäische Projekte musste sich zunächst ergeben. Das Archiv wird jedoch nach Möglichkeit Stück für Stück international erweitert. Die konkrete Auswahl, bei aller Reflexion und Abfrage bei den Gestaltern und Museumsdenkern selbst, bleibt ein wenig subjektiv. Vielleicht haben wir so aber doch einen ersten Zugang zu einem Panorama eines ganzen Jahrhunderts an Expositionen gefunden. Wir freuen uns also auf poetische Gespräche und Gedanken dazu, auf neue spannende Projekte und feine Ausstellungen mit intressanten Entdeckungen und guten Folgen.

The book offers a brief overview of the development of exhibition design in the last century. To this end, the analytical exploration of historical and typological examples is equally as important as searching for experimental exhibition forms that have had a lasting effect on the further development of the format. We at edi, the Exhibition Design Institute in Düsseldorf, have worked intensively for more than three years gathering material and conducting research on the history of the exhibition. We repeatedly discussed and reflected on the interim results with various experts from all over Europe.

The search for information and photographs was often so painstaking that it is barely possible to offer a complete picture. We were first forced to concentrate solely on German/European projects. However, we will be successively expanding the archive little by little to include international projects as far as possible. The actual selection, despite intense reflection and inquiry among the designers and museum thinkers themselves, remains a little subjective. Yet perhaps in this way we have found an initial entry point into a panorama of an entire century of expositions. Thus we are looking forward to poetic conversations and ideas on the subject, to new exciting projects and fine exhibitions with interesting discoveries and good results.

>>> author p.210–211

synchronous
optical history
of exhibition
1900–2000

synchronoptische
ausstellungs
geschichte

Zeitverläufe: Historische Horizonte

Passages of time: Historical Horizons

Kai-Uwe Hemken

Die folgenden Exkurse in die Geschichte Deutschlands/Europas im 20. Jahrhundert dienen einer groben Orientierung, in welchem gesellschaftlichen Klima die jeweilige Ausstellung stattfand. Die Texte stellen synoptische Hinweise auf das kulturelle Klima, kollektive Befindlichkeiten, politische, wirtschaftliche wie soziale Entwicklungen und künstlerische wie kunstbetriebliche Tendenzen dar, in die sich die jeweiligen Ausstellungsprojekte jener Jahre einfügen. Es konnte eine Vielzahl von Einzelinformationen nicht berücksichtigt werden, hätte es doch das Konzept und den Rahmen der vorliegenden Publikation gesprengt. Weiterführende Angaben über die Ausstellungen wurden ebenfalls weggelassen, da sich die zentralen – beispielhaft und ausführlich besprochen – in diesem Band wiederfinden. Die Orientierung an Dekaden ist eine rein formale Gliederung, die lediglich einem raschen Zugriff auf Informationen dienen soll. Eigentlich müssten die politischen, wirtschaftlichen, kulturellen wie künstlerischen Tendenzen in größeren Zeitverläufen geschildert werden, um sie in ihrem Entwicklungsgang, ihren Bedingungen, Möglichkeiten und Kausalstrukturen sichtbar zu machen.

The following elaborations on the history of Germany and Europe in the 20th century serve to provide a rough idea of the social climate in which the exhibitions in question took place. The texts represent synoptic references to the cultural climate, the collective mind-set, the political, economic and social developments and artistic trends which together form the backdrop to the relevant exhibition projects of those years. A number of individual pieces of information have been omitted, as this would otherwise have exceeded the concept and scope of this publication. Details of the exhibitions have likewise been left out since the key elements can be found in this volume – outlined by way of example and in detail. The orientation by decade is a purely formal categorization, which merely serves to enable quick access to information. In actual fact, the political, economic, cultural and artistic trends should really be outlined over longer time periods to make them evident in their development processes, the conditions surrounding them, their possibilities and their causal structures.

>>> author   p.211

Exposition Universelle et internationale
de Paris

Wiener Secession 1902:
Die Ausstellung als Gesamtkunstwerk

1900

1902

15.04.1900–12.11.1900
Paris, F
temporary exhibition

Zur Jahrhundertwende wurde in Paris eine Zusammenstellung aus Kunst, Technik und Wissenschaft des
letzten Jahrhunderts gezeigt. Die Ausstellungsmacher,
inspiriert vom barocken Bühnenbild und angeregt von
den neuesten technischen Möglichkeiten, inszenierten
bühnenhafte Illusionen. Im »Salle des Fêtes« von
Edouard Loviot und im »Salle des Illusions« von Eugène
A. Hérnard schienen sich die Gewölbe unendlich fort-
zusetzen – ein Effekt aus Spiegeln, elektrischem Licht
und perspektivischer Malerei.[1]

*At the turn of the 20th century, Paris hosted an exposition
that took stock of the achievements in art, technology
and science in the prior century. Inspired by Baroque
stage design and animated by the latest technological
advancements, the exhibition organizers created a grand
display of theatrical illusions. In the »Hall of Village«
designd by Edouard Loviot and the »Hall of Illusions« by
Eugène A. Hernard, for example, the vaults appeared to
continue infinitely – an effect created by a combination
of mirrors, electric lighting and perspectival painting.[1]*

2.1

15.04.1902–27.06.1902
Wien, A
Josef Hoffmann
temporary exhibition

Mit den vier unter einem Thema vereinten Künsten
Architektur, Malerei, Skulptur und Musik drehte sich
1902 bei der Wiener Secession alles um Ludwig van
Beethoven. Durch das Zusammenspiel der Architektur
des Ausstellungshauses, Klimts Beethovenfries und
Klingers Beethovenskulptur wurde die Ausstellung
zum Gesamtkunstwerk. Das Konzept wurde mit 60.000
Besuchern belohnt.

*With architecture, painting, sculpture and music united
as the four arts under a common theme, everything at
the 1902 Vienna Secession revolved around Ludwig van
Beethoven. The interplay of the exhibition building's
architecture, Klimt's Beethoven Frieze, and Klinger's
Beethoven Torso transformed the exhibition into a true
synthesis of the arts. And the concept was a resounding
success, pulling 60,000 visitors.*

2.2

1 *Cf. expo2000.de: The History of
the World's Fair, URL: http://www.
expo2000.de/expo2000/geschichte/
detail.php?wa_id=8&lang=1&s_
typ=20, 02.09.2011.*

2.1 *Brooklyn Museum Archives.
Goodyear Archival Collection. Visual
materials (6.1.015): Paris Exposition
lantern slides. Paris Exposition: Salle
des Fetes, Paris, France, 1900*

2.2 *Beethoven-Skulptur von Max
Klinger, Photographie aufgenommen
während der 14. Ausstellung der
Wiener Secession, 1904
Beethoven sculpture by Max Klinger,
photographed during the 14th exhibition
by the Vienna Secession, 1904
© IMAGNO / Austrian Archives*

Kai-Uwe Hemken

1900–1910

Kennzeichen des politischen Geschehens in Europa: Kriegstreiberei, Militarismus und Imperialismus – Wettrüsten seit den 1880er Jahren, maßgeblich von Deutschland forciert – Verbund Deutschlands, Österreich-Ungarns und Italiens gegen England, Frankreich und Russland – Startschuss für den Krieg: Attentat in Sarajevo am 28. Juni 1914 – Wirtschaftlicher Aufschwung, besonders der Schwerindustrie, im Zuge des Wettrüstens – Immenses Anwachsen der Stadtbevölkerung – Folgen der Wohnungsnot und der unzumutbaren Lebensverhältnisse: soziale Unruhen, Streiks und Radikalisierung politisch-kontroverser Positionen – Industriali-sierung und Technisierung des Alltags: Elektrizität, Telefon, Rundfunk, Automobil, erster selbstgelenkter Motorflug, Farbfotografie, Trickfilm – Innovationen in den Wissenschaften: Radiologie, Relativitätstheorie, Psychoanalyse, Gestalttheorie – Aufbruchstimmung in der Kunstszene: Gründung der expressionistischen Künstlergruppe »Die Brücke« (1905), Formierung der Gruppe »Der Blaue Reiter« (1911) mit Wassily Kandinsky, Franz Marc und Alexej Jawlensky, Entstehung des italienischen Futurismus um Umberto Boccioni, Filippo Marinetti und Luigi Russolo (ab 1909) sowie des Kubismus um Pablo Picasso, Albert Gleizes und Georges Braque (ab 1907), Formierung des niederländischen Neoplastizismus um Piet Mondrian (ab 1920), Gründung der Wiener Secession (1897) sowie des Deutschen Werkbunds (1907) in München – Im Ausstellungswesen: allgemein kritisierte Inflation der Veranstaltungen sowie der messebe-zogenen Kunstproduktion – Fortführung der Museumsreform: Museum als Volksbildungsstätte

1900–1910

Characteristics of political happenings in Europe: Warmongering, militarism and imperialism – arms race since the 1880s, driven predominantly by Germany – alliance between Germany, Austria-Hungary, and Italy against England, France, and Russia – shot that triggered World War I: attack in Sarajevo on June 28, 1914 – economic upturn, particularly in heavy industry, on the back of the arms race – immense growth in urban population – result of a lack of housing and unacceptable living conditions: social unrest, strikes and radicalization of politically controversial positions – industrialization and mechanization of everyday life: electricity, telephone, radio, automobile, first self-piloted powered flight, color photography, cartoons – innovations in science: radiology, Theory of Relativity, psychoanalysis, Gestalt psychology – sense of new beginnings in the art scene: founding of the Expressionist group of artists »Die Brücke« (1905), forming of the group »Der Blaue Reiter« (1911) with Wassily Kandinsky, Franz Marc and Alexej Jawlensky, Emergence of Futurism in Italy with Umberto Boccioni, Filippo Marinetti and Luigi Russolo (from 1909) and Cubism with Pablo Picasso, Albert Gleizes and Georges Braque (from 1907), forming of neo-Plasticism with Piet Mondrian (from 1920), founding of the Viennese Secession (1897) and the German Werkbund (1907) in Munich – with regard to exhibitions: generally criticized inflation of events and trade fair-related production of art – continuation of the museum reform: museums to be places of national education

1908

1911

14.05.1908–31.10.1908
White City, London, GB
political, temporary exhibition

18.12.1911–01.01.1912
München, D
Wassily Kandinsky, Franz Marc
art, temporary exhibition

Die Ausstellung galt der Festigung des politischen Ab-
kommens »Entente cordiale« zwischen dem Vereinigten
Königreich und Frankreich. Der Bevölkerung wurden
gemeinsame soziale und wirtschaftliche Errungenschaften präsentiert, die fernen Kolonien wurden vorgestellt und acht Millionen Besucher entdeckten unter
anderem neue Gewürze und exotische Lebensmittel.

Die Ausstellung entstand aus der Idee heraus, ein
offenes Podium für neue Kunstströmungen zu schaffen.
50 Werke von 15 Künstlern, u. a. Matisse und Picasso,
zeigten neue künstlerische Intentionen – von Abstrak-
tionstendenzen über expressionistische Ansätze bis
hin zum Naturalismus. Sie gilt als Geburtsstunde der
Moderne in Deutschland.

This exhibition was intended as a consolidation of the
political »entente cordiale« agreements between the
United Kingdom and France. Social and economic
achievements were showcased and the public offered
a visualization of their distant colonies. In this way,
the eight million visitors were able to discover new
spices, exotic foods, and much more besides.

This exhibition was the result of an idea to crweate
a public platform for new art movements. A total of
50 works by 15 artists, including Matisse and Picasso,
presented new intentions in art – from tendencies
towards abstraction, to Expressionist approaches,
to Naturalism. Today the show is widely regarded
as the birth of German Modernism.

2.3

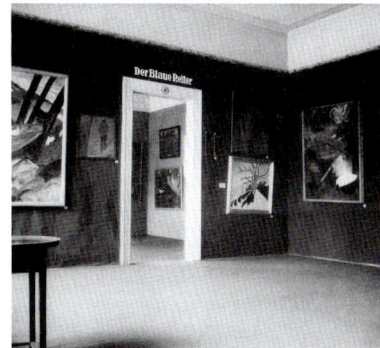

2.4

1912

1913

30.04.1911–1914
Mailand, I
experimental, traveling exhibition

Kannte man den Futurismus bisher nur von den zahlreichen provozierenden Manifesten, so konnte man
sich 1911 in dieser Ausstellung von seiner Vielfältigkeit
und seiner Eindringlichkeit überzeugen. Die Ausstellung
wurde groß in den Medien angekündigt. Riesige Leucht-
reklamen mit den Namen der Künstler begrüßten die
Besucher und standen im Kontrast zur eher konventi-
onellen Hängung und Rahmung der Bilder. Mit großem
Erfolg wanderte die Ausstellung bis 1914 durch Europa.

*While the public presence of Futurism had hitherto been
limited to their numerous provocative manifestos, in 1911
this exhibition afforded the movement an opportunity to
highlight its diversity and intensity thus winning over the
public. The exhibition was all over the press and visitors
were greeted by enormous neon lights boasting the artists'
names and providing a stark contrast to conventional
hanging and framing techniques. A huge success, the
exhibition toured throughout Europe until 1914.*

2.5

17.02.1913–15.03.1913
Sixty-ninth Regiment Armory, New York, USA
art, traveling exhibition

Die »Armory Show«: Der Beginn der Moderne in Amerika. Die Ausstellung, von einem kleinen Künstlerteam
organisiert, zeigte neue internationale Kunst. Dank
guter Pressearbeit wurde sie zum Medienereignis und
hatte viel Einfluss auf die Entwicklung der amerikanischen Kunst.

*The »Armory Show« is considered the beginning of
Modernism in the USA. The exhibition was organized
by a small team of artists who wanted to spotlight new
international art. Thanks to well-orchestrated press
relations, it became a massive press event and thus
strongly influenced the subsequent development of
American art.*

2.6

Kai-Uwe Hemken

1910–1920

Ausbruch des Ersten Weltkriegs – Schlacht in Verdun (1916) als strategischer Wendepunkt im Kriegsverlauf: Ermattung der deutschen Armee, Eintritt der USA in das Kriegsgeschehen (1917), Oktoberrevolution (1917) in Russland, Ende des Ersten Weltkriegs – September 1918: Deutsche Heeresleitung ersucht Waffenstillstand – November 1918: Alliierte stellen Kapitulations-bedingungen – Unterzeichnung des Versailler Vertrages (1919) und offizielle Beendigung des Ersten Weltkriegs – Zusammenkunft des ersten deutschen Parlaments nach 1916 – Aufstände linksorientierter Gruppen (Novemberrevolution) – Ausrufung der sogenannten Räterepublik – Erfolgloser Putsch rechtsradikaler Kreise 1920 in Berlin (Kapp-Putsch) – Politische und wirtschaftliche Instabilität als Kennzeichen der gesellschaftlichen Entwicklung der Weimarer Republik bis 1923, u. a. aufgrund von Reparationszahlungen Deutschlands an die Alliierten sowie der hohen Inflation, die die Bevölkerung am Existenzminimum leben lässt – Besetzung des Ruhrgebiets durch die Alliierten als große Herausforderung für die Bevölkerung – Normalisierung und Stabilisierung der Wirtschaft in der Weimarer Republik erst ab der Klärung der Reparationsfrage – Kritische Reaktionen auf das Kriegsgeschehen in der Kunstszene: Gründung des Cabaret Voltaire in Zürich durch Tristan Tzara, Hugo Ball, Hans Arp, Richard Huelsenbeck u. a. als Reaktion auf die Schlacht von Verdun im Jahre 1916; Veranstaltung absur-der Aufführungen und Gestaltung von Kunstwerken mit kunstfremdem Material unter Einfluss der Futuristen und unter geistiger Patenschaft von Marcel Duchamp – Formierung einer dada-istischen Gruppe um Hannah Höch und Raoul Hausmann (mit Assoziierten wie Kurt Schwitters, zeitweise Theo van Doesburg und Max Ernst) in Berlin nach dem Ende des Ersten Weltkriegs mit stärker politisch ausgerichteter Programmatik – Einführung der Fließbandarbeit in Detroit – Öffentliche Vorstellung der Zwölftonmusik von Arnold Schönberg, Avancieren des Rundfunks zum Massenmedium und Uraufführung des ersten Lichttonfilms – Neben dem Dadaismus Formierung anderer Strömungen (Verismus, Konstruktivismus) und Etablierung von Institutio-nen (Staatliches Bauhaus in Weimar) in der Kunstszene, die das Kunstgeschehen der folgenden Jahre mitprägen sollten

Kai-Uwe Hemken

1910–1920

Outbreak of the First World War – Battle of Verdun (1916) as strategic turning point in the course of the War: exhaustion of the German army, USA enters the war (1917), October Revolution (1917) in Russia, end of the World War I – September 1918: German army command calls for cease-fire – November 1918: allies set capitulation conditions – signing of the Treaty of Versailles (1919) and official end of the First World War – first German Parliament after 1916 convenes – uprisings by groups with left-wing tendencies (November Revolution) – proclamation of the so-called Workers' Republic – unsuccessful putsch by extremist right-wing circles in 1920 in Berlin (Kapp Putsch) – political and economic instability as characteristics of social trends in the Weimar Republic until 1923, in part on account of reparations payments by Germany to the allies and high inflation rate, meaning the population has to exist on the breadline – allied occupation of the Ruhr as major challenge for the population – normalization and stabilization of the economy in the Weimar Republic only after clarification of the reparations question – critical response to the War in the art scene: founding of Cabaret Voltaire in Zurich by Tristan Tzara, Hugo Ball, Hans Arp, Richard Huelsenbeck et al in response to the Battle of Verdun in 1916; organization of absurd performances and creation of works of art using materials not associated with art under the influence of the Futurists and the intellectual patronage of Marcel Duchamp – forming of a Dadaist group with Hannah Höch and Raoul Hausmann (and associates such as Kurt Schwitters, at times Theo van Doesburg and Max Ernst) in Berlin following the end of the First World War with a heavily political program – introduction of assembly line work in Detroit – public presentation of Arnold Schönberg's twelve-tone technique, radio advances to become a mass medium and the first sound movie premieres – alongside Dada, forming of other currents (Verism, Constructivism) and establishing of institutions (State Bauhaus in Weimar) in the art scene, which were to help shape art in the following years

1914

2 Cf. Werner, Frank R. (Ed.): Hans
Dieter Schaal. In-Between. Ausstellungsarchitektur. Stuttgart, London
1999, p.299.

2.7 © Herwarth Walden

2.8 © Dokumenten-Sammlung
Werkbundarchiv – Museum der Dinge

20.09.1913–01.12.1913
Der Sturm, Berlin, D
Herwarth Walden
art, temporary exhibition

Herwarth Walden, ein Vorkämpfer der Moderne, holte
das Pariser Ausstellungskonzept »Salon d'Automne«
1913 nach Deutschland. In seiner Galerie zeigte er
einen Überblick der neuen Kunst. 366 Bilder und Skulpturen von 85 Künstlern aus aller Welt genießen bis heute
den Ruf, Teil einer der bedeutendsten Übersichtsaus-
stellungen vor dem Ersten Weltkrieg gewesen zu sein.

In 1913, Herwarth Walden, a pioneer of Modernism,
brought the exhibition concept that had been used for
the Parisian »Salon d'Automne« to Germany. He used his
own gallery to host an exhibition providing an overview of
new art. Even today, those 366 pictures and sculptures
by 85 artists from all over the world that were included
in the exhibition enjoy the kudos of having been part of
one of the most significant art exhibitions to take place
before the outbreak of the First World War.

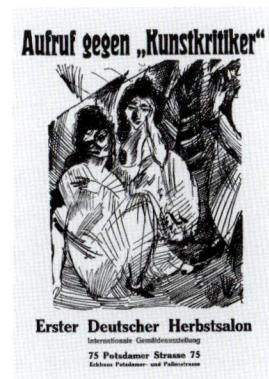

2.7

15.05.1914–08.08.1914
Köln, D
Deutscher Werkbund
industrial, temporary exhibition

Die erste Leistungsschau des Deutschen Werkbunds
war ein Wendepunkt der europäischen Ausstellungs-
entwicklung. Verfolgte man bis dahin noch, auf
Jugendstil reflektierend, den Gedanken, »ein schönes
Gesamtbild zu schaffen«, setzte Bruno Taut mit seinem
Glashaus den Grundstein der modernen Inszenierung
und erreichte eine mediale Verknüpfung der Exponate
zu einer theatralen Erzählung.[2]

Deutscher Werkbund's first exhibition represents a
pivotal point in the development of exhibition concepts
in Europe. Up to that point, the industry had adhered to
the ideal of »creating an aesthetically-pleasing overall
image« reflective of Art Nouveau. By contrast, with his
glass pavilion Bruno Taut laid the foundations for modern
presentation techniques and, with regards to the medium
used, successfully forged a link between the exhibits and
a theatrical narrative.[2]

2.8

1920

1922

30.06.1920–25.08.1920
Berlin, D
experimental, temporary exhibition

Mit Maschinen statt Seelen und objektiven Materialien anstelle individueller Pinselführung war die Ausstellung der Höhepunkt der aktionistischen Anti-Kunst der Dadaisten. Lärmmusik, Fotomontagen, Collagen und Installationen aus Alltagsgegenständen provozierten, schockierten und inspirierten zugleich.

With machines in place of souls and objective materials instead of individual brushwork, this exhibition was the highlight of the Dadaists' actionist anti-art. Noise music, photo montages, collages and installations made up of everyday objects all served to provoke, shock and yet likewise inspired its visitors.

2.9

15.10.1922–31.12.1922
Galerie van Diemen, Berlin, D
temporary exhibition

Von Gemälden und Skulpturen über Architektur bis hin zu Theaterentwürfen bot die Berliner Ausstellung erstmals einen breiten Überblick über Kunst aus Russland. Lange plante man eine Ausstellung dieser Art und ein Jahr nach dem Russischen Bürgerkrieg war es so weit. Konzipiert als Verkaufsausstellung sollte sie den Hungernden in Russland helfen. Dank des großen öffentlichen Interesses und positiver Presse wurde sie mehrmals verlängert.

From paintings and sculptures, to architecture, to designs for theaters, the Berlin exhibition unveiled the first-seen overview of Russian art. The exhibition had been a long time in the planning and just one year after the Russian Civil War the time had come. Conceived as a sales exhibition, it was intended to raise money to help those starving in the Russian famine. Thanks to a great deal of public interest and a positive response from the press, its run was extended a number of times.

2.10

2.9 Kunstwerke von Raoul Haus-mann, George Grosz, John Heartfield, Hannah Hoech usw.
Works by Raoul Hausmann, George Grosz, John Heartfield, Hannah Hoech et al.
© bpk, VG Bild-Kunst, Bonn 2014, Estate of George Grosz, Princeton, N.J., The Heartfield Community of Heirs

2.10 © bpk / Kunstbibliothek, SMB, Photothek Willy Romer / Willy Romer

Kai-Uwe Hemken

1920–1930

Licht- und Schattenseiten der »Goldenen Zwanziger«: der durch den Ersten Weltkrieg
verursachte Reformstau auf allen gesellschaftlichen Gebieten, die Einführung eines neuen
Staatssystems, das eine Entfaltung und Lebensverbesserung des Einzelnen wie der Masse
verspricht, die Impulse durch die amerikanische Kultur (Jazzmusik, Club-Kultur, Revuen,
exotische Tanzvorführungen) und die Verbreitung einer neuen, bunt schillernden Unterhaltungs-
kultur (Kinoszene mit Filmen wie »Nosferatu«, »Metropolis«, »Moderne Zeiten« oder dem
Trickfilm) als Faktoren, die für das erstaunlich hohe Maß an allgemeiner Aktivität und
Experimentierfreudigkeit in allen gesellschaftlichen Sphären mit positiven wie negativen Auswirkungen verantwortlich sind – Die Kehrseite: sichtbare Auswirkungen des Weltkriegs wie
Kriegsversehrte, Leben am Rande des Existenzminimums und Arbeitslosigkeit – Beschluss
über den Beitritt des Deutschen Reiches zum Völkerbund (1926) – 15 Staaten erklären den
Angriffskrieg als völkerrechtswidrig (Briand-Kellogg-Pakt, 1928) – SPD als stärkste Partei bei
den Reichstagswahlen 1928 – Historischer Niedergang der internationalen Wirtschaft mit dem
sogenannten Schwarzen Freitag 1929 – Der Börsensturz in New York als Ausgangspunkt für
eine Weltwirtschaftskrise: Massenentlassungen, immens hohe Arbeitslosigkeit, allgemeine
Verelendung, Ein- und Zusammenbruch des Welthandels sind in den kommenden Jahren an der
Tagesordnung und nähren den allgemeinen Wunsch nach einem autoritären Staatssystem –
Schwere Auseinandersetzungen zwischen linken und rechten Kräften, Destabilisierung
der Demokratie durch häufige Regierungswechsel – Mitte der 1920er Jahre: Stabilisierung
der Wirtschaft und infolgedessen Erneuerung des Ausstellungswesens sowie Etablierung der
Werbebranche als wichtige Einnahmequelle für Künstler – Wiedererstarken der Industriepro-
duktion; eine nicht geringe Zahl von Künstlern fühlt sich der Industriekultur zugehörig –
Gründung des Staatlichen Bauhauses in Weimar (1919) und Umzug nach Dessau (1925) –
Etablierung der Fotografie und des Films als neue künstlerische Medien unter dem Stichwort
»Das Neue Sehen« – Etablierung einer Formensprache in der Architektur, die einem Elementa-
rismus in Farbe und Form sowie einer industrienahen Ästhetik (Material, Bauweise) verpflichtet
ist (Walter Gropius, Mies van der Rohe, Le Corbusier, Gerrit Rietveld u. a.) – Gründung der
Künstlergruppen des Surrealismus, Konstruktivismus, De Stijl, der Neuen Sachlichkeit, des
politischen Dadaismus, Art Concret oder »Cercle et Carré« – Wiederaufgreifen alter Reformpläne
in der Museumsszene: Umbauten und Neuordnungen in zahlreichen Museen (Hannover, Essen,
Köln, München, Hagen), die das Museum als allgemeine Bildungsstätte etablieren sollen

Kai-Uwe Hemken

1920–1930

Positive and negative aspects of the »Roaring Twenties«: the reform backlog in all areas of society caused by the First World War, the introduction of a new political system that promised development for individuals and improved living conditions for the masses, impetus from American culture (jazz music, club culture, reviews, exotic dance performances) and the spread of a new, vibrant entertainment culture (cinema with films such as »Nosferatu«, »Metropolis«, »Modern Times« and cartoons) as factors responsible for the astonishingly high level of general activity and willingness to experiment in all areas of society, with positive and negative effects – the downside: visible impact of the World War, e. g., war-wounded, living on the breadline and unemployment – resolution on the accession of Germany to the League of Nations (1926) – 15 countries declare aggressive war to be contrary to international law (Briand-Kellogg Pact, 1928) – Social Democrats (SPD) the strongest party in the Reichstag elections in 1928 – Historical slump of the international economy with the so-called Black Friday 1929 – stock exchange crash in New York triggers the Great Depression: Mass layoffs, extremely high unemployment, general impoverishment, crash in and collapse of world trade are par for the course in the coming years and fuel the general wish for an authoritarian political system – heavy clashes between left and right-wing forces, destabilization of democracy through frequent changes of government – the mid-1920s: Stabilization of the economy and subsequent revival of exhibitions and establishing of the advertising sector as an important source of income for artists – industrial production regains strength; a not insignificant number of artists feels associated with industrial culture – founding of State Bauhaus in Weimar (1919) and relocation to Dessau (1925) – establishment of photography and cinema as new artistic media »New Vision« – creation of a formal language in architecture bent on Elementarism in color and form and aesthetics related to industry (material, construction method) (Walter Gropius, Mies van der Rohe, Le Corbusier, Gerrit Rietveld et all) – founding of groups of artists associated with Surrealism, Constructivism, De Stijl, New Objectivity, political Dada, Concrete Art and »Cercle et Carré« – re-instigation of old reform plans in the museum scene: Conversion work and restructuring measures in numerous museums (Hanover, Essen, Cologne, Munich, Hagen) intended to establish museums as places of general education

1924

1925

1924
Musik- und Theaterfest, Konzerthaus, Wien, A
Friedrich Kiesler
topical, temporary exhibition

1924 beschäftigte sich Friedrich Kiesler mit der räumlichen Analyse und der Idee von transportablen Syste-
men und entwickelte für die Theaterausstellung das
»L- und T-System«. Dieses Leger- und Trägersystem
war eine flexible, frei stehende Konstruktion, die er
für die Ausstellung mit Objekten und Bildern aus der
Theaterwelt bespielte, und wurde Vorbild für zahlreiche
Ausstellungssysteme im 20. Jahrhundert.

In 1924, Friedrich Kiesler spent a great deal of time
looking into spatial analysis and concepts for portable
systems, and resultantly developed the »L and T System«
for this exhibition. This radical hanging system was a
flexible, free-standing structure, which at this particular
exhibition he covered with objects and images from the
world of theater. It subsequently became a template for
numerous 20th-century exhibition systems.

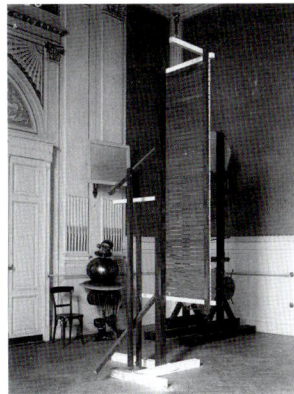

2.11

1925
Exposition Internationale des Arts Décoratifs
et Industriels Modernes, Grand Palais, Paris, F
Friedrich Kiesler
temporary exhibition

Dank dem Erfolg seiner Wiener Ausstellung von 1924
bekam Friedrich Kiesler von Josef Hoffmann den Auftrag für den österreichischen Pavillon. Hierfür verfolgte
er die Vision einer Megastadt und konstruierte eine
flexible, im Raum schwebende Struktur, die sogenannte
»City in Space« (Raumstadt): Bühnenmodelle, Theater-
pläne, Szenen- und Kostümentwürfe konnten einfach
und rhythmisch integriert werden.[3]

Thanks to the success of the Vienna exhibition in 1924,
Friedrich Kiesler was commissioned by Josef Hoffmann
to create the Austrian pavilion at the Exposition Inter-
nationale des Arts Décoratifs et Industriels Modernes.
Here, he took his cue from the vision of a mega-city
and constructed a flexible structure that hovered in
the space – the so-called »City in Space«: It was quite
simple to integrate stage models, theater plans, sets and
costume designs to form a clear rhythm within the main
structure.[3]

2.12

> 013
GeSoLei
Große Ausstellung für Gesundheit,
soziale Fürsorge und Leibesübungen

> 014
Die Wohnung

1926

1927

08.05.1926–15.10.1926
Düsseldorf, D
topical, temporary exhibition

Infolge der zunehmenden Industrialisierung wuchs
die Bevölkerung und soziale Probleme entstanden.
Ausstellungen ermöglichten u. a., diesen zu begegnen:
Die »GeSoLei« griff medizinische, soziale und hygieni-
sche Probleme auf und zeigte den rund 7,5 Millionen
Besuchern moderne, fortschrittliche Lösungen.

*As a consequence of increasing industrialization around
this time, the population had mushroomed and many
new social problems had emerged. Among other things,
exhibitions provided an opportunity to address these
issues: The »GeSoLei« looked at a range of medical, social and hygiene problems and presented the around 7.5
million visitors with advanced, modern solutions to them.*

2.13

23.07.1927–09.10.1927
Stuttgart, D
Deutscher Werkbund
industrial, temporary exhibition

Neben neun Hallen war auch die bis heute existieren-
de Weißenhofsiedlung ein Teil der Ausstellung. Hier
legte Lilly Reich bei der Gestaltung den Fokus auf das
Produkt und seine Funktion. Sie unterteilte die Hallen
nicht wie sonst üblich in Kojen, sondern stellte Warengruppen zusammen, sodass z. B. Haushaltsprodukte
vergleichend betrachtet werden konnten.

*Besides nine halls, also the Weissenhof Estate, which
still exists today, formed one integral part of this exhibition. In her project, Lilly Reich placed emphasis on the
product and its function. She did not divide the halls into
booths, one for each company, as was common for the
time but instead clustered the products into groups, e. g.
household products, such that visitors could consider
them comparatively.*

2.14

>> 014 reviews p.100

21.09.1927–16.10.1927
Berlin, D
Lilly Reich
industrial, temporary exhibition

Ob Industrie oder Mode, Lilly Reich bewies auch in
Berlin ihren eigenwilligen und geschickten Umgang
mit Materialien und Exponaten: Lange, bis zum Boden
reichende Vorhänge bildeten Raumteiler für das »Café
Samt und Seide«, das sie zusammen mit Mies van der
Rohe als zentralen Punkt der Ausstellung »Die Mode
der Dame« entworfen hatte.

Be it in heavy industry, manufacturing or fashion, Lilly
Reich evidenced her individual and highly sophisticated
approach to materials and exhibits once again in Berlin:
Long curtains that skimmed the floor were used as
room-dividers in the »Velvet and Silk Café«, which she
designed together with Mies van der Rohe as the high-
light of the »Ladies' Fashion« exhibition.

2.15

10.1927–1930
Provinzialmuseum, Hannover, D
Alexander Dorner (curator); El Lissitzky (design)
experiment, permanent exhibition

1927 entwickelte El Lissitzky für das Museum in
Hannover den »Raum der Abstrakten«. Mit ihm löste
er das Ordnungsprinzip der einreihigen Hängung auf,
das seit Anfang des 20. Jahrhunderts in Museen domi-
nierte. Flexible Elemente forderten die Besucher auf,
aktiv mitzuwirken und die Kunstwerke in immer wieder
neue Zusammenhänge zu stellen, sodass sich ständig
wechselnde neue Raumbilder ergaben.

El Lissitzky designed the »Abstract Cabinet« for the
museum in Hanover in 1927. He used this opportunity
to deconstruct the traditional principle of arranging
exhibits that reigned in museums at the start of the 20th
century, and proscribed the hanging of artworks in single
rows. Instead, flexible elements required the visitor to
become actively involved in the exhibition, placing the
artworks in new contexts over and over again and creating
new ever-changing constellations.

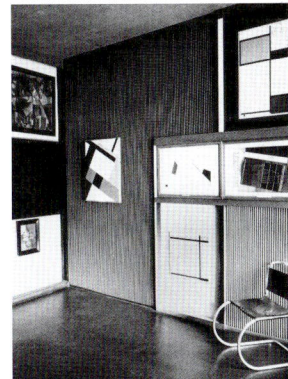

2.16

>> 016 reviews p.104

1928

1929

12.05.1928–10.1928
Köln, D
El Lissitzky
topical, temporary exhibition

Die neue Macht der Massenmedien demonstrierte El
Lissitzky mit dem »Russischen Pavillon«, für den er eine
beeindruckende Raum-Zeit-Collage schuf: Fotomon-
tagen, skulpturale Objekte, dreidimensionale Kulissen,
rotierende Apparate und ausgeklügelte Lichteffekte.
El Lissitzky verfolgte Raumwirkungen experimenteller
Art und bediente sich hier erstmals kinematografischer
Mittel.

El Lissitzky demonstrated the true extent of the newly-
discovered power of the mass media with his design
for the Russian Pavilion. There he created an impres-
sive space/time collage consisting of photo montages,
sculptural objects, three-dimensional scenery, rotating
contraptions and elaborate lighting effects. El Lissitzky
aimed here to create experimental spatial effects and
made use of the medium of cinema for the first time.

2.17

>> 017 reviews p.110

18.05.1929–07.07.1929
Stuttgart, D
Deutscher Werkbund
photo, temporary exhibition

Die Ausstellung »Film und Foto« war eine der wichtigsten ihrer Art. Die Werke wurden zum Teil an einfachen
Lattenkonstruktionen präsentiert oder ohne Rahmen
mit einem Nagel befestigt. Die Ausstellung zeigte die
historischen und aktuellen internationalen Entwicklungen und ermöglichte den Vergleich von Themen,
Anwendungsmöglichkeiten und Stilmitteln in den
Bereichen Kunst, Werbung, Propaganda und Presse.

The »Film and Photo« exhibition was one of the most
important of its kind. In parts, the works were mounted
upon simple thin boards or nailed to the walls unframed.
The exhibition displayed historical achievements and
contemporary developments in international photo-
graphy and facilitated a comparison between topics,
possible uses and stylistic devices in the areas of art,
advertising, propaganda and the press.

2.18

2.17 El Lissitzky: Pressa Pavillon der
Sozialistischen Sowjetrepubliken
USSR, 1928
El Lissitzky, Pressa Pavillon of the
Soviet Socialist Republics USSR, 1928
© Privatbesitz, Deutschland

2.18 Kunstwerke von Laszlo Moholy-
Nagy
Works by Laszlo Moholy-Nagy
© bpk / Kunstbibliothek, SMB, VG Bild-
Kunst, Bonn 2014

20.05.1929–15.01.1930
Exposición Internacional de Barcelona, Barcelona, E
Ludwig Mies van der Rohe
architecture, temporary exhibition

Mies van der Rohe überzeugte auf der Weltausstellung
mit einem neuen Raumkonzept für den Deutschen
Pavillon. Dieses basierte auf einem dynamisierenden
Prinzip, das eine streng geometrische Anordnung
verfolgte. Alle Linien standen entweder parallel oder
senkrecht zueinander; selbst die Form und Anordnung
der Möbel unterlag diesem Ordnungssystem. So entstand
das erste Gebäude mit einem »freien Grundriss«.

Mies van der Rohe wowed the art world with the new
spatial concept that he created for the German Pavilion.
It was based upon a dynamic principle that followed
a strict geometric arrangement. All lines were positioned
either parallel or perpendicular to one another; this
arrangement even determined the shape and positioning
of the furniture. In this way, van der Rohe created the
very first building with a »free ground plan«.

2.19

14.05.1930–13.07.1930
Exposition de la Société des Artistes Décorateurs,
Grand Palais, Paris, F
Deutscher Werkbund
temporary exhibition

Das Team des Deutschen Werkbunds stellte in der
deutschen Abteilung ein neues Gesellschaftsmodell
vor: die Vision modernen Lebens im Hochhaus. Herbert
Bayer untersuchte dazu das Seh- und Wahrnehmungs-
feld und entwickelte für einen Teil der Ausstellung sein
sogenanntes »Field of Vision«. Diese Ausstellungstechnik bezog Wände, Decken und Böden mit ein und sollte
das Blickfeld des Betrachters erweitern.

The Deutscher Werkbund team used the German section
to present a new model of society: a vision of modern
life in a high-rise. When creating the concept, Herbert
Bayer examined our fields of vision and perception and
developed his own, so-called »field of vision« for the
exhibition. The concept not only made use of the walls
but the ceilings and flooring as well and thus aimed to
extend the beholder's field of perception.

2.20

>> 020 reviews p.114

1931

17.05.1930–12.10.1930
Deutsches Hygiene-Museum, Dresden, D
information, temporary exhibition

Anfang des 20. Jahrhunderts entwickelte sich die
Tendenz, die Resultate der Forschung zu veranschaulichen. So auch in Dresden: Auf der 2. Hygiene-Ausstellung wurden erstmals ein lebensgroßer »Gläserner
Mensch« und die einzelnen Bausteine des menschlichen
Körpers gezeigt. Organe, Nervensystem, Kreislauf und
Muskulatur waren farbig und differenzierend beleuchtet
und veranschaulichten so die Komplexität des Gesamt-
organismus.[4] Bis heute dient das Modell der wissenschaftlichen Aufklärung.

At the start of the 20th century a trend had emerged in
Western society to visualize scientific findings. And the
situation was no different in Dresden: The 2nd Hygiene
Exhibition became the venue for the first-ever display
of a life-size »glass man« and the individual elements
that go to make up the human body. Organs, the nervous
system, the circulatory and muscular systems were
illuminated using colored lighting and a variety of other
lighting techniques, visualizing the complexity of the
entire human organism for visitors. Even today this is
still considered the best model for scientific education.[4]

2.21

>> 021 reviews p.122

09.05.1931–02.08.1931
Deutsche Bauausstellung, Berlin, D
Deutscher Werkbund
temporary exhibition

Inspiriert durch die Fotografie schufen Walter Gropius
und sein Team eine neue Sicht auf das Thema »Arbeiter-
Bildung«. Erhöhte Laufgänge verschafften einen Blick
aus der Vogelperspektive, bewegliche Lamellenkon-
struktionen verkörperten neue Visionsstandpunkte,
versteckte Exponate und Gucklöcher ergaben neue
Perspektiven.

Inspired by the medium of photography, Walter Gropius
and his team created a new perspective on the topic of
»workers' education«. Raised walkways provided visitors
with a bird's eye view, moving louver-blade constructions
embodied new angles on things, and hidden exhibits and
peepholes offered a range of new perspectives.

2.22

4 *Cf. Schriefers, Thomas: Ausstellungs-*
architektur: Geschichte, wiederkehrende
Themen, Strategien. Bramsche 2004,
p.89f.

Kai-Uwe Hemken

Prägung der Jahre zwischen 1932 und 1945 in Deutschland durch die systematische Zerstörung der Demokratie seitens der Nationalsozialisten, die Einrichtung der Diktatur Hitlers in allen Bereichen des gesellschaftlichen Lebens, die rassenideologische Ausrichtung und systematische Vernichtung der jüdischen Bevölkerung sowie den Zweiten Weltkrieg – Ernennung Adolf Hitlers zum Reichskanzler am 30. Januar 1933 – Die folgenden Jahre nationalsozialistischer Diktatur in Deutschland lesen sich wie ein Horrorszenario – Abschaffung der Länderparlamente aufgrund des Erlasses zum »Neuaufbau des Deutschen Reiches« – Einrichtung des Volksgerichtshofs – Reichsparteitage in Nürnberg – Austritt des Deutschen Reiches aus dem Völkerbund – Verabschiedung der »Rassengesetze«: Legalisierung der Judendiskriminierung – Boom der Automobilindustrie – Ausbau der Film- und Rundfunkindustrie im Rahmen der Propaganda – Gleichschaltung aller kulturellen und künstlerischen Bereiche sowie aller Bereiche des gesellschaftlichen Lebens – Angriff der deutschen Fliegerstaffel Legion Condor auf das Dorf Guernica aufseiten der spanischen Faschisten – Einmarsch deutscher Truppen in Österreich – Landesweite Zerstörung von Synagogen durch Nationalsozialisten – Überfall deutscher Truppen auf Polen – Beginn des Zweiten Weltkriegs – Besetzung Frankreichs bis Paris, der Niederlande, Belgiens, Luxemburgs, Dänemarks, Norwegens und der Balkanländer – Überfall der deutschen Wehrmacht auf die Sowjetunion – Eintritt der USA in den Weltkrieg – Mobilisierung der deutschen Wirtschaft und Industrie – Massenmord an der jüdischen Bevölkerung beschlossen (»Wannsee-Konferenz«) – Landung der Alliierten in Italien und Frankreich – Attentat auf Hitler – Kapitulation Deutschlands (1945) – Schließung des Staatlichen Bauhauses in Dessau auf Drängen rechtsradikaler Kräfte im Gemeinderat Dessau (1932) – Neugründung des Bauhauses als Privatinstitut in Berlin – Schließung des Bauhauses in Berlin – Gründung des New Bauhaus in Chicago (1937) – Gründung der School of Design in Chicago (1939) – Eröffnung der Großen Deutschen Kunstausstellung 1937 in München als Propaganda-Ausstellung nationalsozialistischer Kunst – Eröffnung der Ausstellung »Entartete Kunst«, ebenfalls 1937, zur Diffamierung moderner Kunst

Kai-Uwe Hemken

1930–1950

In Germany the years between 1932 and 1945 were shaped by the systematic destruction of democracy by the Nazis, the penetration of all areas of social life by Hitler's dictatorship, its racist ideology, the systematic annihilation of the Jewish population and the Second World War – appointment of Adolf Hitler as Chancellor of the Reich on January 30, 1933 – the following years of Nazi dictatorship in Germany read like a horror scenario – abolition of the state assemblies and the decree for the »Rebuilding of the German Reich« – establishment of the People's Court – the Nuremberg Rallies – the exit of Germany from the League of Nations – the passing of the Nuremberg Race Laws: Legalization of discrimination against the Jews – boom in the automobile industry – expansion of the cinema and broadcasting for propaganda purposes – forcible coordination (Gleichschaltung) of all cultural and artistic fields and all areas of social life – on the side of the Spanish fascists the German Legion Condor squadron attacks the village of Guernica – German troops march into Austria – nationwide destruction of synagogues by Nazis – German troops attack Poland – start of the Second World War – occupation of France as far as Paris, of the Netherlands, Belgium, Luxembourg, Denmark, Norway, and the Balkan countries – German army attacks the Soviet Union – the USA enters the War – mobilization of the German economy and industry – mass murder of the Jewish population decided (»Wannsee Conference«) – allied troops land in Italy and France – assassination attempt on Hitler – capitulation of Germany (1945) – closure of Staatliches Bauhaus in Dessau on pressure from extreme right-wing forces in Dessau municipal council (1932) – Bauhaus reestablished as a private institute in Berlin – closure of Bauhaus in Berlin – founding of New Bauhaus in Chicago (1937) – founding of the School of Design in Chicago (1939) – opening of the Major German Art Exhibition in 1937 in Munich, an exhibition of Nazi art for propaganda purposes – opening of the »Degenerate Art« exhibition 1937, for the purpose of defaming modern art

1932

21.08.1931–30.08.1931
Berlin, D
information, temporary exhibition

Neuheiten und innovative Ideen für Funk und Fernsehen wurden 1924 auf der Funkausstellung in Berlin zum ersten Mal gezeigt. 1931 fand dort die erste vollelektronische Fernsehübertragung statt und die Ausstellung verzeichnet die meisten Besucher vor dem Zweiten Weltkrieg. Bis heute ist sie eine der wichtigsten internationalen Ausstellungen für alle Arten von Unterhaltung, Elektronik, Kommunikation und in Deutschland eine der ältesten Industriemessen.

In 1924, new products and innovative ideas in the area of radio and television were presented together for the first time at the Radio and Television Exhibition in Berlin. The exhibition enjoyed its highest attendance figures prior to the Second World War and in 1931, the first fully electronic television broadcast took place here. Today, it remains one of the most important exhibitions for all kinds of entertainment, electronics, and communication media, and is also one of Germany's oldest trade fairs.

2.23

29.10.1932–29.10.1934
Mostra della Rivoluzione Fascista,
Palazzo delle Esposizioni, Rom, I
Giuseppe Terragni, Arrigo Arrigotti
propaganda, temporary exhibition

Vor dem Krieg wurden Ausstellungen in Europa zunehmend zu Propagandazwecken der Politik benutzt. Die »Sala 0« überzeugte natürlich nicht wegen der faschistischen Inhalte, sondern durch ihre ungewöhnliche Gestaltung. Eine starke Erzählkraft, auf das Wesentliche reduziert, sowie eine ideale Mischung aus Symbolik und theatralischem Effekt erinnerten an El Lissitzky und waren doch ganz eigen.

In the years prior to the Second World War, politicians increasingly exploited exhibitions for propaganda purposes. »Sala 0« was a convincing display, not of course on account of the fascist contents but thanks to its unusual design. A strong narrative line, reduced to the essentials, not to mention an ideal combination of symbolism and theatrical effects were reminiscent of El Lissitzky and yet quite unique.

> 025
Mostra dell'aeronautica italiana

> 026
Machine Art:
Objects 1900 and Today

1934

1934
Palazzo dell'Arte, Mailand, I
Giuseppe Pagano
topical, temporary exhibition

Technischen Fortschritt, explosive Energie und die
Grenzenlosigkeit des Fliegens vermittelte die »Sala
d'Icaro« von Giuseppe Pagano. Durch ein spiralförmiges
Band, das meterhoch in einer leuchtenden Lichtscheibe
endete, veranschaulichte er die Dynamik wirkender
Aufwinde und zeigte den Drang, sich der energiegela-
denen Sonne immer weiter zu nähern, der bis heute mit
dem Fliegen verbunden wird.[5]

Giuseppe Pagano's »Sala d'Icaro« conveyed technologic-
al advances, explosive energy and the boundlessness
of flying in one single exhibition hall. He used a spiraled
band, which ended meters above an illuminated lens, to
visualize the dynamic nature of the active up-draughts,
in this way demonstrating the human wish to near the
radiant sun, which even today retains its associations
with flight.[5]

2.24

05.03.1934–29.04.1934
Museum of Modern Art, New York, USA
Alfred Barr (curator); Philip Johnson (design)
art, temporary exhibition

1934 entdeckte Philip Johnson die Ästhetik maschinell
hergestellter Objekte. Er wählte 600 von ihnen nach
»Platons Begriff der Schönheit« aus, sortierte sie in
Kategorien und inszenierte sie, inspiriert durch die
Gestaltung von Mies van der Rohe, zu einer Ausstellung,
die Kunstgeschichte schrieb – nicht nur wegen ihrer
minimalistischen Gestaltung, sondern auch durch die
Entdeckung der »Maschinen-Kunst«.

In 1934, Philip Johnson discovered the aesthetic qualities
of mechanically produced objects. He selected 600 such
objects, which corresponded to Plato's notion of beauty,
organized them into categories, and presented them in
an exhibition that was inspired by Mies van der Rohe's
designs. In doing so he truly wrote art history – not only
thanks to his minimalist design but also his discovery
of »machine art«.

5 *Cf. Schriefers, Thomas: Ausstellungs-*
architektur: Geschichte, wiederkehrende
Themen, Strategien. Bramsche 2004,
p.89f.

2.24 *© Fondazione Franco Albini –*
www.fondazionefrancoalbini.com

1936

1937

30.05.1936–10.1936
VI Triennale di Milano, Palazzo dell'Arte, Mailand, I
Franco Albini, Giovanni Romano
temporary exhibition

1936 fand man auf der Triennale in Mailand ein Spektrum von neuen Präsentationslösungen. Dazu gehörte auch die Rasterinstallation von Franco Albini und Giovanni Romano für den Raum »Mostra dell'Antica Oreficeria Italiana«. Durch geschickten Umgang mit Licht und Schatten schienen die zwischen senkrechten und waagerechten Stützen präsentierten Exponate zu schweben.

In 1936, the Milan Triennial unveiled a whole spectrum of new presentation ideas. This also included Franco Albini and Giovanni Romano's grid installation for the »Mostra dell'Antica Oreficeria Italiana« room. The sophisticated use of light and shadow gave the vertical and horizontal supports the appearance that they were swaying.

2.25

05.1937–10.1937
Düsseldorf, D
propaganda, temporary exhibition

Ein fast vergessenes Großereignis stellt die Ausstellung »Schaffendes Volk« dar. Was eine bescheidene Werkbundausstellung werden sollte, wurde durch den Einfluss der NS-Regierung zu einer gigantischen Propagandaschau. Die deutsche und nationale Presse berichteten und über sechs Millionen Besucher kamen, um das »neue deutsche Wohnen«, das »neue deutsche Arbeiten« und die »neue deutsche Kunst« zu sehen.

The »Reich Exhibition of the Productive People« was a major event of its time that has now as good as fallen into obscurity. Intended as a modest Werkbund exhibition, the influence of the Nazi government resulted in the production of a bombastic propaganda show. The German and the international press turned out to report on the event and over six million visitors flocked to see this show of »new German lifestyle«, »new German labor« and »new German art«.

2.26

18.07.1937–1944
Haus der Deutschen Kunst, München, D
art, temporary exhibition

Diese erste von acht Ausstellungen war der Versuch, nationalsozialistische Kunst zu definieren. Sie sollte Vermittler und Wegweiser für die »neue deutsche Kunst« sein. Aktbilder, Landschaften, Arbeiter- und Industriebilder sowie Plastiken des »neuen artreinen Menschen« wurden auf zwei Stockwerke verteilt und nach Themen geordnet. Jedes Bild und jede Plastik wurden im großzügigen Salonstil des 19. Jahrhunderts inszeniert.

This, the first of eight exhibitions, was an attempt to define Nazi art – as an agent and pioneer for »New German Art«. Nudes, landscapes, paintings of workers and industry as well as sculptures of the »New ›Aryan‹ man« were spread over two floors, arranged by theme. Each and every picture and sculpture in the exhibition were presented in the lavish salon style of the 19th century.

2.27

19.07.1937–04.1941
München, D
Joseph Goebbels, Adolf Ziegler
propaganda, traveling exhibition

Im Zuge der NS-Kunstpolitik sollte für eine Neuordnung des künstlerischen Schaffens gesorgt werden. Dazu gehörte auch die Ausstellung »Entartete Kunst«, die als gezielte Gegendarstellung einen Tag nach der »Großen Deutschen Kunstausstellung« eröffnet wurde. Massen von Werken der Moderne, zuvor aus allen deutschen Museen konfisziert, wurden wahllos eng an- und über- einander gehängt. Große Schriftzüge wetterten gegen die »verbotene Kunst«.

The Nazi's art policy called for a realignment of art and artistic activity in Germany. Measures taken to achieve this end included the orchestration of the »Degenerate Art« exhibition, which was conceived as a strategic re- sponse to »The Great German Art Exhibition« and opened its doors just one day after its counterpart. Masses of Modernist works that had been confiscated from museums all over Germany were hung in no particular order, so close to each other that they even overlapped at times. Large lettering covered the walls, raging against the vices of this »forbidden art«.

2.28

>> 030 reviews p.130

1938

1938
Museum of Modern Art, New York, USA
Herbert Bayer
temporary exhibition

Das Bauhaus und seine Bedeutung wurden in Amerika vorgestellt. Bei der Gestaltung lag der Fokus auf Abfolge und Gliederung der Arbeiten. In verschieden großen Kojen wurden sie nach Themen sortiert und untergebracht. Eine Bemalung des Fußbodens in verschiedenen Farben und mit richtungsweisenden Formen half den Besuchern, sich zu orientieren.

This exhibition served to introduce Bauhaus and its significance in Germany and Europe to an American audience. In terms of design, great emphasis was placed on the sequence and arrangement of the works. Presented in booths that varied in size, they were organized according to their thematic focus. The floor was painted with a range of shapes and colors, pointing the visitors in the right direction and helping them to find their way among the works.

2.29

17.01.1938–22.02.1938
Paris, F
experimental, temporary exhibition

Bei dieser Totalinszenierung handelt es sich um ein surrealistisches Gesamtkunstwerk, das Geschichte schrieb. Die Besucher tauchten ein in ein Ambiente, das alle ihre Sinne forderte: Schaufensterpuppen sowie wilde Kombinationen aus Natur und Kunstobjekten zeigten ihnen die Tiefen des Unbewussten und machten sie zu einem Teil des räumlichen Bildes. Neu definiert wurde nicht nur das Medium Ausstellung, sondern auch das Verhältnis zwischen Besucher und Ausstellung.

This all-round production was a Surrealist synthesis of the arts that wrote art history. Visitors stepped into a setting that exercised every single one of their senses: Mannequins and wild combinations of natural elements and man-made objects confronted them with the depths of the unconscious and made them a part of the overall installation. The show not only redefined the medium of the exhibition, but also the relationship between viewer and exhibition.

1939

06.05.1939–29.10.1939
Zürich, CH
propaganda, temporary exhibition

Diese Ausstellung der Schweiz diente zur Kriegsvor-
bereitung. Hauptanziehungspunkt neben dem
»Schifflibach«, auf dem man in kleinen Booten durch
das Ausstellungsgelände treiben konnte, war die
»Höhenstraße«, ein Weg, der durch seinen Aufbau beim
Besucher Schritt für Schritt Optimismus wecken und
so das Vertrauen ins Vaterland stärken sollte.

The Swiss National Exhibition was intended as prepara-
tion for war. Alongside the »Schiffli« brook, which carried
visitors through the exhibition grounds in small boats,
the main attraction was the »Höhenstraße«, a pathway
whose construction functioned to inspire increasing
optimism in the visitor with each step they took, and was
thus supposed to enhance their faith and confidence in
their home country.

30.04.1939–27.10.1940
New York, USA
Henry Dreyfuss
temporary exhibition

Das Thema der New Yorker Weltausstellung war »die
Welt von morgen«. Die Attraktion: ein 210 Meter hoher,
dreieckiger Turm und eine Kugel; in ihr die Ausstellung
»Democracity«. Eine inszenierte Welt aus Megacitys,
vernetzt durch fortschrittliche Transportsysteme, vermittelte den experimentierfreudigen Geist der Zeit.

The focus at the New York World's Fair was firmly on the
world of tomorrow. The main attraction: a 210-meter-
tall, triangular tower and a sphere; and inside it the
exhibition – Democracity. A highly-orchestrated world of
mega-cities was connected by technologically advanced
transportation systems, a clear expression of the zeit-
geist and its characteristic joy in experimentation.

2.30 © Walter Mittelholzer

2.30

> 035
Mostra del Pittore Scipione
e del Bianco e Nero

> 036
Road to Victory

1941

1942

1941
Pinacoteca di Brera, Mailand, I
Franco Albini
graphic, temporary exhibition

Im Ausstellungssystem von Franco Albini für die Grafik-
ausstellung »Mostra del Pittore Scipione e del Bianco
e Nero« kamen auch kleine Exponate gut zur Geltung.
Es handelte sich dabei um eine Konstruktion aus Stützen, in die großflächige Glaswände und Auslagen zur
Präsentation der Exponate integriert wurden.

The system developed by Franco Albini for the prints
exhibition »Mostra del Pittore Scipione e del Bianco
e Nero« made sure that even the smallest exhibits came
into their own. The exhibition concept included large
glass walls and display stands, which were integrated
into a complex construction of pillars.

2.31

09.1942
MoMA, New York, USA
Edward Steichen (concept); Herbert Bayer (design);
Carl Sandburg (text)
propaganda, photo, traveling exhibition

»Road to Victory« hatte als Propagandaausstellung
die Mission, das Vertrauen in die US-Armee zu stärken.
Konzipiert von Edward Steichen und inszeniert von
Herbert Bayer zeigte sie Fotografien von der Nation im
Krieg. Große Fototafeln – kombiniert mit Texten von Carl
Sandburg – wurden mit Bayers Ausstellungstechnik
»Field of Vision« angeordnet.

As a propaganda exhibition, »Road to Victory« had been
charged with the mission of boosting the public's con-
fidence in the US Army. Conceived by Edward Steichen
and staged by Herbert Bayer, it exhibited a collection of
photographs of the nation at war. Large-format photo
panels were combined with texts composed by Carl
Sandburg and arranged according to Bayer's »Field of
Vision« exhibition technique.

1946

20.10.1942–05.1947
The Art of This Century Gallery, 30 West 57th Street,
New York, USA
Friedrich Kiesler
art, permanent exhibition

Die »Art of This Century Gallery« von Peggy Guggenheim
war 1947 ein Ort des Zusammentreffens der amerikanischen und europäischen Kunst der Nachkriegsjahre.
Ihren Erfolg verdankt sie auch der visionären Innen-
architektur von Friedrich Kiesler. Er entwickelte neue
Präsentationssysteme, ein multifunktionales Möbel mit
achtzehn verschiedenen Verwendungsmöglichkeiten
sowie ein Aufhängungssystem, das rahmenlose Bilder
scheinbar frei im Raum schweben ließ.

In 1947, the »Art of This Century Gallery« owned by
Peggy Guggenheim constituted a major venue where
post-war American and European art could meet. Its
great success was in part thanks to Friedrich Kiesler's
visionary interior design. He developed a series of new
presentation systems, multi-functional furniture with
18 potential uses as well as a hanging system, whereby
unframed pictures seemed to float in the space.

2.32

25.08.1946–31.10.1946
Dresden, D
Herbert Volwahsen
art, temporary exhibition

Die erste Allgemeine Deutsche Kunstausstellung war
ein Zusammentreffen von Künstlern aus den Besat-
zungszonen. Als erste und zugleich letzte gesamtdeut-
sche Kunstausstellung bis 1990 zeigte sie viele Werke,
die als »entartet« galten, und dokumentierte Aufbruchs-
euphorie und Schöpferdrang der Künstler nach dem
Zweiten Weltkrieg.

The first General German Art Exhibition provided a mee-
ting point for artists from the occupation zones. As the
first and last united German art exhibition until 1990, it
presented many works that had been considered »dege-
nerate« under the Nazis and documented the elation felt
by artists following the end of Second World War and the
creative impulse this unleashed.

2.33

Kai-Uwe Hemken

1950–1960

Zerrissenheit der Kunst- und Kulturentwicklung in Deutschland in den 1950er Jahren: Kollektive Schwermut aufgrund der Grenzerfahrungen der nationalsozialistischen Diktatur, des Holocaust und des Zweiten Weltkriegs versus Aufbruchsituation, angetrieben von dem Willen, die Leistungen der Moderne vor den genannten historischen Ereignissen wieder ins Bewusstsein zu rufen und den Anschluss an die internationale Wertegemeinschaft zu erringen – Re-Education, Entnazifizierung und Entideologisierung als zentrale Stichworte einer demokratisch gesinnten Neuorientierung, forciert durch die Alliierten und die progressiven Kräfte mit deutschem Hintergrund – Ende des Zweiten Weltkriegs: Kapitulation am 8. Mai 1945 – Gründung der Vereinten Nationen (UN) – Abwurf von Atombomben auf Hiroshima und Nagasaki durch die USA (1945) – Befreiung der Konzentrationslager durch alliierte Truppen – Belastung Mitteleuropas durch Flüchtlingsströme – Nürnberger Prozesse gegen zahlreiche Nationalsozialisten der Führungselite – Verkündung des Marshallplans zum Wiederaufbau in Deutschland – Einführung der Deutschen Mark als neue Währung – Ost-West-Konflikt (»Kalter Krieg«) als Leitlinie der Weltpolitik – Staatsgründung im Westen (Bundesrepublik Deutschland) und Osten (Deutsche Demokratische Republik) im Mai 1949 – Arbeiteraufstand in der DDR (1953) – NATO integriert die Bundesrepublik Deutschland – Gründung des Warschauer Pakts mit Aufnahme der DDR: Besiegelung der Teilung Deutschlands – Ab Mitte der 1950er Jahre Boom der deutschen Wirtschaft (»Wirtschaftswunder«) – Etablierung des Fernsehens – Gründung der Europäischen Wirtschaftsgemeinschaft (EWG) – Forcierung der Weltraumfahrt in Ost und West, Wettlauf um die Vorherrschaft im All – Erste Demonstrationen gegen atomare Aufrüstung: »Ostermärsche« in Deutschland – Weltausstellung in Brüssel – Revolution in Kuba durch die Truppen von Fidel Castro – Gründung der »Gruppe 47« – Gründung der Ulmer Hochschule für Gestaltung und des »Kulturbundes zur demokratischen Erneuerung Deutschlands« (1945–47) – Tagungen mit überregionaler Bedeutung, wie etwa die Darmstädter Gespräche zu den Themen »Menschenbild in unserer Zeit« oder »Ökonomisierung der Kunst« – Ausstellungstätigkeit der Alliierten: Wanderausstellungen sowie Ausstellungen mit moderner amerikanischer oder französischer Kunst – Gründung von Künstlergruppen wie »Quadriga« (1952), »junger westen« (1948), ZEN 49 (1949), ZERO (1958) und Neuer Realismus (1960) mit unterschiedlichen Konzepten – Gründung und Ausstellungstätigkeit von Kunstgalerien wie Galerie Rosen (Berlin), Galerie Breuer (Berlin), Galerie Schuler (Berlin), Galerie Frank (Berlin), Galerie Stangl (München), Galerie Probst (Mannheim) – Öffentlicher Disput zwischen Will Grohmann und Karl Hofer zu Grundsatzfragen der Kunst in der modernen, industrienahen Kultur – Eröffnung des Guggenheim Museums in New York (Architekt: Frank Lloyd Wright, 1959) – documenta 1 und 2 in Kassel

Kai-Uwe Hemken

1950–1960

Inner turmoil with regard to art and culture in Germany in the 1950s: collective melancholy on account of the extreme limits experienced under Nazi dictatorship, the Holocaust and the Second World War versus a new beginning, driven by the will to rekindle awareness of the achievements of the modern age prior to the historical events mentioned and to be adopted again by the international community of values – re-education, denazification and liberation from ideology as the keywords of democratically-minded reorientation, pushed forward by the allies and the progressive forces with a German background – end of the Second World War: capitulation on May 8, 1945 – founding of the United Nations (UN) – USA drops atomic bombs on Hiroshima and Nagasaki (1945) – liberation of concentration camps by allied troops – Central Europe strained by flow of refugees – Nuremberg trials of numerous leading Nazis – declaration of the Marshall Plan to rebuild Germany – introduction of the Deutsche Mark as the new currency – East-West conflict (»Cold War«) as the guideline for world politics – states founded in the West (Federal Republic of Germany) and the East (German Democratic Republic) in May 1949 – workers' uprising in East Germany (1953) – NATO integrates the Federal Republic of Germany – founding of the Warsaw Pact including East Germany: Division of Germany sealed – from the mid-1950s boom in the German economy (»economic miracle«) – television established – founding of the European Economic Community (EEC) – space travel pushed ahead within the East and West, race for supremacy in space – first demonstrations against nuclear armament: »Easter marches« in Germany – Expo in Brussels – revolution in Cuba by Fidel Castro's troops – founding of »Gruppe 47« (Group 47) – founding of the Ulm Design Academy and the »Kulturbund zur demokratischen Erneuerung Deutschlands« (Cultural Association for the democratic Renewal of Germany) (1945–47) – conferences of national importance such as the »Darmstädter Gespräche« on, for example, »The Conception of Man in our Time« or »The Economization of Art« – exhibition activity on the part of the allies: touring exhibitions and exhibitions featuring modern American or French art – founding of artists' groups such as »Quadriga« (1952), »junger westen« (young west) (1948), ZEN 49 (1949), ZERO (1958) and Neuer Realismus (new realism) (1960) with different concepts – founding of and exhibitions by art galleries such as Galerie Rosen (Berlin), Galerie Breuer (Berlin), Galerie Schuler (Berlin), Galerie Frank (Berlin), Galerie Stangl (Munich), Galerie Probst (Mannheim) – public dispute between Will Grohmann and Karl Hofer on basic questions about art in a modern culture with close associations with industry – opening of the Guggenheim Museum in New York (Architect: Frank Lloyd Wright, 1959) – documenta 1 and 2 in Kassel

1948

1948
Italienischer Pavillon, XXIV Biennale di Venezia,
Giardini di Castello, Venedig, I
Carlo Scarpa
art, temporary exhibition

Schlichte Eleganz – so hat man die Gestaltung Carlo
Scarpas in Erinnerung, z. B. die »Retrospektive« Paul
Klees. Große, weiß und schwarz bezogene Paneele,
vertikal oder horizontal angeordnet, verliehen dem
Raum durch das abwechselnde Spiel der Kontraste
eine klare Struktur. Die Paneele waren eingesetzt als
Passepartouts und gaben den Bildern Raum zum Wirken.

Simple elegance – this is how Carlo Scarpa's exhibition
design is remembered today, one example being the
Paul Klee retrospective. Large, black-and-white panels,
arranged vertically or horizontally, created an alterna-
ting interplay of contrasts, which lent the space a clear
structure. The panels were used to mount the artist's
pictures, providing them with sufficient space to be seen
to their full effect.

1948–1951
Marshall Plan, Westeuropa
OEEC – Organisation für Europäische Wirtschaftliche
Zusammenarbeit
information, traveling exhibition

Im Rahmen des Wiederaufbau-Programms der Amerikaner fuhr diese Ausstellung durch ganz Europa.
Der »Europazug« zeigte in sieben Waggons bewegliche
Modelle, besondere Beleuchtungs- und Toneffekte
sowie einzigartige, auf Knopfdruck reagierende Apparaturen, die die Besucher faszinierten. Die Ausstellung
sollte ein Beweis für die fortschreitende Entwicklung
Europas sein.

This exhibition made its way around Europe as part of
the US reconstruction program, the Marshall plan. The
»Europazug« filled seven wagons with moving models,
special lighting and sound effects, and unique gadgets
that responded at the press of a button, all fascinating
visitors. The exhibition was intended as a demonstration
of the progress made in rebuilding Europe.

2.34

1949

1950

07.05.1949–17.05.1949
Schweizer Mustermesse Basel, Basel, CH
Max Bill
graphic, traveling exhibition

Die Ausstellung »Die gute Form« entstand aus der
These Max Bills, dass sich »Form aus Funktion und
Schönheit« zusammensetze. 80 Ausstellungstafeln
zeigten Entwürfe aus allen Bereichen der Gestaltung,
die als Vorzeigebeispiele für eine gelungene Formgebung
galten. Befestigt waren sie an einer Dachlattenkons-
truktion, die zwischen Boden und Decke eingespannt
wurde und so an alle Raumverhältnisse angepasst
werden konnte. Als Wanderausstellung konzipiert tourte
sie durch Europa und war Vorreiter für viele weitere
Ausstellungen.

The »Gute Form« exhibition was the product of a theory
developed by Max Bill, which presented »design as a
product of function and aesthetics«. 80 exhibition panels
showcased designs from all areas of the discipline,
serving as prime examples of accomplished design work.
These were hung on thin slats that spanned the space
between floor and ceiling, thus fitting perfectly to the
dimensions of the room. Conceived as a traveling exhi-
bition, it toured throughout Europe and served as a role
model for many subsequent exhibitions.

2.35

>> 041 reviews p.134

1950
Padiglione Montecatini, Fiera di Milano, Mailand, I
Erberto Carboni
information, temporary exhibition

In der Halle der Chemie, einem technischen Traum-
land, verwendete Erberto Carboni originelle Elemente
zur Darstellung der Chemie. Mit seinen analytisch und
plastisch umgesetzten Ideen stellte er Bezüge her, die
sehr starke Eindrücke hinterließen und die Besucher in
das komplexe wissenschaftliche Thema einführten.

Erberto Carboni employed original exhibition elements
to present the science of chemistry in the scientific won-
derland that was the Chemistry Hall. With his analytical
and sculptural concepts he created associations that
left strong impressions on the visitors and provided them
with an introduction to this complex scientific subject.

1951

1951
IX Triennale di Milano, Palazzo dell' Arte, Mailand, I
Max Bill, Rosemarie Schwarz, Hans G. Conrad
temporary exhibition

In dieser Ausstellung über Qualitätsarbeit und
Handwerk aus der Schweiz wurden Industrietextilien,
Handwebstoffe und Keramik gezeigt. Der gesamte
Raum war dunkel, lediglich die von innen leuchtenden
Trommelvitrinen setzten Akzente. Durch die außerge-
wöhnliche Präsentation wurden die Exponate besonders
in den Vordergrund gestellt.

At this show presenting Swiss quality craftsmanship,
exhibits included industrial and hand-woven textiles,
and ceramics. The entire room was unlit apart from the
barrel display cases, which illuminated from inside set
the accent throughout the space. The unusual pre-
sentation technique served to place the exhibits, quite
literally, in the spotlight.

1951–1955
Museum of Modern Art, New York, USA
Edward Steichen
photo, traveling exhibition

Ein Porträt der Menschheit: 503 Aufnahmen von 273
internationalen Fotografen sollten nach den schreck-
lichen Erfahrungen des Krieges Helfer und Vermittler
für eine bessere Welt und mehr Verständnis zwischen
den Menschen sein. Die beeindruckende Ausstellung
reiste von Land zu Land und erreichte über neun Millionen Besucher.

A portrait of humanity: Following the harrowing experi-
ences of the Second World War, the 503 images by 273
international photographers on display here were intend-
ed as an encouraging force conveying the sense of a
better world and of increased understanding among the
people. The captivating exhibition traveled from country
to country and attracted over nine million visitors.

2.36

61

1953

1953–1954
Padiglione Montecatini, Fiera di Milano, Mailand, I
Erberto Carboni
information, temporary exhibition

Betrat man den Montecatini-Pavillon, die »Phantasie-welt eines technischen Wunders«[6], befand man sich mitten in der komplexen technischen Welt des Mediums Fernsehen. Die aussagekräftige gewölbte Form des Geräts wurde in den Raum übertragen und mit weiteren typischen Elementen ergänzt. Der Pavillon wurde zum Symbol der gesamten Fernsehausstellung.

From the moment they set foot in the Montecatini pavilion, or the »fantasy world of a technical wonder«,[6] visitors found themselves at the center of the complex, technical world of television. The appliance's highly ex-pressive curved shape was translated into the exhibition context and augmented with other elements typical to the mass medium. This particular pavilion became a symbol for the entire Television exhibition.

1954

20.04.1954–16.05.1954
Brooklyn Museum, New York, USA
graphic exhibition, traveling exhibition

Mit dieser Ausstellung wurde Skandinavisches Design in den USA zum Mythos. Viele Jahre tourte sie durch die USA und war Vorreiter für viele folgende Designaus-stellungen. Die Ausstellung war nicht nur Leistungs-schau, sondern auch Designkampagne und eine der erfolgreichsten Marketingaktionen in der Geschichte der USA.

This exhibition made Scandinavian design legendary in the USA. It spent many years touring the USA and was the forerunner of many subsequent design exhibitions. »Design in Scandinavia« not only displayed the Nordic achievements in the field but also functioned as a design campaign and one of the most successful marketing actions in US history.

2.37

2.38

6 *Bayer, Herbert: »Foreword«, in: Carboni, Erberto: Exhibitions and Displays. Italien 1957, p.16.*

2.37 *Aufzeichnungen des Fach-bereichs Fotografie: Ausstellungen. Skandinavisches Design. (20.04.1954–16.05.1954). Ausstellungsansicht. Records of the Department of Photography: Exhibitions. Design in Scandinavia. (04/20/1954–05/16/1954). Installation view. © Brooklyn Museum Archives*

2.38 *Aufzeichnungen des Fach-bereichs Malerei und Skulptur: Ausstellungen. Skandinavisches Design. (20.04.1954–16.05.1954). Ausstellungsansicht. Records of the Department of Painting and Sculpture: Exhibitions. Design in Scandinavia. (04/20/1954–05/16/1954). Installation view. © Brooklyn Museum Archives*

> 047
<u>Il Labirinto dei ragazzi</u>

> 048
<u>documenta. Kunst des XX. Jahrhunderts.
Internationale Ausstellung</u>

2.39 *Gunther Becker*
© documenta Archiv

1954
IX Triennale di Milano, Mailand, I
Studio Architetti BBPR
experiment, temporary exhibition

Der Ausstellungsort war eine Art Labyrinth mit rotati-
onssymmetrischer Grundrissform, in dem Wandzeich-
nungen ausgestellt wurden. Anfang und Ende lagen
nah beieinander, der Weg des Besuchers war sehr
direkt und eindeutig vorgeschrieben. Das Labyrinth war
ein Beispiel für das Experiment »sens unique«. Durch
sein Ein-Weg-System sollten die Besucher das Thema
schneller und besser erfassen können.

*The exhibition venue itself was a kind of labyrinth, with
a rotationally symmetric ground plan displaying an array
of wall illustrations. The beginning and end were set
close to each other, while the path pointing visitors in
the right direction was very direct and clearly marked.
The labyrinth was exemplary of the »sens unique«
experiment. A one-way system was supposed to make
the subject at hand easier and faster to grasp.*

15.07.1955–18.09.1955
Museum Fridericianum, Friedrichsplatz, Neue Galerie,
Kassel, D
Arnold Bode
art, temporary exhibition

Die erste documenta 1955 in Kassel war eines der
ersten Ausstellungskonzepte mit einem professionellen
kuratorischen Management. Organisatorisch wie auch
betriebswirtschaftlich ging sie neue Wege und erstmals
wurde eine Stadt zum Ausstellungsraum. Die Ausstellung war ein Medienereignis und zeigte eine Zusammenfassung der Kunst der Moderne.

*The first documenta held in Kassel in 1955 was one of
the first exhibition concepts to have professional curatorial management. It broke new ground in terms of both
organization and business aspects, and was the first
instance of a town being transformed into an exhibition
space. The exhibition was a media event and presented a
summary overview of Modernist art.*

2.39

>> 048 reviews p.140

> 049
This Is Tomorrow

> 050
Le poème électronique

1956

1958

09.08.1956–09.09.1956
Whitechapel Gallery, London, GB
art, temporary exhibition

Die Ausstellung »This Is Tomorrow« gilt als die Geburtsstunde der Pop-Art. Inspiriert von Mode, Stadtleben
und Massenmedien stellte die Independent Group
ihre Ideen der Öffentlichkeit vor und interpretierte das
Medium Ausstellung neu: »Sie war provisorisch, ortsge-
bunden, nicht käuflich und in besonderer Weise durch
die Wahrnehmungsformen der Besucher definiert.«[7]

*Now, the »This Is Tomorrow« exhibition is considered
the birth of Pop Art. Inspired by fashion, city life and the
mass media, the Independent Group presented their
ideas to the public and reinterpreted the exhibition as
a medium in its own right: »It was provisional, location-
bound, non-commercial and defined by the visitors'
modes of perception in a rather unique way.«[7]*

2.40

17.04.1958–19.10.1958
Philips-Pavillon, Exposition universelle et internatio-
nale de Bruxelles, Brüssel, B
*Büro Corbusier: Le Corbusier, Edgar Varèse (concept);
Iannis Xenakis (architecture)*
temporary exhibition

Le Corbusier verwischte im »Philips-Pavillon« auf der
Expo 1958 die Grenzen zwischen Ausstellungsarchi-
tektur und Exponat. Das »Elektronische Gedicht«, ein
Zusammenspiel aus Architektur, Projektion, Licht und
Musik, zeigte die Geschichte der Menschheit als Pano-
rama und war ein technisches Meisterwerk als erste
elektronisch gesteuerte Multimedia-Umgebung in der
Geschichte der Ausstellung.

*Le Corbusier used the »Philips Pavilion« at the Expo
1958 to blur the boundaries between exhibition architecture and the exhibit. The »electronic poem« was an
interplay of architecture, projection, light and music,
unveiling a panorama of the history of humanity and as
the first electronically-controlled multimedia environment
in the history of the World Expos constituted a technical
masterpiece.*

2.41

>> 050 reviews p.148

7 *Klüser, Bernd; Hegewisch, Katharina
(Eds.): Die Kunst der Ausstellung. Eine
Dokumentation dreißig exemplarischer
Kunstausstellungen dieses Jahrhun-
derts. Frankfurt am Main, Leipzig
1991, p.126.*

Kai-Uwe Hemken

1960–1970

Konflikt zwischen den Generationen in den 1960er Jahren: Die Jugend verlangt Liberalismus, Toleranz, Frieden und das Aufgeben konservativer Wertvorstellungen, während die ältere Generation, an den Schalthebeln der Macht sitzend, mit aller Härte gegen die Forderungen vorgeht – Ernennung John F. Kennedys zum US-Präsidenten am 20. Januar 1961 – Ermordung John F. Kennedys am 22. November 1963 – Protestmarsch gegen Rassendiskriminierung in den USA, Martin Luther Kings Rede »I have a dream«, Beginn der Bürgerrechtsbewegung in den USA, Aufhebung der Rassentrennung in den USA – 17 afrikanische Staaten erhalten ihre Unabhängigkeit – Beginn einer Welle der Zwangskollektivierung in der DDR – Mauerbau in Berlin, erste Todesschüsse an der Mauer – Invasion in der Schweinebucht vor Kuba scheitert, Kuba-Krise – Vatikanisches Konzil: Innerkirchliche Reformen nach gesellschaftlichen Veränderungen – Studentische Protestbewegung in Deutschland kritisiert gesellschaftliche Verhältnisse und führt zu Umbrüchen in der gesellschaftlichen Entwicklung – Kalter Krieg wird in Asien weitergeführt: Vietnam-Krise – Konservative Kulturrevolution in China – Koalition von CDU/CSU und SPD (Große Koalition) – Studentenproteste in ganz Europa, studentische Demonstrationen in Deutschland, Tod des Studenten Benno Ohnesorg, Radikalisierung des Studentenprotestes: Sachbeschädigung – Formierung der Roten Armee Fraktion – »Prager Frühling« durch sowjetische Truppen gestoppt – Landung auf dem Mond durch die USA – Woodstock-Festival und Etablierung der Hippiebewegung – Erste sozialliberale Koalition, Willy Brandt wird Bundeskanzler – Beginn der Entspannungspolitik – Friedensbewegung formiert sich – Rasanter Innovationsschub der westeuropäischen Kunstentwicklung, Entstehung einer Vielzahl von Kunstströmungen in den USA und Europa: Pop-Art, Land-Art, Minimal Art, Concept-Art, Aktionskunst – Fundamentale Akzentverschiebungen in den kunsttheoretischen Grundlagen: Kritik an gesellschaftlichen Prozessen und Strukturen, Kritik am Kunstbetrieb (Handel, Museen, Kunstkritik etc.), Wandel des Kunstbegriffs – Grundsteinlegung für die Nationalgalerie, ein Museum für die Kunst des 20. Jahrhunderts (Architekt: Ludwig Mies van der Rohe, 1968) in West-Berlin – Teilnahme Deutschlands an der Biennale in Venedig in den Jahren 1960, 1962, 1964 und 1968 – Einweihung der Neuen Philharmonie in Berlin (Architekt: Hans Scharoun) – Boom der Modewelle »Swinging London« – Die Musik der Beatles und Rolling Stones wird frenetisch gefeiert – Filme wie »Die Vögel«, »James Bond« und »Cleopatra« erobern die Leinwand, Filme wie »Psycho« werden heftig diskutiert – Etablierung der Pille als Mittel der Empfängnisverhütung – Juri Gagarin als erster Mensch im Orbit

1960–1970

Conflict between the generations in the 1960s: the youth demands liberalism, tolerance, peace and the abandoning of conservative ideals, whereas the older generation, which was in charge in the corridors of power, dealt with the demands with an iron hand – John F. Kennedy sworn in as US President on January 20, 1961 – assassination of John F. Kennedy on November 22, 1963 – Protest march against racial discrimination in the USA, Martin Luther King's speech »I have a dream«, start of the civil rights movement in the USA, abolition of racial segregation in the USA – 17 African countries are given independence – beginning of a wave of compulsory collectivization in East Germany – building of the Wall in Berlin, first fatal shots by the Wall – invasion in the Bay of Pigs in Cuba fails, Cuban crisis – Vatican Council: Reforms within the Church following changes in society – student protest movement in Germany criticizes social conditions and leads to upheavals in society – Cold War continued in Asia: Vietnam crisis – Conservative cultural revolution in China – coalition of Conservatives (CDU/CSU) and Social Democrats (SPD) (Grand Coalition) – student protests throughout Europe, student demonstrations in Germany, death of the student Benno Ohnesorg, radicalization of the student protest: material damage – formation of the Red Army Faction – »Prague spring« halted by Soviet troops – the USA puts a man on the moon – Woodstock festival and emergence of the Hippie movement – first Social Democrat/Liberal coalition, Willy Brandt becomes Federal Chancellor – beginning of the policy of détente – peace movement forms – Rapid innovation surge in Western European art, emergence of a number of art movements in the USA and Europe: Pop Art, Land Art, Minimal Art, Concept Art, Action Art – fundamental shifts of accent in the basic theories of art: criticism of social processes and structures, criticism of the art business (tradeart, museums, criticism etc.), change in the perception of art – laying of the foundation stone for the »Nationalgalerie«, a 20th-century art museum (architect: Ludwig Mies van der Rohe, 1968) in West Berlin – Germany attends the Venice Biennale in 1960, 1962, 1964 and 1968 – official opening of the »Neue Philharmonie« in Berlin (architect: Hans Scharoun) – boom in the »swinging London« fashion wave – the music of The Beatles and The Rolling Stones frenetically received – films such as »The Birds«, »James Bond« and »Cleopatra« conquer the big screen, while films such as »Psycho« are the subject of intense discussion – the pill becomes established as a method of contraception – Yuri Gagarin is the first person to journey into outer space

1961

8 *Cf. Koenig, Gloria: Eames. Köln, London et al. 2005, p.73.*

9 *Cf. kunstwissen.de: Claes Oldenburg, URL: http://www.kunstwissen.de/ fach/f-kuns/o_mod/oldenb0.htm., 29.06.2010.*

1961
California Museum of Science and Industry,
Los Angeles, USA
Eames Office: Ray Eames / Charles Eames
information, temporary exhibition

Die »Mathematica« war ein ungewöhnliches Beispiel für die Vermittlung von Wissenschaft durch intellektuelle Unterhaltung. Unterstützt von IBM, gestaltete das Büro Eames einen Themenpark zu mathematischen Problemen und deren Lösungen, die durch Schrifttafeln, Anschauungsmaterial und interaktive Erklärungshilfen vermittelt wurden.[8]

»Mathematica« is an unusual example of the promotion of science by means of intellectual entertainment. With support from IBM, the Eames' company created a theme park consisting of mathematical puzzles and their solutions; these were displayed using panels, illustrative materials and interactive explanations.[8]

01.12.1961–31.12.1962
East Second Street, New York, USA
Claes Oldenburg
experiment, temporary exhibition

Auf die Proteste gegen serienmäßig hergestellte Waren 1961 in New York City reagierte Claes Oldenburg mit einem »Galerie-Performance-Environment-Atelier-Laden«[9]: The Store. Hier präsentierte er dreidimensionale Objekte aus Draht, Gips und Farbe und erzielte mit seiner Kunstausstellung einen szenografischen Wendepunkt, indem er die Exponate wie in einem Gemischtwarenladen inszenierte.

The 1961 protests against the mass production of consumer goods in New York City certainly evoked a response from Claes Oldenburg – with him choosing the form of a »gallery-performance-environment-studio-store«[9]: The Store. There he exhibited three-dimensional objects made of wire, plaster cast and paint; in this way, he brought about a scenographic watershed, in that he showcased the exhibits in the same way a general store would present its goods.

> 053
Dylaby.
Ein dynamisches Labyrinth

> 054
Vie d'acqua da Milano al mare

1962

1963

09.1962
Stedelijk Museum, Amsterdam, NL
*Willem Sandberg (curator); Jean Tinguely, Niki de Saint
Phalle, Daniel Spoerri, Martial Raysse, Per Olof Ultvedt,
Robert Rauschenberg (artist)*
art, temporary exhibition

Wie eine Schaubude wurde »Dylaby« von sechs Künstlern mit zuvor gefundenen Materialien vom Trödel,
Schrottplätzen oder der Straße direkt im Museum
geschaffen. »Eine künstliche Strandszene mit Jukebox,
ein stockdunkles Labyrinth, ein Schießstand, ein auf die
Seite gekippter Museumssaal und andere Überraschungen«[10] forderten die Besucher zum Mitmachen auf.

*Like a show booth, »Dylaby« was created on site at the
Stedelijk museum by six artists using materials they
had found at flea markets, scrap yards or on the street.
»An artificial beach scene with a jukebox, a pitch-black
labyrinth, a firing range, a museum hall turned on its
side, among other surprises,«[10] required the visitors to
interact with the exhibition itself.*

>> 053 reviews p.156

15.10.1963–30.11.1963
Palazzo Reale, Mailand, I
Achille Castiglioni, Piergiacomo Castiglioni
topical, temporary exhibition

Als Lösung für ein Wirtschaftsproblem entstand ein
effizientes Binnenschifffahrt-System, das in Mailand
räumlich erlebbar war. Raue Holzbretter an Böden und
Wänden bildeten Räume, Gänge, Öffnungen, Fenster
und Borde, auf denen die bunte Masse an Exponaten
ihren Raum fand, und erzählten ihre Geschichte.

*An efficient cargo system for inland waterways was
created as the solution to an economic problem, and
then made into a spatial experience in Milan. Raw
wooden beams on the floor and walls formed rooms,
walkways, openings, windows and decks, on which the
colorful mass of exhibits were displayed, and were
able to tell their stories.*

10 *Cf. Schneede, Uwe M.: Die
Geschichte der Kunst im 20. Jahrhun-
dert: Von den Avantgarden bis zur
Gegenwart. München 2001, p.207.*

2.42 *Beuys' Stallausstellung /*
Photo: Fritz Getlinger, VG Bild-Kunst,
Bonn 2014

26.10.1963–24.11.1963
Hause van der Grinten, Kranenburg Niederrhein, D
Hans van der Grinten, Franz Joseph van der Grinten,
Joseph Beuys
art, temporary exhibition

Die legendäre Beuys-Ausstellung zeigte 282 Werke in
den leer stehenden Ställen der Familie van der Grinten.
Sie hingen an Nägeln, standen in Nischen oder auf Käs-
ten und Vorsprüngen. Typische Anordnungsmuster wurden nicht beachtet, denn Beuys nutzte zur Präsentation
einfach alles, was vorhanden war und wo er Platz fand.

This legendary Beuys exhibition unveiled 282 works in a
series of empty stables belonging to the van der Grinten
family. They were hung using nails, placed in niches, on
boxes or balanced on ledges. Taking no notice of conven-
tional arrangement patterns, Beuys simply used anything
available to him, any free space, to display his exhibits.

2.42

1964
Sezione Italiana, XIII Triennale di Milano, Palazzo dell'
Arte, Mailand, I
Gae Aulenti, Carlo Aymonino
temporary exhibition

13. Architektur-Triennale in Mailand: Gae Aulenti gestaltete den preisgekrönten italienischen Pavillon und
stellte das Thema Freizeit kritisch und gleichzeitig sinnlich dar. Invasion und Zerstörung der Landschaft, aber
auch Momente des Glücks wurden auf provozierende
Weise gezeigt, zum Beispiel der Weg zum Meer, lebens-
froh durch dynamische Figuren Picassos symbolisiert.

The 13th Architecture Triennial in Milan: Gae Aulenti
designed the prize-winning Italian pavilion, critically revi-
siting the fair's theme (recreation) while simultaneously
stimulating the senses. The invasion and destruction
of the countryside, but moments of happiness too,
appeared in a provocative display, for example the route
to the sea, symbolized full of life using dynamic figures
painted by Picasso.

> 057

Exposition nationale suisse de 1964

30.04.1964–25.10.1964
Lausanne, CH
temporary exhibition

Die Expo 64 präsentierte ihren zehn Millionen Besuchern eine moderne Schweiz. Sie nutzte futuristisch wirkende Fortbewegungsmittel, brachte ihre Besucher mit dem Unterseeboot Mesoscaphe von Auguste Piccard in die Tiefen des Genfersees und setzte das Medium Film offensiv und sehr kreativ ein.

Expo 64 presented a modern Switzerland to its ten million visitors. The show included futuristic means of transportation, used the Mesoscaphe submarine by Auguste Piccard to transport visitors to the depths of Lake Geneva, and made powerful and highly creative use of the medium of film.

> 058

Chemistry – for a safer Future: Looking Ahead to the Year 2000

1967

1967
Montecatini Pavillon, Fiera di Milano, Mailand, I
Achille Castiglioni, Piergiacomo Castiglioni
temporary exhibition

Im ersten, scheinbar leeren Raum der Ausstellung über den Chemiekonzern Montecatini und seine Visionen gestalteten die Castiglioni-Brüder in der bis auf 2 m abgehängten Decke ein umgekehrtes »Labyrinth«. Der Boden des zweiten Raumes war verspiegelt und wirkte unendlich. Die überraschten und faszinierten Besucher wurden Teil der Ausstellung.

In the first, seemingly empty hall in this exhibition on the Italian chemical company Montecatini, the Castiglioni brothers installed an upside-down »labyrinth« from the ceiling, which had been lowered to only two meters. The floor in the second hall was mirrored and so appeared infinite, leading the surprised and fascinated visitors to become part of the exhibition themselves.

1969

2.43 Hugo Kükelhaus und sein
Strudelgerät auf der Interschul 1967
in Dortmund.
*Hugo Kükelhaus and his strudel device
at Interschul 1967 in Dortmund*
© Stadtarchiv Soest, Nachlass Hugo
Kükelhaus (VG Bild-Kunst, Bonn 2014),
P 56.83

28.04.1967–27.10.1967
Deutscher Pavillon, Universal and International
Exhibition Montreal. Expo 67, Montreal, CA
Hugo Kükelhaus
experimental, temporary exhibition

Mit dieser als »Naturkundliches Spielwerk« erlebnis-
pädagogisch angelegten Ausstellung sollten die Sinne
der Besucher spielerisch »reaktiviert« werden. Etwa
35 ausgetüftelte Spielgeräte forderten den Besucher
auf, seine Sinne zu nutzen, zu experimentieren und
zu erproben. Hugo Kükelhaus entwickelte einen ganz
eigenen Zugang zu Erfahrungsfeldern und wurde
Wegbereiter der heutigen »Mitmachausstellungen« und
Science-Center.

*This exhibition, entitled a »Field of Experience to Develop
the Senses«, was based upon experiential learning and
set out to »reactivate« the visitors through play. Around
35 elaborate »experience stops« encouraged the visitor
to use their senses, experiment and explore. Hugo Kükelhaus had developed a very unique approach to fields
of experience and became a pioneer for what we today
know as »interactive exhibitions« and science centers.*

02.03.1969–27.04.1969
Kunsthalle Bern, Bern, CH
Harald Szeemann
experimental, traveling exhibition

Viele Arbeiten der legendären Wanderausstellung
»Wenn Attitüden Form werden« entstanden erst vor
Ort im Museum. Harald Szeemann schuf mit ihr eine
neue Form der Inszenierung. Die chronologische oder
thematische Darstellung stand nicht im Vordergrund,
vielmehr stellte die ungewöhnliche Konzeption die
Arbeiten in einen neuen, spannungsreichen Dialog
zueinander.

*Many works from the legendary traveling exhibition
»When attitudes become form« were site-specific, produced in the museum. Harald Szeemann used them to
create a new system for exhibition presentation. It was
not the chronological or thematic representation that
took pride of place, but instead this unusual exhibition
concept sought to present the works in a new, exciting
dialogue with one another.*

2.43

>> 059 reviews p.160

> 061
Kugelauditorium

> 062
Musée d'Art Moderne, Départment des Aigles:
Section des Figures:
Der Adler vom Oligozän bis heute

1970

1972

15.03.1970–13.09.1970
Deutscher Pavillon, Nippon Bankoku Hakurankai
Japan World Exposition. »Expo 70«, Osaka, J
Karlheinz Stockhausen, Otto Piene
experimental, temporary exhibition

Der bislang einzigartige kugelförmige Konzertsaal
ermöglichte zum ersten Mal die dreidimensionale Wie-
dergabe von Musik: Bach, Beethoven und Live-Konzerte
wurden als elektro-akustische Raumkompositionen
wiedergegeben. Hunderte von Lautsprechern gestalteten
die Ausstellung.

The spherical concert hall, which remains unique in
shape to this day, enabled organizers to have music
played three-dimensionally for the very first time: Bach,
Beethoven, and live concerts were to be heard as electro-
acoustic spatial compositions. The exhibition itself was
outfitted with hundreds of loudspeakers.

16.05.1972–09.07.1972
Kunsthalle Düsseldorf, Düsseldorf, D
Marcel Broodthaers
temporary exhibition

Das »Musée d'Art Moderne, Départment des Aigles«,
1968 gegründet, war ein fiktives Museum auf Zeit.
Der Adler war nicht nur Inhalt, sondern Konzept und
Sammlungsmethode. 1972 zeigte Broodthaers die
»Section des Figures«: 300 Exponate, die einen Adler
darstellten oder abbildeten, ohne chronologische oder
inhaltliche Ordnung.

The »Musée d'Art Moderne, Départment des Aigles«,
founded in 1968, was a temporary, fictional museum.
The eagle not only made for its content, but also the
concept and collection methodology. In 1972, Marcel
Broodthaers presented his »Section des figures«:
300 exhibits representing or depicting eagles, with no
systematic arrangement, be it chronological or in terms
of content.

2.44

Kai-Uwe Hemken

1970–1980

Kennzeichen der 1970er Jahre in Deutschland: die Entspannungspolitik Willy Brandts, der Linksterrorismus und eine allgemeine Protestbewegung, u. a. die Frauenemanzipation sowie die Kritik an der Kernenergie und der Umweltzerstörung – Erste Erfolge der Entspannungspolitik Willy Brandts zwischen Ost und West, dennoch heftige Kritik in Deutschland – Gründung und erste Aktionen der Umweltorganisation Greenpeace – Die deutsche Frauenbewegung wird bundesweit aktiv und findet breite Unterstützung in der Bevölkerung – Terroranschlag während der Olympiade in München (1972) – Ölkrise in Deutschland – Landung einer unbemannten russischen Raumkapsel auf dem Mond – Die USA und Vietnam beenden ihren Krieg – Watergate-Affäre in den USA – Willy Brandt tritt als Bundeskanzler wegen der Guillaume-Spionageaffäre zurück – Unterzeichnung der KSZE-Schlussakte zur internationalen Friedenssicherung – Aktionen der RAF-Gruppe und die staatliche Terrorbekämpfung (Rasterfahndung) weiten sich aus – Entführung eines deutschen Flugzeugs nach Mogadischu und Erpressung der Freilassung von inhaftierten Mitgliedern der RAF (»Deutscher Herbst«) – Erste Direktwahlen des Europäischen Parlaments – Rückzug der USA aus Vietnam, Militärputsch in Chile und Portugal – Einleitung eines Friedensprozesses im Nahen Osten auf der Konferenz in Camp David (USA) – Der Iran wird ein islamischer Gottesstaat – Amerikanische und sowjetische Raumschiffe treffen sich im All – Keine Gruppenbildungen oder neuen Strömungen in der Kunst, sondern Diskursthemen wie Feminismus, Körperlichkeit, Politik, Sexualität, Homosexualität und Gewalt – Eröffnung der documenta 5 und 6 in Kassel, die Ausstellung »Spurensicherung« initiiert eine fortgesetzte künstlerische Auseinandersetzung mit der deutschen Geschichte – Entlassung Joseph Beuys' als Professor an der Kunstakademie Düsseldorf – Eröffnung des »Centre National d'Art et de Culture Georges Pompidou« in Paris – Entdeckung der Terrakotta-Armee in China

1970–1980

Characteristics of the 1970s in Germany: Willy Brandt's policy of détente, left-wing terrorism and a general protest movement, including women's liberation and criticism of nuclear energy and the destruction of the environment – first success for Willy Brandt's policy of détente between East and West, though hefty criticism in Germany – founding of the environmental organization Greenpeace and first direct actions – the German women's liberation movement becomes active nationwide and enjoys wide support among the population – terrorist attack during the Olympic Games in Munich (1972) – oil crisis in Germany – an unmanned Russian space capsule lands on the moon – the war between the USA and Vietnam ends – Watergate affair in the USA – Willy Brandt resigns as Federal Chancellor because of the Guillaume espionage affair – signing of the Final Act of the Conference on Security and Co-operation in Europe to secure international peace – RAF activity and state combating of terrorism (profiling) increase – a German aircraft is hijacked to Mogadishu and held to ransom to secure the release of imprisoned members of the RAF (»Deutscher Herbst« (German Autumn)) – first direct elections to the European Parliament – the USA withdraws from Vietnam, military putsch in Chile and Portugal – initiation of a peace process in the Middle East at the conference in Camp David (USA) – Iran becomes an Islamic theocracy – American and Soviet spaceships meet in space – no formation of groups or new currents in art, but rather topics of discourse such as feminism, physicality, politics, sexuality, homosexuality and violence – opening of documenta 5 and 6 in Kassel, the exhibition »Spurensicherung« (Forensics) initiates a present-day artistic investigation of German history –Joseph Beuys dismissed as Professor at the Düsseldorf Academy of Art – opening of the »Centre National d'Art et de Culture Georges Pompidou« in Paris – discovery of the Terracotta Army in China

1975

30.06.1972–08.10.1972
documenta 5, Museum Fridericianum, Kassel, D
Herbert Distel
art, permanent exhibition

Auf der documenta bekam man einen ersten Eindruck vom kleinsten Museum jener Zeit: Ein alter Nähseidenspulenkasten mit 20 Schubladen und jeweils 25 Fächern bildete 500 kleine Ausstellungsräume, die von zeitgenössischen Künstlern gestaltet wurden. 1977 wurde das Schubladenmuseum fertiggestellt und zeigt bis heute moderne Kunst des 20. Jahrhunderts.

At the documenta, visitors were afforded a first glimpse at the smallest museum of its time: An old sewing spool cabinet with 20 drawers each containing 25 compartments made for 500 small exhibition spaces, which were filled with works by contemporary artists. In 1977, the Museum of Drawers was completed and continues to be used to display modern 20th-century art to this day.

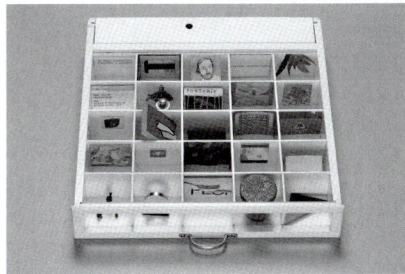

2.45

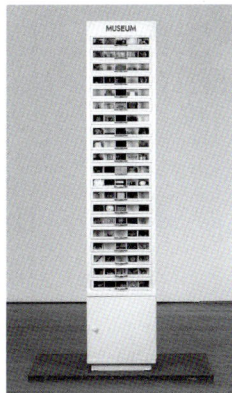

2.46

05.07.1975–17.08.1975
Kunsthalle Bern, Bern, CH
Harald Szeemann
experimental, traveling exhibition

Die visionäre Wanderausstellung reiste quer durch Europa. Kurator Harald Szeemann visualisierte »geistesgeschichtliche Hintergründe technischer und gesellschaftlicher Umwälzungen« über den Mythos der Junggesellenmaschine und leistete als »Regisseur« Pionierarbeit für zukünftige Ausstellungsinszenierungen.

This visionary traveling exhibition toured the entire European continent. Curator Harald Szeemann visualized »intellectual backdrops to technological and social change« on the myth of the »bachelor machine« and as the »director« created an exhibition that would prove pioneering for exhibition presentation of the future.

2.47

1976

1977

1976
Wiener Festwochen, Wien, A
Coop Himmelb(l)au
temporary exhibition

Der Wiener »Supersommer« war ein Konzept zur
Stadtveränderung. Das Thema Ausstellungsarchitektur
wurde in den freien Stadtraum verlagert. Ausstellungen
im öffentlichen Raum sollten »Spielplatz für die Bürger«
sein, sie sollten die Stadt wieder in Besitz nehmen
und aus ihrer Starre lösen. Die Aktionen haben Spuren
hinterlassen und prägen Wien bis heute.

*The Viennese »Super Summer« was a concept for urban
change. Exhibition architecture as a theme was thus
relocated outdoors and into the urban space. Such
exhibitions held in the public sphere were intended as
»playgrounds for their citizens« with the idea being
that they reclaimed the city and shook the citizens out
of their perspectival stupor. These interventions left a
lasting mark on the city, still evident in Vienna of today.*

2.48

2.49

26.03.1977–05.06.1977
Württembergisches Landesmuseum,
Stuttgart, D
historic, temporary exhibition

Diese Ausstellung war die erste große Geschichtsschau
über die Staufer. Sie zeigte viele Elemente aus der
Geschichte, Kunst und Kultur dieser Epoche. Die un-
zähligen Ausstellungsexponate füllten fünf Bände des
sehr beeindruckenden Kataloges und erstmals kamen
hunderttausende Besucher zu einer einzigen Wechsel-
ausstellung.

*This exhibition was the first large-scale presentation of
the history of the Hohenstaufen dynasty and unveiled
elements of the period's history, art and culture. The
seemingly endless exhibits filled five volumes of a highly
impressive exhibition catalog, while the one-time, temporary exhibition itself attracted hundreds of thousands
of visitors.*

2.50

1978

1979

02.1978–heute
Berkeley Art Museum, California, USA
James Elliott
art, experimental, permanent exhibition

Das Konzept dieser permanenten, sich aber stetig ver-ändernden Ausstellung sieht sechs bis acht individuelle Ausstellungen mit zeitgenössischer Kunst pro Jahr vor. So wurden in den letzten dreißig Jahren über 230 Matrix-Shows von internationalen avantgardistischen Künstlern gezeigt; die erste mit dem Titel »Matrix 1: Cones« im Jahr 1978 von Kurator Michael Auping und Künstlerin Ursula Schneider.

The concept behind this permanent yet continually evolv-ing exhibition is designed to host six to eight individual exhibitions of contemporary art each year. And so, over 230 Matrix shows by international artists of the avant-garde have been displayed there of the past 30 years; the first of them, entitled »Matrix 1: Cones«, took place in 1978 and was organized by curator Michael Auping and artist Ursula Schneider.

2.51

2.52

18.03.1979–29.04.1979
Kölnischer Kunstverein, Köln, D
Marie-Louise Plessen, Daniel Spoerri,
Cologne college students
historic, temporary exhibition

Die Ausstellung, in der Geschichte mit Geschichten erzählt wurde, war Querschnitt und Streifzug durch die Stadtgeschichte Kölns. Die 250 Exponate zu rund 120 Stichworten waren alphabetisch geordnet von Adenauer bis Zoo. Das »Musée Sentimental« ist bis heute als Aus-stellungsprinzip bekannt.

Using individual stories to convey history, the exhibition provided a cross-section of Cologne's history as well as taking visitors on a journey through it. The 250 exhibits corresponding to around 120 key words were arranged in alphabetical order – from Adenauer to Zoo. The »Musée Sentimental« remains a well-known exhibition principle even today.

2.53

>> 068 reviews p.168

1980

1980
I Mostra internazionale d'architettura, Corderie,
Venedig, I
architecture, temporary exhibition

Die Strada Novissima war eine kulissenartige Straße
aus Fassaden internationaler Architekten. Ihre Gestaltung brach mit der bis dahin sehr zurückhaltenden
Ausstellungsarchitektur und setzte neue Maßstäbe.
Je nach Blickwinkel war sie »eine schaurig-schöne,
grässlich-ordinäre, populistisch-aggressive Angelegen-
heit«[11] und erinnerte an die »Straßen der Nationen« der
Weltausstellungen Ende des 19. Jahrhunderts.

The Strada Novissima was a street resembling those
found on film sets, made up of a series of façades
designed by a number of international architects. These
designs broke away from the hitherto, rather restrained
conventions of exhibition architecture and set new
standards in the field. Depending on the angle, it was a
»spookily-beautiful, ghastly-ordinary, populist-aggres-
sive subject matter«[11] and reminiscent of the »streets of
nations« at the world expositions that took place at the
end of the 19th century.

27.06.1980–05.10.1980
Linz, A
Helmuth Gsöllpointner, Angela Hareiter,
Laurids Ortner, Peter Baum
experimental, temporary exhibition

Wie beeinflusst Design den Menschen im Alltag? Das
»Forum Design« entwickelte dazu einen provisorisch
wirkenden Ausstellungsbau mit waggonähnlichen
Pavillons, die zum Schutz mit einer weißen Kunststoff-
haut überzogen waren. Es entstand eine Einführung ins
Thema mit der Vorstellung von Konzepten und Entwürfen
führender Designer. Das Forum war ein Meilenstein in
der Geschichte des Designs.

How does design influence people's everyday lives?
In answer to this question, »Forum Design« constructed
a seemingly makeshift exhibition building with wagon-like
pavilions fitted with white plastic covers to protect them
from the elements. The result was an introduction to the
theme that presented concepts and designs by leading
designers. The forum is now considered a milestone in
design history.

11 *Werner, Frank R. (Ed.): Hans Dieter*
Schaal. In-Between. Ausstellungsarchi-
tektur. Stuttgart, London 1999, p.23.

2.54

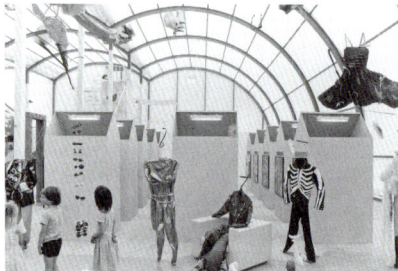
2.55

Kai-Uwe Hemken

1980–1990

Prägung der 1980er Jahre in Deutschland durch die sogenannte »geistig-moralische Wende« (Helmut Kohl): Konservatismus, Primat der Ökonomie und Rückzug des Sozialstaatsprinzips, Wirtschaftsboom, allgemeine Technisierung – Machtwechsel in Bonn: Helmut Kohl (CDU) wird Bundeskanzler – Fall der Mauer (1989), Öffnung der innerdeutschen Grenze – Zugleich Formierung der Postmoderne als kritische Revision des bisherigen Moderne-Konzeptes und ihr Vordringen in alle Sparten des gesellschaftlichen Lebens (Kunst, Design, Architektur, Wissenschaft, Politik, Philosophie) – Jugendbewegung des Punk und New Wave, besonders in Berlin – Öffentliche Debatte um die Freiheit der Kunst, ausgelöst durch den »Sprayer von Zürich«, Harald Naegeli – Jahrzehnt der Museumsneugründungen in Deutschland: Frankfurt, Stuttgart, Köln; besondere Rolle des »Museumsufers« in Frankfurt am Main mit zahlreichen Museumsbauten – Boom der Pop-Musik, Verbreitung der Punk- und New-Wave-Musik, Etablierung der Kunstbewegung »Neue Wilde«, Wiederentdeckung der Malerei und Abgrenzung zur »Verwissenschaftlichung« der Kunst, insbesondere der amerikanischen Kunstszene – Skandal: Aufdeckung der Fälschung von Hitler-Tagebüchern, die der »Stern« veröffentlicht hatte – Ausstrahlung der Programme erster kommerzieller Fernsehsender (Pro7, Sat.1, RTL, 3sat) – Boom von Musical-Aufführungen: »Cats« (Hamburg), »Starlight Express« (Bochum) – Öffentliche Austragung des Historikerstreits um die Singularität der nationalsozialistischen Judenvernichtung (Hauptkontrahenten: Jürgen Habermas und Ernst Nolte) – Massenproteste gegen Rüstung sowie Friedenskundgebungen in Deutschland – Wettlauf im Weltraum: USA und die Sowjetunion ringen um die technische Vormachtstellung im All – Mordanschlag auf Papst Johannes Paul II. – Misslungener Putschversuch des Militärs in Spanien – Michail S. Gorbatschow wird Generalsekretär der KPdSU und leitet die weltweit bedeutsame Reformpolitik ein – USA greifen Libyen an – Atomunfall im Kernkraftwerk Tschernobyl – Massiver Anstieg von Aids-Erkrankungen – Wiedereröffnung der Semperoper in Dresden nach ihrer Zerstörung im Zweiten Weltkrieg – Versteigerung des Gemäldes »Schwertlilien« von Vincent van Gogh in New York für 90 Millionen Dollar – Einweihung der Glaspyramide des Louvre in Paris

1980–1990

The 1980s in Germany were dominated by what was known as the »intellectual and moral turnaround« (Helmut Kohl): Conservatism, the primacy of the economy and the withdrawal of the welfare state principle, an economic boom, general mechanization – change of power in Bonn: Helmut Kohl (CDU) becomes Federal Chancellor – the Wall comes down (1989), opening of the inner-German border – at the same time emergence of post-Modernism, a critical revision of the previous concept of Modernism that penetrated all facets of social life (art, design, architecture, academia, politics, philosophy) – the youth embraces Punk and New Wave, especially in Berlin – public debate about the freedom of art, triggered by the »Sprayer of Zurich«, Harald Naegeli – decade of new museums being founded in Germany: Frankfurt, Stuttgart, Cologne; special role of the »Museumsufer« (museum river bank) in Frankfurt/Main with numerous museums – boom in Pop music, spread of Punk and New Wave music, the art movement »Neue Wilde« (new wild things) established, rediscovery of painting and differentiation from an increasingly academic approach to art, in particular the American art scene – scandal: revelation that Hitler's diaries published by »Stern« magazine were a fake – the first commercial TV stations go on air (Pro7, Sat.1, RTL, 3sat) – boom in musical productions: »Cats« (Hamburg), »Starlight Express« (Bochum) – public »Historians' Debate« on the singularity of the Nazi annihilation of the Jews (major voices for and against: Jürgen Habermas and Ernst Nolte) – Mass protests against armament, and peace rallies in Germany – space race: the USA and the Soviet Union fight for technical supremacy in space – assassination attempt on Pope John Paul II – failed military putsch in Spain – Mikhail Gorbachev becomes Secretary-General of the Communist Party of the Soviet Union and introduces the policy of reform that becomes significant for the world as a whole – USA attacks Libya – nuclear accident in the power station in Chernobyl – massive rise in the number of cases of AIDS – Having been destroyed in the World War II the Semper Opera House reopens in Dresden – Vincent van Gogh's painting »Irises« auctioned in New York for US$ 90 million – official opening of the glass pyramid at the Louvre in Paris

1981

1983

12 Cf. Ein Gespräch mit Gottfried Korff.
in: Reinhardt, Uwe J.; Teufel, Philipp:
Neue Ausstellungsgestaltung 01 / New
Exhibition Design 01. Ludwigsburg
2007, p.34.

2.56 © Margret Nissen

2.57 © Luc Bernard, VG Bild-Kunst,
Bonn 2014

2.58 © Georg Riha

15.08.1981–15.11.1981
Martin-Gropius-Bau, Berlin, D
Manfred Schlenke, Gottfried Korff,
Karl Ernst Herrmann, Jan Fiebelkorn
historic, temporary exhibition

»Preußen« war eine der ersten kulturhistorischen
Ausstellungen, die versuchten, sich von den »Wand-
tapeten« zu lösen und »begehbare Raumbilder zu
produzieren«, die aus originalen Relikten, nicht nur aus
Kunstwerken, sondern auch aus trivialen und alltäglichen Dingen der Vergangenheit arrangiert waren.[12]

»Prussia« was one of the first exhibitions on cultural
history that sought a break out of the mold of »wall-
paper« and instead »produce walk-through exhibits«.
These were arranged using original relics from the time;
not only artworks but trivial and everyday objects from
the past, too.[12]

2.56

1983
Künstlerhaus Wien, Wien, A
Hans Hollein
historic, temporary exhibition

Der 300. Jahrestag des Sieges über die Türken wurde
groß gefeiert. Hans Hollein verwandelte das Wiener
Künstlerhaus in ein überdimensionales Türkenzelt
und erzählte im Inneren die Geschichte mit beeindruckenden Panoramen und Bühnenbildern. Er gestaltete
eine kulturhistorische Ausstellung, die alle bisherigen
Maßstäbe sprengte.

The 300th anniversary of the victory over the Turks was
cause for great celebration and Hans Hollein transform-
ed the Viennese Künstlerhaus into a monumental
Turkish tent for the occasion. Using the tent's interior
to tell the story with breathtaking panoramas and set
designs, he in the process designed an art-history exhi-
bition that superseded all previous models.

2.57

2.58

1984

1985

29.09.1984–02.12.1984
Messe Düsseldorf, Düsseldorf, D
Kaspar König (curator); Hermann Czech (design)
art, temporary exhibition

In einer Messehalle zeigte die Ausstellung »Neue deutsche Kunst« Plastiken, Gemälde, Grafik, Objektkunst und Installationen. Das Besondere war die Ausstellungsarchitektur: eine Stadtlandschaft mit Straßen, Plätzen und Cafés, erschlossen über eine Außentreppe, von der die Besucher sich einen Überblick verschaffen und dann durch die Ausstellung flanieren konnten.

In 1984, a trade fair hall in Düsseldorf became the venue for the exhibition »New German Art«, which presented sculptures, paintings, prints, object art and installations. The exhibition's eye-catching feature was its architecture: a cityscape complete with streets, plazas and cafés, accessed via an external staircase, from which visitors were able to gain an overview of the exhibition before ambling through it.

03.1985–10.1985
Künstlerhaus Wien, Wien, A
Hans Hollein
temporary exhibition

Diese Ausstellung zeigte den Jugendstil in Wien mit dem Ziel, nicht nur Informationen, sondern auch Atmosphäre zu vermitteln. Traum und Wirklichkeit sprachen alle Sinne an und thematisierten nicht nur Kulturhistorisches, sondern zeigten auch die Stimmung dieser Zeit.

This exhibition presented examples of Art Nouveau to be found in Vienna and in doing so its objective was not only to convey the information but the atmosphere, too. Dream and reality appealed to each and every one of the senses, and with art history the very theme of the show, a strong attempt was made to recreate the mood of the time.

2.59–**2.60** *Messe Düsseldorf*

2.61–**2.62** *© Georg Riha*

2.59

2.61

2.60

2.62

> 075
Les Immatériaux

> 076
Berlin. Berlin.
Die Ausstellung zur Geschichte der Stadt

1987

2.63 © Centre Pompidou, Mnam,
Bibliothèque Kandinsky, Jean Claude
Planchet

2.64–2.65 © Reinhard Görner, Berlin

28.05.1985–15.07.1985
Centre Georges Pompidou, Paris, F
Jean-François Lyotard (curator); Thierry Chaput,
Philippe Délis (design)
topical, temporary exhibition

Obgleich ein Philosoph im Museum ungewöhnlich
scheint, setzte Jean-François Lyotard Zeichen für eine
neue Präsentationsästhetik und stellte seine philosophischen Ideen in den Vordergrund. Die Ausstellung
sprach Gefühle an; Sinn und Bedeutung sollte sich
jeder Besucher selbst erschließen.

Although a philosopher in the museum world may seem
a little strange, Jean-François Lyotard paved the way
for a new exhibition aesthetic and in doing so placed
great emphasis on his philosophical ideas. The exhibition
appealed to the visitors' emotions, although they were
left to reach their own conclusions on the sense and
meaning of it all.

2.63

>> 075 reviews p.176

15.08.1987–22.11.1987
Martin-Gropius-Bau, Berlin, D
Hans Dieter Schaal (design); Bodo-Michael Baumunk,
Gottfried Korff, Reinhard Rürup, Wolfgang Weik,
Marie-Louise von Plessen (curator)
temporary exhibition

Architektur, Lichtführung und 3.000 Exponate bildeten
das Bühnenbild der Stadtgeschichte Berlins. Die Architektur spielte im Ausstellungskonzept eine tragende
Rolle. Sie war sehr dominant, gab aber gleichzeitig den
Exponaten Raum, sodass trotz der Masse an Informationen die Neugier immer wieder geweckt wurde.

Architecture, lighting and a total of 3,000 exhibits came
together to create this set for the history of Berlin.
The architecture in particular played an eminent role
in the exhibition concept. On the one hand dominating
the space, it simultaneously afforded the exhibits
sufficient room to continually kindle the visitors' curiosity
and interest, despite the potentially overwhelming mass
of information.

2.64

2.65

1988

1987–1990
Grande Halle de La Villette, Paris, F
François Confino
traveling exhibition

Wie Statisten bewegten sich die Besucher in dieser Kinostadt, die aus Kulissen von Städteszenen großer Filme inszeniert und rekonstruiert worden war. In einen anderen Raum und eine andere Zeit versetzt erlebten sie die begehbaren Inszenierungen und wurden Teil der Ausstellung.

Like extras on a film set, visitors swarmed through this cinema city, made up of reconstructions of city scenes well-known to them from the great moments of the silver screen. Transported to another place and time, they were free to roam and explore the sets and thus became a part of the exhibition itself.

2.66

1988
Boijmans Van Beuningen, Rotterdam, NL
Harald Szeemann
art, temporary exhibition

Eine Sammlung mal anders präsentiert: »a-Historische klanken« zeigte eine Auswahl der Sammlung des Boijmans Van Beuningen Museums: Werke von Rubens, Bruegel, Beuys und anderen Meistern des 20. Jahrhunderts in ungewöhnlichen Kompositionen. Gemälde und Objekte sowie zahlreiche Stühle und Skulpturen lenkten die Aufmerksamkeit auf den Raum zwischen den Exponaten und bekamen eine neue Bedeutung.

Not your usual collection presentation: »a-Historische klanken« unveiled selected works taken from the Boijmans Van Beuningen Museum collection: works by Rubens, Bruegel, Beuys and other 20th-century art masters were presented in unusual compositions. Paintings and objects as well as numerous chairs and sculptures drew visitors' attention to the space between the exhibits and were thus given an entirely new meaning.

2.66 *© Atelier Confino / François Confino*

> 079
Stationen der Moderne:
Die bedeutenden Kunstausstellungen
des 20. Jahrhunderts in Deutschland

> 080
Machines à communiquer

1992

06.1988–08.1988
Berlinische Galerie, Berlin, D
Eberhard Roters, Bernhard Schulz, Jörn Merkert
art, temporary exhibition

In einer Ausstellung über Ausstellungen zeigte man
1988 in Berlin die bedeutendsten Kunstausstellungen
Deutschlands. Die Auswahl von 20 Ausstellungen aus
dem 20. Jahrhundert wurde im Gropius-Bau gezeigt
und zum Teil rekonstruiert.

In 1988, an exhibition about exhibitions presented the
most important art shows in Germany. This selection of
20 exhibitions from the 20th century were exhibited and
in part reconstructed for the event in Berlin's renowned
Martin Gropius Building.

2.67

12.07.1992–25.10.1992
Cité des Sciences et de l'Industrie, Paris, F
Ruedi Baur, Philippe Delis, Bob Stern
temporary exhibition

Die Kommunikationsmaschine, ein Zusammenspiel
aus Architektur, Grafik und Exponat, zeigte das Unter-
richtsthema »Informationsraum« der Ecole Nationale
Supérieure des Beaux-Arts. Alles wurde mit Texten
und Informationen bespielt, nur der Raum, der die Ein-
samkeit des Menschen als Konsequenz der Maschine
darstellte, enthielt keinen Text.

Machines à Communiquer (machines for communica-
tion) was an interplay of architecture, graphic design and
exhibits, and presented the Ecole Nationale Supérieure
des Beaux-Arts' curriculum theme: »information space«.
All exhibits were accompanied by text and information,
only the hall, which was intended as a portrayal of man's
loneliness as a consequence of machines, lacked any
form of commentary.

2.68

1993

01.10.1992–08.11.1992
Hofburg, Wien, A
Peter Greenaway
temporary exhibition

Die Ausstellung war ein Versuch, die Welt enzyklopädisch darzustellen. »Es sollte nichts ausgelassen werden – kein Material, keine Technik, keine Art, keine Wissenschaft, keine Kunst und keine Disziplin, keine Entwürfe, keine Illusion, kein Trick und Behelf …«.[13] Eine Idee, ein Thema, 100 Objekte als Repräsentation der Welt.

This exhibition was an attempt to depict the world in the same way as an encyclopedia. »Nothing should be omitted – no material, no piece of technology, no type, no science, no art and no discipline, no designs, no illusion, no trick or substitute…«[13] One idea, one theme, 100 objects to represent the world.

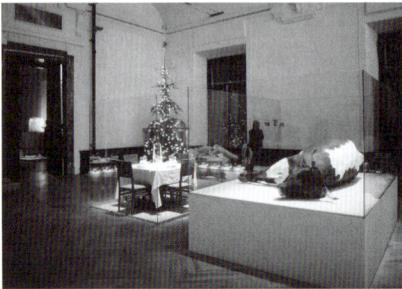
2.69

>> 081 reviews p.184

04.1993–today
Washington, D. C., USA
Ralph Appelbaum Associates
museum, permanent exhibition

Das grauenvolle Thema des Holocausts wird mit Geschichten aus dem wahren Leben erzählt. Die Wegführung, absichtlich eingeengt, lässt nur eine Richtung zu und führt an tausenden authentischen Artefakten vorbei. Die Ausstellung macht den Holocaust für die Besucher erlebbar.

A harrowing theme, the Holocaust, told using real-life stories. The route is clearly marked out for visitors, visibly narrowed, and only allows them to move in one direction. It leads them past thousands of genuine artifacts and thus makes the Holocaust palpable to the viewer.

2.70

>> 082 reviews p.192

13 *Greenaway, Peter: Einleitung, in: Greenaway, Peter: 100 Objekte zeigen die Welt. 100 Objects to represent the World. Wien 1992.*

2.69 *© Peter Greenaway*
Photo: Manu Luksch

2.70 *© Ralph Appelbaum Associates*

Kai-Uwe Hemken

1990-2000

Zentrale Ereignisse in Deutschland, die die gesellschaftlichen Prozesse bestimmen: der Fall der Mauer und die Wiedervereinigung der beiden deutschen Staaten – Zerfall der Sowjetunion, Jugoslawiens und der Tschechoslowakei – Erhebliche Zunahme rechtsextremer Gewalt (Hoyerswerda, Solingen), vornehmlich gegen Ausländer – Abzug alliierter Truppen aus Deutschland – Wahljahr mit insgesamt 19 Wahlen – Tod von Prinzessin Diana – Im Januar 1998 erhält die SPD die Mehrheit im Bundestag und löst den »Einheitskanzler« Helmut Kohl ab – Entscheidung für die Europäische Währungsunion – Spendenskandal in der CDU – Katastrophen: Concorde-Absturz, Explosion einer Feuerfabrik in Enschede, Atom-U-Boot Kursk sinkt – Filme von Steven Spielberg werden Kassenschlager – Wiederwahl von Bundeskanzler Gerhard Schröder – Massenhafte Verbreitung der Computertechnologie: Ausrufung der »digitalen Revolution« in Medienwissenschaft, Kunst, Philosophie, Museum und Privathaushalten – Bau des Eurotunnels zwischen Großbritannien und Frankreich – Der amerikanische Künstler Christo verhüllt den Reichstag in Berlin – Eröffnung der Weltausstellung »Expo« in Hannover

Kai-Uwe Hemken

Major events in Germany that determine social processes: the fall of the Wall and unification of the two German states – collapse of the Soviet Union and Yugoslavia – considerable increase in extreme right-wing violence (Hoyerswerda, Solingen), primarily against foreigners – collapse of Czechoslovakia – withdrawal of allied troops from Germany – election year with a total of 19 elections – death of Princess Diana – in January 1998 the Social Democrats gain a majority in the Federal Parliament and replace the »unification Chancellor« Helmut Kohl – decision in favor of a European currency union – donations scandal in the Conservative CDU party – disasters: Concorde crashes, explosion in a fireworks factory in Enschede, nuclear submarine Kursk sinks – films by Steven Spielberg are box office hits – Federal Chancellor Gerhard Schröder reelected – spread of computer technology on a massive scale: proclamation of the »digital revolution« in the media, art, philosophy, museums and private households – construction of the Eurotunnel between Great Britain and France – the American artist Christo wraps the Reichstag in Berlin – opening of the »Expo« exhibition in Hanover

1994

1993–1994
Arsenal Pavillon, Paris, F
Agence Confino
temporary exhibition

Die Ausstellung von Stadtgeräuschen war ein Versuch,
den Pariser Sound zu identifizieren. Die spezifischen
Klänge der Stadt wurden als Spaziergang inszeniert.
So konnte man Paris vom Süden bis zum Norden akus-
tisch erleben.

Presenting the noises of the city, this exhibition was an
attempt to identify the sound of Paris. Sounds and tones
specific to the French capital were orchestrated as a
walk through the city, enabling visitors to experience
Paris acoustically, from the south up to the north.

1994–today
Muséum nationale d'Histoire Naturelle de Paris,
Paris, F
Paul Chemetov, Borja Huidobro
museum, permanent exhibition

Die Grande Galerie de l'Evolution ist bis heute ein
großes begehbares Gesamtkunstwerk mit präparierten
Tieren als Stars. Die Evolution des Lebens bildet den
roten Faden der Ausstellung. Das wissenschaftliche
Thema wird den Besuchern mit unterschiedlichen
Präsentationsformen nahegebracht; so findet man
klassisch museale, aber auch Bereiche, die an das
Wunderkammer-Prinzip erinnern.

The Grande Galerie de l'Evolution is a huge, walk-through
artistic synthesis with stuffed animals as its stars. The
evolution of life forms is the central theme that runs like
a red thread through the exhibition – made accessible to
visitors with a variety of different approaches to presen-
tation. And so one finds both classic museum techniques
and areas reminiscent of the principle of a »cabinet of
curiosities« in one and the same place.

2.71

>086
ohne Titel. Sichern unter …
Unbeständige Ausstellung der Bestände des
Werkbund-Archivs

1995

22.07.1994–01.11.1994
Gasometer, Oberhausen, D
Ulrich Borsdorf, Franz-Josef Brüggemeier,
Gottfried Korff, Jürg Steiner
temporary exhibition

Vor dem Abriss gerettet, wurde der Gasometer zum
Ausstellungsort. Eine Videoinstallation, persönliche
Erinnerungsstücke, Statistiken und »Helden« des
Ruhrgebiets sowie der Gasometer selbst erzählten über
Geschichte, Leben und Arbeit im endenden Industrie-
zeitalter. Die Verbindung von Ort, Inhalt und musealer
Umsetzung begeisterte 200.000 Besucher.

The gasometer was saved from demolition and given
a new role as an exhibition venue. Video installations,
personal mementos, statistics and »heroes« from the
Ruhr region, not to mention the gasometer itself, were
combined to document the history of the region and tell
the story of life and work there in the outgoing industrial
age. This convincing relationship between location, con-
tent and curatorial approach attracted and fascinated
200,000 visitors.

2.72

2.73

2.74

13.01.1995–02.07.1995
Martin-Gropius-Bau, Berlin, D
Renate Flagmeier, Eckhard Siepmann, Angelika
Thiekötter (concept); Detlef Saalfeld (design)
temporary exhibition

Als inszeniertes Archiv wurden Gegenstände und
Dokumente aus zwei Jahrzehnten in austauschbaren
Räumen gestapelt, aufgereiht, angesammelt, gruppiert,
zugeordnet, inventarisiert, katalogisiert, eingeschweißt
und in ihrem inhaltlichen Kontext neu zusammengefügt.
Den Besuchern bot sich eine neue Sicht auf die Dinge
des Alltags.

As an archive made to be displayed, objects and docu-
ments from two decades were placed in interchangeable
rooms stacked, lined up, amassed, grouped, ordered,
inventoried, catalogued, shrink-wrapped and reassem-
bled according to their content. In this way visitors were
encouraged to see everyday items with new eyes.

2.75

>> 086 reviews p.198

> 087
Aroma, Aroma –
Versuch über den Geruch

> 088
Eine un-heimlich schöne Begegnung
mit Licht und sich selbst

1997

14 *Götz, Matthias; Haldner, Bruno
(Eds.): Aroma, Aroma. Versuch über
den Geruch. Museum für Gestaltung
Basel. Basel, Muttenz 1995. p.2.*

2.76–2.78 © Ingo Maurer

20.05.1995–07.01.1996
Museum für Gestaltung Basel, Basel, CH
Matthias Götz, Bruno Haldner (concept);
Ursula Gillmann (design); Bruno Kaspar (graphic)
topical, temporary exhibition

»Der Duft ist eine Dimension der Dinge, die ungreifbar
bleibt, so aufdringlich sie manchmal sein mag.«[14] Das
Museum für Gestaltung stellte nicht-visuelle Themen
aus und verwandelte sich 1996 in ein »Duftmuseum auf
Zeit«. Die Ausstellung als olfaktorischer Versuch war
vor allem riechend zu erkunden.

»Scent is one dimension that remains intangible, as intru-
sive as it may be.«[14] In 1996, the Museum für Gestaltung
added an array of non-visual elements to its holdings and
was thus transformed into a »temporary scent museum«.
As an olfactory experiment, visitors experienced the
exhibition first and foremost with their noses.

1997
Deutzer Brücke, Köln, D
Ingo Maurer
temporary exhibition

400 m voller Licht waren bei der Inszenierung von Ingo
Maurer im Hohlraum der Deutzer Brücke in Köln zu
sehen. 16.000 Besucher entdeckten ein Lichtereignis,
das Freude, Spaß und Unterhaltung vermitteln sollte.

400 meters of light was assembled in a display created
by Ingo Maurer in the hollow arch of the Deutz Bridge
in Cologne. 16,000 visitors were able to experience this
light sensation; its aim: to spread joy and fun and provide
a little entertainment.

2.76

2.77

2.78

1998

07.05.1997–30.10.1998
Speicherstadt, Hamburg, D
Atelier Brückner; Götz, Schulz, Haas Architekten
temporary exhibition

Elemente aus Theater, Film und Literatur wurden zu
einer Reise durch Themenräume und Rauminstallationen
inszeniert, die das Schicksal der Menschen sichtbar
machten und die Besucher zu eigenen Interpretationen
ermutigten. Der Mythos Titanic wurde emotional erlebbar.

Elements from theater, film and literature were combined
to create a journey through the particular themed spaces
and installations of this exhibition, which made the fate
of the passengers quite apparent and encouraged visitors
to make their own interpretations. Here, the legend of the
Titanic was made tangible on an emotion level.

06.09.1998–31.01.1999
Alte Völklinger Hütte, Völklingen, D
Hans Dieter Schaal
temporary exhibition

Mit Prometheus im UNESCO Weltkulturerbe wurde das
Industriedenkmal Alte Völklinger Hütte zum Kunstwerk.
H. D. Schaal zeigte anhand von multimedial inszenierten
Bühnenbildern den Wandel der Menschen sowie ihre
Ideale und Vorstellungen im Laufe der Jahrhunderte.

The exhibition »Prometheus« held on the UNESCO World
Heritage Site of the Alte Völklinger Hütte transformed the
industrial monument into a work of art. H. D. Schaal used
a variety of multimedia elements to produce an image of
the changes man has undergone down through the cen-
turies as well as shifts in human ideals and perception.

2.79

2.80

2.81

2.82

1999

26.06.1998–20.09.1998
Salomon R. Guggenheim Museum, New York, USA
Frank O. Gehry Associates
traveling exhibition

Die Motorräder im Guggenheim mit ihren funkelnden, chromähnlichen Materialien und Formen symbolisierten Geschwindigkeit, Freiheit und Bewegung. Die Maschinen, die scheinbar unsichtbar auf Straßen befestigt waren, simulierten Bewegung und erzählten ihre Geschichte. Die Ausstellung wanderte von New York nach Bilbao und Las Vegas.

With their gleaming, chrome-like surfaces and forms, the motorbikes on display in the Guggenheim were destined to be symbols of speed, freedom and movement. The vehicles, fixed to the exhibition streets by seemingly invisible fastenings, simulated movement, and each of them told their own story. The exhibition moved from New York to Bilbao and then on to Las Vegas.

2.83

22.04.1999–08.08.1999
Deutsches Hygiene-Museum, Dresden, D
Nicola Lepp (curator); Martin Kohlbauer (design)
temporary exhibition

Der Mensch der Zukunft, wie sollte er sein? Dynamisch, kraftvoll, naturverbunden oder perfekt funktionierend … Die Vielfalt an Ideen und die Versuche des 20. Jahrhunderts, sie in die Praxis umzusetzen, zeigten rund 800 Exponate aus Wissenschaft, Kunst und Kulturgeschichte. Es entstand eine inszenierte Reise durch fünf Labore des Neuen Menschen.

Humans of tomorrow, what will they be like? Dynamic, powerful, at one with nature or functionalized to perfection … The plethora of ideas and attempts throughout the 20th century to make such notions a reality was demonstrated with around 800 exhibits from the areas of science, art and cultural history. The result: an orchestrated journey through five laboratories exploring the new human being.

2.84

2.85

> 093

1 Monde Réel — Master/Slave.
Collection de Robots de Rolf Fehlbaum

> 094

Museum für Kommunikation

2000

30.06.1999–14.11.1999
Fondation Cartier pour l'art contemporain, Paris, F
Diller + Scofidio: Elizabeth Diller, Ricardo Scofidio
temporary exhibition

Der Besucher als stiller Beobachter wurde auf Abstand gehalten und war trotzdem mittendrin in einer inszenierten Spielzeug-Robotersammlung. Auf knapp 10 m² tummelte sich eine Gruppe von Robotern, die sich bewegten, anhielten und wieder weiterfuhren. Nichts blieb verborgen: Zahlreiche Monitore zeigten Bilder aus jedem Blickwinkel, sogar von ihrem mechanischen Innenleben.

As a silent observer, the visitor was kept at a distance yet simultaneously found themselves at the heart of a carefully arranged collection of toy robots. On an area just under 10 m² in size, a group of robots could be seen bustling around: starting, stopping and then restarting. There wasn't a single element that wasn't shown: A mass of monitors presented images from every conceivable angle, even revealing their mechanical innards.

2000–today
Berlin, D
hg merz architekten
museum, permanent exhibition

Zur Eröffnung des Museums für Kommunikation entstand eine Dauerausstellung über die Post- und Kommunikationsgeschichte. Das Museum präsentiert und dokumentiert historische sowie technische Entwicklungen, zeigt Veränderungen im privaten und öffentlichen Leben und in seiner Schatzkammer die »Blaue Mauritius«.

The inauguration of Berlin's Museum für Kommunikation was marked by a permanent exhibition on the history of postal correspondence and communication. The museum presented and documented historical and technological developments as well as changes within the public and private spheres in its treasure chamber, aptly called the »Blue Mauritius«.

2.86

> 095
Le temps, vite …

> 096
7 Hügel. Bilder und Zeichen des
21. Jahrhunderts

2.87 © Atelier Confino / François
Confino

2.88 Kern im Lichthof
Nucleus in the atrium
© Detlev Schilke

13.01.2000–17.04.2000
Centre Georges Pompidou, Paris, F
François Confino, Daniel Soutif
temporary exhibition

Zeit kann man zwar nicht sehen, nicht fühlen und nicht
hören, aber man kann sie ausstellen: Daniel Soutif
und François Confino vereinten 400 wissenschaftliche
Objekte, Kunstwerke und Dokumente in einem Museum
für moderne Kunst und zeigten etwas scheinbar nicht
Darstellbares – die subjektive und die objektive, die
freie, die gemessene, die erlebte und die erinnerte Zeit.

We may not be able to see time, feel or hear it, but we
can put it on display: Daniel Soutif and François Confino
brought together 400 scientific objects, artworks and
documents in a museum of modern art and presented
something that is seemingly impossible to actually show
– subjective and objective, free, measured, experienced
and recalled time.

2.87

14.05.2000–29.10.2000
Martin-Gropius-Bau, Berlin, D
Lebbeus Woods, Bodo-Michael Baumunk, Ken Adam,
Gereon Sievernich
temporary exhibition

»7 Hügel« zeigte sieben Visionen der Zukunft mit einer
Art theatralischer Ideenschau: Grand Opéra, begehbare
Filme, Licht- und Toninszenierungen … Die Ausstellung
war eine Zusammenfassung der szenischen und tech-
nischen Möglichkeiten der letzten 100 Jahre. Sie war
Kunst- und Wunderkammer des 20. Jahrhunderts.

»7 Hills« presented seven visions of the future in an
almost theatrical display of ideas: Grand opera, films you
could walk through, lighting and sound arrangements …
The exhibition was a summary of the possibilities in
stagecraft developed over the previous hundred years:
a cabinet of curiosities from the 20th century.

2.88

> 097
<u>Vision Machine</u>

> 098
<u>Expo 2000 Hannover</u>
<u>Mensch, Natur und Technik —</u>
<u>Eine neue Welt entsteht</u>

05.2000–09.2000
Musée des Beaux-Arts, Nantes, F
Nox: Lars Spuybroek
temporary exhibition

Mit der »Vision Machine« wurde Friedrich Kieslers Idee
aus den 1930er Jahren neu interpretiert. Das Konzept
beschäftigte sich mit dem Prozess visueller Wahrnehmung von Kunst. Die Installation im Lichthof des Musée
des Beaux-Arts erinnerte an ein Papier-Modell und
zeigte 250 Werke aus Architektur und bildender Kunst
des 20. Jahrhunderts.

*The »Vision Machine« was a reinterpretation of Friedrich
Kiesler's idea from the 1930s. The concept dealt with the
process involved in the visual perception of art. The installation, reminiscent of a paper model was housed in the
atrium of the Musée des Beaux-Arts and displayed 250
works from 20th-century architecture and the visual arts.*

01.06.2000–31.10.2000
Hannover, D
temporary exhibition

Die erste Expo-Weltausstellung in Deutschland hat
die alten Weltausstellungen neu interpretiert. Innovative Themenparks mit Erlebnislandschaften wurden
genutzt, um Zukunftsvisionen zu vermitteln. Zudem
war ein neuer Trend sichtbar: Natur- und Biowissen-
schaften wurden immer mehr zu Impulsgebern für
museale Gedanken.

*The first World Exposition to be held Germany provided
an opportunity to reinterpret the notion of the world fair
used in the past. Innovative theme parks complete with
experience fields were used to convey visions of the
future. And the exhibition presented a new trend, too:
the ever-increasing influence of the natural and biological
sciences on thought in the museum world.*

2.89–2.91 *MVRDV / Rob't Hart*

2.89

2.90

2.91

> 099
Fashion will go out of Fashion

> 100
Mutations:
Evènement culturel sur la ville
contemporaine

2.92 »Rudi Gernreich – Fashion will go
out of Fashion«, Ausstellungsansicht,
Neue Galerie Graz im Künstlerhaus,
im Rahmen des Festivals steirischer
Herbst, 2000
»Rudi Gernreich – Fashion will go out
of Fashion«, installation view, Neue
Galerie Graz im Künstlerhaus,
displayed in conjunction with the
steirischer herbst festival, 2000
© Markus Pillhofer

2.93 © Philippe Ruault /
arc en rêve centre d'architecture

08.10.2000–26.11.2000
Künstlerhaus Graz, Landesmuseum Joanneum, Graz, A
Brigitte Felderer (curator); Coop Himmelb(l)au (design)
temporary exhibition

Rudi Gernreich, ein Modestar der 1960er, war mit seiner
Oben-ohne-Mode, dem Total Look und der Unisex-Mode
ungewöhnlich, mutig und provozierend. Seine Popula-
rität wurde vermittelt durch Artikel, Schlagzeilen und
Pressefotos an Wänden und Boden sowie verschiedene
Medienstationen und seine wichtigsten Entwürfe waren
real erlebbar.

With his topless fashion, Total Look and unisex vogues,
Rudi Gernreich, a star of the 1960s fashion scene, was
unconventional, courageous and provocative. Newspaper
articles, headlines and press photographs covered the
walls, floors and a number of »media stations« convey-
ing his popularity, while specimen samples of his designs
allowed visitors to experience his work for themselves.

2.92

11.2000–03.2001
Arc en Rêve, Bordeaux, F
Jean Nouvel, Hans Ulrich Obrist, Rem Koolhaas,
Sanford Kwinter, Stefano Boeri
traveling exhibition

Ein Ausstellungsdesigner, zwei Architekten, ein Fotograf,
ein Kunstkritiker und zwei Philosophen berichteten über
die Veränderungen des Lebensraums Stadt anhand von
Beispielen aus der ganzen Welt und dargestellt durch
verschiedenste Medien.

One exhibition designer, two architects, a photographer,
an art critic and two philosophers reported on the chan-
ges that have taken place in the city as a living space.
Drawing on examples from all around the world, their
ideas were presented making full use of multimedia.

2.93

reviews
rezensionen

Eva Citzler

Werkbund-Ausstellung »Die Wohnung«

Im Juli 1927 wurde die Werkbund-Ausstellung »Die Wohnung« eröffnet.
Ihr Schauplatz und zugleich ihr Ausstellungsobjekt war die Weißenhofsiedlung in Stuttgart, die bis heute existiert. Die Idee für die Ausstellung
war gewagt, ihre Ausmaße und der erforderliche Organisationsaufwand
enorm. Eine Siedlung, bestehend aus 21 Häusern, die von 17 internationalen
Architekten entworfen und von 55 Innenarchitekten eingerichtet wurden,[1]
musste für das Vorhaben in weniger als fünf Monaten erbaut werden.

Während des Ersten Weltkriegs und der darauffolgenden Inflation waren
kaum Ressourcen vorhanden, um staatliche Bauprojekte zu verwirklichen.
Doch ebendiese Knappheit finanzieller Mittel, das Aufkommen von Groß-
städten sowie die zunehmende Technisierung forderten die Auseinandersetzung mit der Frage, wie ein neues Bauen und ein neues Wohnen
aussehen könnten. Neue Wohnungen sollten ökonomisch, funktional und
technisch fortschrittlich sein.

Le Corbusier, der mit seinen Arbeiten die Ausstellung wesentlich mitge-
staltete, prägte den Begriff der »Wohnmaschine«[2] und wies damit darauf
hin, dass ein Haus ebenso konstruiert und durchgeplant sein müsse wie ein
Auto oder ein Flugzeug.[3] Mit dem Bau der Weißenhofsiedlung begegnete
man diesen Anforderungen der Zeit.

Der Deutsche Werkbund führte zusammen mit der Stadt Stuttgart eine
Wohnungsausstellung durch, die über Deutschland hinaus eine wegweisende
Funktion einnehmen sollte und nach ihrer Beendigung dringend benötigten
neuen Wohnraum für die Stuttgarter Bevölkerung bot. Mies van der Rohe,
der 1926 Vizepräsident des Deutschen Werkbunds wurde, oblag die künstlerische Leitung der gesamten Ausstellung. In der Denkschrift und dem Programm der Ausstellung vom Dezember 1926 heißt es: »Ein systematischer
Lösungsversuch für die neue Wohnung und aller damit zusammenhängenden
organisatorisch-räumlichen, konstruktiven, technischen und hygienischen
Probleme ist die geplante Werkbund-Ausstellung [...].«[4]

Die Weißenhofsiedlung als wesentlicher Schauplatz wurde von drei
weiteren Ausstellungen begleitet und ergänzt. »Die Internationale Plan- und
Modellausstellung Neuer Baukunst« ließ das Neue Bauen, das in der
Weißendorfsiedlung umgesetzt wurde, in ihrem internationalen Kontext
erscheinen. Gezeigt wurde sie in den städtischen Ausstellungshallen
auf dem Interimstheaterplatz beim Neuen Schloss.[5] Das ursprüngliche
Vorhaben, Pläne und Modelle auszustellen, konnte allerdings nicht

Werkbund-Exhibition »Die Wohnung«

*The Deutscher Werkbund exhibition »Die Wohnung« was opened to the public
in July 1927, whereby the Weissenhof Estate in Stuttgart, which still exists
today, doubled up as both the setting and the exhibit. The exhibition concept
was certainly bold, the sheer scale and organizational input enormous. It
took five whole months to complete this project, to build an estate consisting
of 21 houses, designed by 17 international architects and decorated by
55 interior designers.[1]*

*During the First World War and the subsequent period of rampant inflation
the resources required to realize state-funded construction projects were
certainly few and far between. But it was precisely this scarcity of funds,
augmented by the emergence of big cities and increasing mechanization
which caused attention to be paid to the question: What might a new kind
of construction and a new kind of living be like? New dwellings needed to be
economic, functional and technically advanced.*

*Le Corbusier who made a major contribution to the exhibition with his work
coined the term »a machine for living«[2] and in doing so pointed out that a
house should be constructed and planned down to the smallest detail in just
the same way as a car or an airplane.[3] By building the Weissenhof Estate, the
organizers hoped to find a solution to these requirements of the day.*

*The Deutscher Werkbund together with the City of Stuttgart held an exhibition
of homes which had been intended to blaze the trail in terms of housing and
which upon completion would offer Stuttgart's citizens the additional housing
they so desperately needed. Mies van der Rohe was appointed Vice President of the Deutscher Werkbund in 1926 and thereby was assigned artistic
direction of the entire exhibition. The exhibition's memorandum and program
made in 1926 said: »The Werkbund exhibition is a systematic attempt to find
a solution to provide new housing and solve all problems associated with that
task in terms of organization, space, construction, technical elements and
hygiene [...].«[4]*

*Firmly in the public eye, the Weissenhof Estate was accompanied by three
additional exhibitions. Firstly, »The International Plan and Model Exhibition
of New Architecture« provided an international stage for the new kind of
architecture implemented in the Weissenhof Estate. It was displayed in the
municipal exhibition rooms in the Provisional Theater at the New Palace in
Stuttgart.[5] However, the organizers were unable to realize their original
proposal to exhibit plans and models there; in place of these, over 100*

3.1   3.2   3.3

umgesetzt werden. Stattdessen wurden über 100 großformatig reproduzierte Fotografien neuer internationaler Baukunst museal anmutend präsentiert. Zu den vertretenen Ländern gehörten Deutschland, die Tschechoslowakei, Russland, die USA, die Schweiz, Frankreich, Belgien und Österreich. Überzeugend wurde dargelegt, dass sich die Architekten des Weißenhofs mit ihrer Baukunst in eine weltweite Bewegung einreihten. Im Anschluss an die Ausstellung in Stuttgart wurden die sogenannten Stuttgarter Tafeln als Wanderausstellung in 17 weiteren Städten gezeigt.[6]

Die Hallenausstellungen am Gewerbehallenplatz und die Ausstellung im Stadtgartenumgang begleiteten die Präsentation der Weißenhofsiedlung insofern, als umfassendes Material zur Einrichtung und zur technischen Ausstattung von Wohnungen gezeigt wurde. Die Verantwortung für die Gestaltung der Hallen wurde Lilly Reich übertragen. Sie unterteilte die Hallen nicht in Kojen, in denen Unternehmen ihre Produkte unabhängig voneinander hätten präsentieren können, sondern sie stellte Warengruppen zusammen, sodass Produkte vergleichend betrachtet werden konnten. ›3.1 Folgende Ausstellungsobjekte wurden in den insgesamt neun Hallen präsentiert: Herde und Öfen, elektrische Haushaltsgeräte, Waschräume und Badezimmer, Einbauküchen wie die Stuttgarter Kleinküche, die Eschebachsche Reformküche und die Frankfurter Küche, Linoleum, Textilien, Möbel, Tapeten und Beleuchtungskörper. ›3.2

Besonders hervorzuheben ist Halle 4, in der Mies van der Rohe und Lilly Reich gemeinsam eine Spiegelglashalle gestalteten. ›3.3 Diese wird als Vorläufer des Barcelona-Pavillons angesehen, den Mies van der Rohe zwei Jahre später erbauen ließ. Im Stadtgartenumgang waren unter anderem Baumaterialien, Konstruktionselemente, Fenster und Gartenzäune ausgestellt.[7]

Der dritte begleitende Ausstellungsort war ein Experimentiergelände, das am Weißenhof lag. Hier konnten Baumethoden und Materialien ebenso wie Fertighäuser besichtigt werden. Die Weißenhofsiedlung war das eigentliche Anschauungsobjekt der Ausstellung. Der Weißenhof mit seiner weitläufigen und ansprechenden Aussicht erschien als der optisch ästhetischste Standort, um eine neuartige Siedlung in Stuttgart zu erbauen, mit der die Stadt und der Werkbund weltweite Beachtung finden wollten.[8] Die Herausforderung lag vor allen Dingen darin, eine Siedlung zu gestalten, die den individuellen Vorstellungen der verschiedenen Architekten gerecht wurde, ohne dass dies zu Lasten eines einheitlichen Gesamtbildes ging.

large-format photographs of new international architecture were presented in a museum-like setting. Germany, Czechoslovakia, Russia, the USA, Switzerland, France, Belgium and Austria were among the countries represented. The exhibition convincingly championed the architecture to be seen at Weissenhof and helped place its creators among the ranks of a worldwide movement. In addition to their appearance in Stuttgart, the so-called »Stuttgart Panels« were displayed in 17 other cities in a traveling exhibition.[6]

Indoor exhibitions in the city's Trade Hall and a show held in the arcades surrounding the city gardens can also be considered accompaniments to the Weissenhof Estate in that they presented extensive material on the estate's construction and the dwellings' technical furnishings. Responsibility for the design of these exhibition spaces was handed over to Lilly Reich, who rather than dividing the space up into bays where each company could present their own products chose to cluster the various product groups enabling visitors to make a comparison between the range of products on show. ›3.1 The following exhibits were presented over a total of nine halls: stoves and ovens, electrical household appliances, lavatories and bathrooms, fitted kitchens such as the Stuttgart kitchenette, the Eschebach »Reform Kitchen« and the »Frankfurt Kitchen«, linoleum, textiles, furniture, wallpaper and luminaires. ›3.2

Hall 4 deserves particular attention in this context for it hosted the results of a joint design endeavor between Mies van der Rohe and Lilly Reich: the »mirror glass« hall. ›3.3 It is often cited as the forerunner for the Barcelona pavilion designed by Mies van der Rohe two years later. The arcades surrounding the city's gardens hosted a plethora of exhibits including building materials, structural elements, windows and garden fences.[7]

The location of the third accompanying exhibition was an experimentation area within the Weissenhof site itself, where both construction methods and materials could be viewed by the public as well as complete pre-fabricated homes. But it was the Weissenhof Estate that everybody was there to see. Rambling and rather appealing to the eye, Weissenhof emerged as the most aesthetically-pleasing location to build innovative housing estates in Stuttgart, destined to bring the city and the Deutscher Werkbund worldwide fame.[8] The challenge was above all to design an estate that would do justice to the individual visions of the various architects on the project without causing detriment to the overall image.

So gab es Vorgaben bezüglich des Außenmaterials, beispielsweise der Türen und Fenster, und auch das flache Dach war verpflichtend. ›3.4 Die Innenausstattung hingegen konnte individuell vorgenommen werden. ›3.5

Von den 17 involvierten Architekten seien hier stellvertretend neben Ludwig Mies van der Rohe noch Le Corbusier, Jacobus Johannes Pieter Oud und Walter Gropius genannt. Mies van der Rohe entwarf vier Reihenhäuser zu je sechs Wohnungen für die Weißenhofsiedlung. Grundlegend für seine Wohneinheiten war die Idee eines möglichst variablen Innenraums. Durch einen Skelettbau als Konstruktionssystem, bei dem nur Treppenhaus, Küche und Badezimmer fix angelegt wurden, war die Freiheit der Raumaufteilung nach individuellen Bedürfnissen größtmöglich. Das Abgrenzen der Räume erfolgte durch bewegbare, in verschiedenen Größen verfügbare Stellwände.[9]

Oud, ehemaliges Mitglied der Künstlergruppe »De Stijl«, plante drei Einfamilienhäuser. Seinen oftmals als »puritanisch« bezeichneten Stil begründete er so: »So wird mein Haus in der Benutzung ›lebendig‹. ›Puritanisch‹ scheint es mir nur so lange es noch Besuchsobjekt ist. Das Leben soll sich frei ausleben können und nicht von einem Bau unterdrückt werden: das empfinde ich als das ›moderne‹ dem akademischen gegenüber.«[10]

Le Corbusier, der gemeinsam mit Pierre Jeanneret ein Einfamilienhaus sowie ein Doppelreihenhaus gestaltete, galt bei vielen als der Star der Werkbund-Ausstellung.[11] Dabei erhielt er jedoch nicht nur positive Kritiken. Le Corbusier wurde höchst kontrovers diskutiert;[12] ein Phänomen, das auf die gesamte Ausstellung zutraf. Obwohl Mies van der Rohe politisch links orientierte Architekten für die Ausstellung bevorzugte,[13] gab es viel Kritik von linker Seite. Diese bezog sich auf die hohen Kosten der Ausstellung, mit denen noch eine Vielzahl mehr Wohnungen hätte finanziert werden können. Auch entsprachen die Wohnungen weniger dem Budget der Arbeiterklasse, sondern dem eines gehobenen Mittelstands. Die Lösung des »Wohnungsproblems« der Zeit konnte also aus linker Sicht nicht in einem befriedigenden Umfang geliefert werden.[14] Konservative Kreise hießen den Bruch mit den bewährten, traditionellen Baustilen nicht gut. Auch die Tatsache, dass viele ausländische Architekten für den Bau der Siedlung engagiert wurden, missfiel der rechten Seite. Bei den Nationalsozialisten fand die Weißenhofsiedlung gar keinen Anklang. Nach ihrer Machtübernahme im Jahre 1933 diffamierten sie die Siedlung als »Schandfleck Stuttgarts«, entworfen von »Theater-Architekten«.[15]

For this reason there were a number of specifications regarding the dwellings' exteriors; the uniform doors and windows for example, or the flat roofs, which were also obligatory. ›3.4 The interior designers were on the other hand left completely to their own devises. ›3.5

In addition to the shining example of Ludwig Mies van der Rohe, the 17 architects to make contributions to the estate included no lesser leading lights than Le Corbusier, Jacobus Johannes Pieter Oud and Walter Gropius. Mies van der Rohe designed four terraced blocks for Weissenhof, each containing six apartments. The basic premise for his apartments was that the interior should offer as much variety as possible. A skeleton structure, whereby the arrangement of the staircase, kitchen and bathroom was fixed, allowed for the greatest scope in then dividing and rearranging the rooms to suit the individual's needs, made possible by movable partitions available in various sizes.[9]

Oud, formerly a member of the artists' group »De Stijl«, created the blueprints for three detached houses. His own reasoning behind his unique style, often described as »puritan« was: »My house ›comes to life‹ when lived in. To me it is only ›puritan‹ as long as it remains an exhibit. Domestic life should be free to take its own course and should not be suppressed by a building: I consider that ›modern‹ in comparison to the academic use of the term.«[10]

Le Corbusier, who designed both a detached house and a set of semi-detached houses in collaboration with Pierre Jeanneret, was considered by many the star of the Werkbund exhibition.[11] However, not all the reviews were positive. Le Corbusier became the subject of a highly controversial debate,[12] something that affected the entire exhibition. Despite Mies van der Rohe's clear preference for leftist architects,[13] criticism came from precisely that end of the political spectrum nonetheless. It was sparked predominantly by the high costs associated with the exhibition, which could have been used to finance the construction of a great deal more housing than Weissenhof in fact provided. In addition, the housing was far from in line with a working-class budget, but was definitely more suitable for upper middle class purses. Therefore from a leftist perspective, this project would not be able to deliver a satisfactory solution to the »housing problem« of the period.[14] In conservative circles, on the other hand, it was the break from the traditional, long-established style of construction that met with opposition. The fact that many of the architects involved were foreign did not bode well with the right either. The Weissenhof Estate certainly do not meet the approval of the National Socialists. Following their accession to power in 1933, they denounced the estate as »Stuttgart's black spot«, created by »show architects«.[15]

3.4

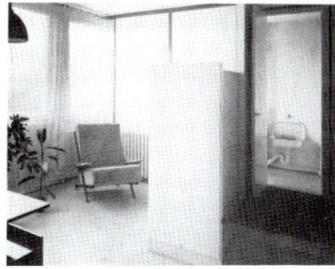

3.5

Während des Zweiten Weltkriegs wurde die Siedlung teilweise zerstört. 1958 wurden die Bauten unter Denkmalschutz gestellt; in den Jahren 1981 bis 1987 wurde die Siedlung renoviert. Heute befinden sich in den erhaltenen Häusern Dienstwohnungen für Beamte und sie sind ein großer Besuchermagnet für Stuttgart.

Mit der Ausstellung »Die Wohnung« wurde eines der zentralen Themen des Werkbunds aufgegriffen: Der Einzug der Gestaltung in die Industrie und der damit einhergehende – immer wieder neu zu lösende – Konflikt der Beziehung von Form und Funktion. Eine »einheitliche[...] Gestaltung aller Lebensformen aus einer gemeinsamen geistigen Orientierung«[16] war das Ziel. Es ist kritisch zu reflektieren, ob die Weißenhofsiedlung diese einheitliche Gestaltung wirklich verkörperte. Das obligatorische Flachdach allein konnte die zum Teil stark divergierenden Vorstellungen von dem neuen Baustil der einzelnen Architekten nicht vereinheitlichen. Von anderen wiederum wurden die Fragen nach der Gestaltung gar nicht erst gestellt, sondern einzig die »Rationalisierung, Typisierung und Verbilligung«[17] von Wohnungen in den Vordergrund gerückt. Die Ziele der Ausstellungen erfuhren deshalb seitens der Architekten, der Presse und auch innerhalb des Werkbunds immer wieder ambivalente Formulierungen.[18] Ein geschlossener, neuer Baustil sowie die Gleichsetzung von Form und Funktion konnten somit in der Weißenhofsiedlung nicht vollständig präsentiert werden. Die Ausstellung bot dadurch jedoch eine große Anzahl wertvoller Ideen, Vorschläge und Entwürfe, um die bestehende Diskussion über die Gestaltung innerhalb der Industrie voranzutreiben und Lösungen, insbesondere für das Wohnungsproblem, zu finden.

During the War various parts of the estate were destroyed. In 1958 the remaining buildings were placed under a preservation order and between 1981 and 1987 the estate underwent renovation works. Today, the surviving houses are used as official residences for civil servants and constitute a major tourist attraction in Stuttgart.

The exhibition »Die Wohnung« seized upon one of the Werkbund's key focuses: The absorption of design into industry and the concomitant conflict in the relationship between function and form, constantly calling for novel solutions. The aim was a »holistic [...] design for all walks of life originating from a common, spiritual position.«[16] It is crucial to reflect upon whether the Weissenhof Estate did in fact embody this concept of holistic design. The mandatory flat roof alone was not sufficient to unite what were in some cases highly divergent notions of a new style of construction held by the individual architects. On the other hand, there were others who did not even pose the design question in the first place, but focused solely on the »rationalization, typification and cost effectiveness« of the homes.[17] Thus on the side of the architects, with both the press and the Deutscher Werkbund, the project's objectives were constantly subject to ambivalent commentaries.[18] It was for this reason that in the end the Weissenhof Estate was unable to provide as the canvas for a new, cohesive style of construction or a unification of function and form in its entirety. However, the exhibition did as a consequence contribute a plethora of valuable ideas, suggestions and designs to public dialogue; attempts to drive forward the running discussions on design within German industry, to find solutions, in particular to the housing problem so rampant at the time.

>>> author p.212

1 Cf. Kirsch, Karin: Die Weißenhofsiedlung: Werkbund-Ausstellung »Die Wohnung« – Stuttgart 1927. Stuttgart 1987, p.43.
2 Corbusier, Le; Conrads, Ulrich (Ed.): Bauwelt Fundamente 2. Ausblicke auf eine Architektur, Berlin 1969, p.23.
3 Cf. Kirsch, Karin: Die Weißenhofsiedlung: Werkbund-Ausstellung »Die Wohnung« –

Stuttgart 1927. Stuttgart 1987, p.128.
4 Denkschrift und Programm der Ausstellung in der Formulierung vom Dezember 1926. in: Kirsch, Karin: Die Weißenhofsiedlung: Werkbund-Ausstellung »Die Wohnung« – Stuttgart 1927. Stuttgart 1987, p.22.
5 Cf. ibid., p.27.

6 Cf. ibid., p.31.
7 Cf. ibid., p.40.
8 Cf. ibid., p.44.
9 Cf. ibid., p.59.
10 Oud an Wedepohl, approx. Sept./Okt. 1927, Oud-Archiv, Rotterdam. in: Kirsch, Karin: Die Weißenhofsiedlung: Werkbund-Ausstellung »Die Wohnung« –

Stuttgart 1927. Stuttgart 1987, p.99.
11 Cf. ibid., p.112.
12 Cf. ibid., p.124.
13 Mies an Stotz, 11.09.1925, Bundesarchiv Koblenz. in: Kirsch, Karin: Die Weißenhofsiedlung: Werkbund-Ausstellung »Die Wohnung« – Stuttgart 1927. Stuttgart 1987, p.53.

14 Cf. ibid., p.52.
15 Cf. ibid., p.207.
16 Winfried Nerdinger: Neues Bauen – Neues Wohnen. in: Nerdinger, Winfried (Ed.): 100 Jahre Deutscher Werkbund 1907–2007, München 2007, p.142–145.
17 Cf. ibid., p.142.
18 Cf. ibid., p.142.

Ines Katenhusen
Moderne Ästhetik muss zur Selbstveränderung werden. Das Abstrakte Kabinett El Lissitzkys und Alexander Dorners 1926/27 in Hannover

Hannover im Oktober 1927: Vertreter aus Kommunal- und Provinzialverwaltung finden sich zu den Feierlichkeiten anlässlich des 75-jährigen Bestehens des Provinzialmuseums ein. Besondere Würdigung findet die Arbeit Alexander Dorners, des Leiters der Kunstabteilung. Der 34-Jährige steht auf dem Höhepunkt seiner bisherigen Karriere, was seinen Ausdruck in der Aufnahme in den Deutschen Museumsbund findet, dessen Jahrestagung 1927 zugleich in Hannover stattfindet.[1] An der Stätte seines Schaffens also kann Dorner den Kollegen aus dem ganzen Reich sein Neuordnungskonzept für eine Kunstsammlung präsentieren, die nicht mehr wie bisher darauf abzielt, ohne erkennbare Ordnung möglichst viel Museumsbesitz zu zeigen, sondern ausgewählte Exponate den entwicklungsgeschichtlichen Gang der Kunstgeschichte streiflichtartig illustrieren zu lassen. Stolz führt Dorner die Besucher in den letzten Raum auf dem Parcours durch die abendländische Kunstgeschichte: das Abstrakte Kabinett, das aus diesem Anlass der Öffentlichkeit übergeben wird.[2]

Der russische Konstruktivist El Lissitzky, den Dorner mehr als ein Jahr zuvor damit beauftragt hat, diesen rund 24 m² großen Raum zu konzipieren, ist selbst nicht anwesend. So liegt es am Museumsleiter, Funktion und Wirkungsweise eines Museumsexperiments zu erläutern, das in dem Jahrzehnt seiner Existenz für viel Furore sorgen, ja das, in den Worten von Alfred H. Barr, dem Gründungsdirektor des New Yorker Museum of Modern Art, gar zum »wahrscheinlich bedeutendsten Einzelraum für die Kunst des 20. Jahrhunderts weltweit« avancieren wird.[3]

Lissitzky, Anfang 1927 in die Sowjetunion zurückgekehrt, wendet sein Interesse recht bald neuen Aufgaben zu. Dorner dagegen propagiert das Abstrakte Kabinett und seinen Anteil an seiner Entstehung nach Kräften – mit Erfolg. Sigfried Giedion etwa, der Schweizer Kunsttheoretiker, verfasst im »Cicerone« einen viel beachteten Aufsatz über den neuen Raum, der exemplarisch für eine neue Ausstellungspraxis sei, die »zu einer lebendigen Chronik der Zeit werden und die Dinge zeigen [werde], so lange sie noch in Bewegung sind und nicht erst, wenn sie anfangen, im historischen Sarg zu liegen«[4]. »Bewegung« oder, wie es an anderer Stelle des Beitrags heißt, »Lebendigmachen des Kunstbesitzes« und »Eingliederung ins Leben« – hiermit sind die bestimmenden Elemente im Konzept des Abstrakten Kabinetts genannt.

Modern aesthetics must become self-transformation. The Abstract Cabinet by El Lissitzky and Alexander Dorner 1926/27 in Hanover

Hanover, October 1927: Representatives of the communal and provincial authorities gathered to celebrate the 75th anniversary of the Provincial Museum. The work of Alexander Dorner, head of the Art Department, was the focus of special recognition. The 34-year-old was at the time at the peak of his career, as can be seen from the fact that he was made a member of the German Museums Association, whose 1927 annual conference was taking place in Hanover at the same time.[1] Thus, in the very place that he had achieved so much, Dorner was afforded the opportunity to present his new concept for the arrangement of art collections to colleagues from across the country. It was a concept that moved away from the common aim which had previously dictated the practice of exhibition design, namely to display as much of a museum's inventory as possible at the detriment of a recognizable order, and instead allowed a careful selection of exhibits to illustrate the development and evolution of art history as if illuminated by a ray of light. Dorner proudly led the visitors into the final stage of this journey through the history of Western art: the Abstract Cabinet, which on this occasion was bestowed to the museum to become public property.[2]

Russian constructivist El Lissitzky himself, commissioned by Dorner to create this approx. 24 m² room more than a year beforehand, was not present. Thus it was left to the Museum's director to explain the function and effect of a museum experiment, which during its single decade of existence, caused a real furor and which, in the words of Alfred H. Barr, the founding director of the New York Museum of Modern Art, was to emerge as »probably the most important single room in 20th century-art worldwide.«[3]

Lissitzky, who had returned to the Soviet Union at the beginning of 1927, soon turned his attention to new things. Dorner on the other hand propagated the Abstract Cabinet and his share in its creation using all possible means – and he did so successfully at that. Sigfried Giedion, the Swiss art theorist, for example, wrote a highly noted essay on the new room for »Cicerone«; according to him the room was exemplary of a new curatorial practice, which »[shall] become a living chronicle of the times and display objects, as long as they are still in motion and not only once they have taken their place in a historical coffin.«[4] »Movement« or as it is dubbed in other parts of the text »bringing art holdings to life« and »integrating into life« were suggested the three determining elements in the concept of the Abstract Cabinet.

3.2–3.4 ©Aline Gwose, Michael Herling, Sprengel Museum Hannover, VG Bild-Kunst, Bonn 2014

3.2

3.3

3.4

Es sind Elemente, die ihr kreativer Schöpfer El Lissitzky so kennzeichnet: Entgegen der üblichen Praxis, Kunstwerke in Ausstellungen einem Zoo gleich zu präsentieren, »wo die Besucher gleichzeitig von tausend verschiedenen Bestien angebrüllt werden«, sollen in seinem Raum »die Objekte den Beschauer nicht alle auf einmal überfallen«. Statt der üblichen Passivität, die sich beim Vorbeiziehen an den Wänden zwangsläufig einstelle, »soll unsere Gestaltung den Mann aktiv machen«.[5]

Diese Aktivierung wird durch dreierlei gewährleistet: einmal durch die Gestaltung der Wände, zum Zweiten durch einen spezifischen kuratorischen Umgang mit den präsentierten Kunstwerken und schließlich – dies ein explizit auf Dorners Anregung hin aufgenommenes didaktisches Element – durch bewegliche Informationstrommeln, in denen die Einflüsse der abstrakten Kunst auf Alltagsgegenstände illustriert werden. In die Wände des Raums sind schmale Zinnstreifen eingelassen, die im rechten Winkel zur Wandfläche stehen. Diese Streifen sind auf der einen Seite schwarz gefärbt, auf der anderen grau und an den in den Raum ragenden Kanten weiß – schnell erhält der Raum die ironisierende Bezeichnung des »Plissee-kämmerchens«. Durch diese Tönung ändern die Wände ihren Ausdruck mit jedem Schritt des Beschauers. Dorner fasst dies mit den Worten zusammen, der Raum habe »viel mehr sinnliche Bildeindrücke« als ein Museumssaal im herkömmlichen Sinn enthalten, »[d]ie Beweglichkeit explodierte ihn sozusagen«.[6] Dieses Moment der Dynamik und Aktivierung wird zudem noch durch eingelassene Kassetten, die jeweils drei Bilder zeigen, gesteigert. Durch vom Besucher zu verschiebende Flächen wird erreicht, dass mehr Werke als in herkömmlichen Museumsräumen gehängt werden können, aber, so Lissitzky, »gleichzeitig sieht man nur die Hälfte davon«.[7] Der Besucher kann sich also nicht nur auf jeweils ein Werk allein konzentrieren, sondern er ist es, der die Entscheidung darüber trifft, welches Werk dies sein soll und welche anderen er dafür verschwinden lässt.

Im Mai 1928 – die Arbeiten werden regelmäßig ausgetauscht – handelte es sich beispielsweise um diese Arbeiten: »Rechts: 2 Aquarelle von Lissitzky in verschiebbaren Wechselrahmen. Dahinter liegen 2 weitere Blätter, die sichtbar werden, wenn man den Rahmen nach rechts oder links schiebt. > 3.3 Darüber und darunter auf glatter schwarzer oder weißer Wandfläche 2 Arbeiten von Mondrian. Links: Unten Léger, oben Picasso, zwischen beiden eine verschiebbare Platte, die ein drittes Bild verdeckt.«[8] > 3.1

Their artistic creator El Lissitzky had identified these elements as follows: In contrast to the common practice of displaying works of art in exhibitions as a zoo would display animals, »where thousands of animals all roar at the visitors at once,« in his exhibition space »the objects [should] not all assail the beholder at one time.« Instead of fostering that ubiquitous passivity which inevitably ensues when perusing the walls of the exhibition, »our design should render the man active.«[5]

Three types of measures were taken to activate the viewer in this way: Firstly in the design of the walls, secondly in the specific curatorial approach to the artworks exhibited and finally (this being a didactic element incorporated explicitly at Dorner's suggestion) in moveable »information drums«, containing illustrations of the influences of abstract art on everyday objects. Thin tin strips were drilled into the walls of the room at right angles to the surface. The strips were black on one side and gray on the other, then white on those edges that protruded into the room – it was not long before the room was ironically dubbed a »pleated cubbyhole«. This metallic shading meant that the walls changed their look with every step the visitor took. Dorner summarizes this by claiming the room makes »many more sensory image impressions« than a traditional museum hall, »whereby movement actually explodes the space, as it were.«[6] In keeping with the second key element, this moment of dynamism and activation was enhanced by integrated panels, each of which contained three images. By installing surfaces that visitors were able to move themselves they were able to hang more artworks than would have been possible in conventional museum spaces, but, as Lissitzky points out, »at the same time, we only ever see half of them in any one moment.«[7] The beholder was therefore unable to concentrate on one particular work at a time and thus forced to decide which work should be visible and which should disappear to make room for the other.

In May 1928 for example the following works were on display (the works were changed regularly): »Right: two watercolors by Lissitzky in sliding clip-on picture frames. Behind them two other works that become visible when the frames are slid to the left or the right. > 3.3 Above and below, mounted on black or white surfaces are two works by Mondrian. Left: Léger below, Picasso above, between them a sliding panel that conceals a third work.«[8] > 3.1

Mithin verfügt die Kunstabteilung des Provinzialmuseums Ende der 1920er Jahre über Arbeiten von einigen der heute profiliertesten Vertretern der Klassischen Avantgarde. Dies ist nicht zuletzt auf das national wie international weit gespannte Netzwerk ihres Leiters Alexander Dorner zurückzuführen, der das Museum und darüber hinaus die hannoversche Kunstszene in das Blickfeld von Freunden der Avantgarde rückt – aber auch von ihren Gegnern.

Das Abstrakte Kabinett lässt schon lange vor der nationalsozialistischen Machtübernahme Kritiker über »Kulturbolschewismus« und »Internationalismus« klagen, die in einem Museum nichts zu suchen hätten. Nach 1933 setzt hier der Hebel einer neuen Kulturpolitik an: Schnell entstehen Pläne lokaler NSDAP-Kunstfunktionäre, den Raum zu einer »Schreckenskammer« zu machen, also nach Vorbild anderer deutscher Museen hier eine Sammlung von als besonders abschreckend gewerteten Beispielen »entarteter« Kunst zu installieren.[9] Drei Jahre lang gelingt es Alexander Dorner, das Abstrakte Kabinett geöffnet zu lassen – Jahre, in denen hier Werke zu sehen sind, die andernorts schon den Weg in die Magazine gefunden haben, Jahre aber auch, in denen Dorner eine für sich selbst wie für die dort ausgestellte Kunst diskreditierende Politik lippenbekennerischer Anpassung entwickelt. Dann, fast zehn Jahre nach seiner Fertigstellung, wird das Abstrakte Kabinett demontiert.[10]

Weder der Künstler noch der Museumsleiter erleben diesen Moment im Juli 1937: El Lissitzky hat Hannover jahrelang nicht mehr besucht, Alexander Dorner befindet sich bereits auf dem Weg in die USA und wird die Stätte, an der er bedeutende Arbeit für die Entwicklung moderner Museologie geleistet hat, nur ganz kurz vor seinem Tod im Herbst 1957 wiedersehen. Bis zu seinem Ende bleibt er überzeugt von der Pionierarbeit, die Lissitzky und er mit seiner Einrichtung geleistet haben. Moderne Ästhetik, so schreibt er noch in den 1950er Jahren, »kann nie mehr im ›Schauen‹ (= Zustand) sich erschöpfen, sondern muss zum Handwerk werden, zur Interaktion, zur Selbstveränderung«.[11]

Gut zehn Jahre später, konkret: Ende Juni 1968, wird das Niedersächsische Landesmuseum, die Nachfolgeeinrichtung des Provinzialmuseums, einem Wunsch von Dorners Witwe entsprechen und, finanziell unterstützt u. a. von der Ehefrau John D. Rockefeller Jrs., einer langjährigen Freundin der Dorners, ein nachgebautes Abstraktes Kabinett eröffnen.[12] In Hannover und weit darüber hinaus wird das Ereignis von Freunden und alten Weggefährten als lange überfällige Ehrung des Künstlers, des Kunsthistorikers und des Momentums ihrer Kollaboration begrüßt.

Indeed, by the end of the 1920s the Provincial Museum's Art Department housed works from (today) some of the most prominent representatives of the classical Modernist avant-garde. This is not least to be attributed to Alexander Dorner, the department's director, and his wide-reaching network that spanned Germany and the world. Dorner brought the museum and the Hanover art scene to the attention of friends of the avant-garde – but also of its opponents.

The Abstract Cabinet had already been a cause of complaint from critics long before the Nazi's accession to power, who all claimed its »cultural bolshevism« and »internationalism« had no place in a museum. And so, post-1933, the powers-that-were introduced a new cultural policy: plans by local Nazi art officials to turn the space into a »Chamber of Horrors« were quick to surface, a collection of particularly dissuasive instances of »degenerate« art was to be installed.[9] Alexander Dorner succeeded in keeping the Abstract Cabinet open for three whole years – years, during which works could be seen here that had already found their way into warehouses in other places, but also years during which Dorner developed a policy of assimilation (one could say he paid lip service to the Nazis) that brought both himself and the art on display into discredit. Then, almost a decade after its completion, the Abstract Cabinet was taken down.[10]

Neither the artists nor the Museum's director were destined to experience this moment in July 1937: El Lissitzky had not set foot in Hanover for many years and Alexander Dorner was already on his way to the USA – not to return to this place where he had made such a hugely significant contribution to the development of modern museology until shortly before his death in 1957. To the very end he remained convinced of the trail-blazing work that he and Lissitzky had achieved with their installation. As he wrote in the 1950s, modern aesthetics »should not be allowed to become mere 'beholding' (= state) ever again, but must now become craftsmanship, interaction, self-transformation.«[11]

Precisely ten years later: At the end of 1968, the Lower Saxony State Museum, which succeeded the Provincial Museum, would grant the wish of Dorner's widow and thanks to the financial support of John D. Rockefeller Jr.'s wife (a long-standing friend of Dorner) opened a replica of the Abstract Cabinet.[12] This was greeted by friends and old companions in Hanover and beyond, as a long-overdue honor to the artist, the art historian and what their collaboration had sparked.

Auch Lissitzkys Witwe Sophie, die es nach einem tragischen Lebensverlauf nach Nowosibirsk verschlagen hatte, gratuliert und erinnert sich an die Anfangsjahre des Abstrakten Kabinetts in Hannover, an eine bessere Zeit, da die dort gezeigten Kunstwerke noch nicht durch einen nationalsozialistischen Bildersturm in alle Welt zerstreut waren.[13] Erst die nachfolgenden Generationen werden nicht nur das Konzept der Rekonstruktion dieses Versuchs eines Gesamtkunstwerks kritischer beleuchten, ihnen wird es auch obliegen, die inneren Widersprüche und Unvereinbarkeiten einer Zusammenarbeit zwischen El Lissitzky, dem visionären Idealisten, und dem aufklärerischen Pragmatiker Alexander Dorner aufzudecken.[14]

Lissitzky's widow Sophie, who found herself in Novosibirsk following a quite tragic biography, also applauded the move and recalled the Abstract Cabinet's opening years and thus better times, before the works of art on show there were left scattered across the world following the Nazi's iconoclasm.[13] It is for succeeding generations to throw a more critical light on the concept surrounding the reconstruction of this attempt at artistic synthesis. It also be incumbent upon them to uncover the inner contradictions and inconsistencies of this collaborative project between the visionary idealist, El Lissitzky, and the enlightened pragmatist, Alexander Dorner.[14]

>>> author p.212

Die Verfasserin dankt folgenden Einrichtungen für Forschungsstipendien und Reisebeihilfen: Fritz Thyssen Stiftung für Wissenschaftsförderung, John Nicholas Brown Center for American Studies/Brown University, Providence, R. I., Institute for Contemporary German Studies, Washington, D. C./DAAD, Fulbright-Kommission, Deutsches Historisches Institut, Washington, D. C., sowie Terra Foundation for American Art, Chicago/John F. Kennedy-Institut für Nordamerikastudien, Berlin. Der Artikel wurde gefördert mit Forschungsmitteln des Landes Niedersachsen (ähnlich erschienen in PLOT #4).
The author would like thank the following institutions for their research and travel grants: The Fritz Thyssen Foundation; John Nicholas Brown Center for American Studies/Brown University, Providence, R. I.; Institute for Contemporary German Studies, Washington, D. C./DAAD; The Fulbright Commission; German Historical Institute, Washington, D. C.; as well as The Terra Foundation for American Art, Chicago/John F. Kennedy-Institute for North American Studies, Berlin. The article was supported by research funding from the State of Lower Saxony (a similar version was published in PLOT #4).

1 Protokoll der Tagung des Deutschen Museumsbundes im Provinzialmuseum Hannover, 11./12.10.1927, Zentralarchiv der Staatlichen Museen zu Berlin, Stiftung Preußischer Kulturbesitz, Akten des Deutschen Museumsbundes, Nr. 285.
Minutes from the meeting of the Deutscher Museumbund at Provinzialmuseum Hannover, October 11-12, 1927, Central Archive of Berlin State Museums, Foundation of Prussian Cultural Heritage, Deutscher Museumbund records, no. 285.
2 Jubiläum des Provinzialmuseums. Die Feier des 75-jährigen Bestehens. Festakt in der Stadthalle, Hannoverscher Kurier, 10.10.1927.
Anniversary of the Provinzialmuseum's opening. Ceremony celebrating 75 years held in the Stadthalle, Hannoverscher Kurier, October 10, 1927.
3 Diese Aussage traf Barr im Zusammenhang mit der Entstehung des Buches von Samuel Cauman: Das lebende Museum. Erinnerung eines Kunsthistorikers und Museumsdirektors. Alexander Dorner, Hannover 1961, S.116.
This statement from Barr was made in relation to Samuel Cauman's book: The living museum: experiences of an art historian and museum director: Alexander Dorner, (New York, 1958), p.116.
4 Giedion, Sigfried: Lebendiges Museum, in: Cicerone, no. 21, 1929, p.103–106.
5 Cf. Lissitzky-Küppers, Sophie (Ed.): El Lissitzky. Maler, Architekt, Typograf, Fotograf. Erinnerungen, Briefe, Schriften. Berlin, Wien et al. 1980, p.362.
6 Dorner, Alexander: Überwindung der »Kunst«. Hanover 1959, p.151.
7 Lissitzky-Küppers, Sophie (Ed.): El Lissitzky. Maler, Architekt, Typograf, Fotograf. Erinnerungen, Briefe, Schriften. Berlin, Wien et al. 1980, p.362.
8 Handschriftliche Rückseitenbeschriftung eines Fotos vom Abstrakten Kabinett, gestempelt am 22.5.1928, Eidgenössische Technische Hochschule Zürich, Archiv des Instituts für Geschichte und Theorie der Architektur, Nachlass Sigfried Giedion, 43 – S – 5 – 9 – F – 1.
Handwritten lettering on the back of a photograph of the Abstract Cabinet, stamped on April 5, 1928, Federal Institute of Technology Zurich, Archives of the Institute for History and Theory of Architecture, bequest of Sigfried Giedion, 43 – S – 5 – 9 – F – 1.
9 Vgl. dazu ein Dokument, das im Niedersächsischen Staatsarchiv aufbewahrt wird. Auf einen Zeitungsartikel aus der Dresdner Zeitungen vom 5.5.1933, der von einer »Ausmusterung der modernen Abteilung der Dresdener Staatsgalerie« und einer »Kunstausstellung zum Abschrecken« berichtete, reagierte Schatzrat Hartmann mit dieser Aktennotiz: »1) Herr Dr. Lambert, voraussichtlich Vorsitzender der Museumskommission, besprach mit mir die nebenstehend mitgeteilten Maßnahmen anderer Museen zum Abschrecken und stellte zur Erwägung, auch im Provinzial-Museum Ähnliches vorzusehen, z. B. das Abstrakte Kabinett als Gegenbeispiel gegen die heutige Auffassung zu bringen. 2) Urschriftlich g. R. Herrn Prof. Dr. Dorner, Prov. Mus. zur Äußerung für das Museum für Kunst pp. Im Laufe dieses Monats ist eine Sitzung der Museumskommission vorgesehen. D.L.D. gez. Hartmann.« Auf diesem Blatt befindet sich diese Rückmeldung Dorners: »Urschriftlich Dorner an Hartmann, 9.5.1933, Mit dem Berichte zurückgereicht, dass nach Rücksprache mit Herrn Lambert eine entsprechende Beschriftung in dem Expressionisten- und Abstrakten Kabinett angebracht worden ist. gez. Dorner.« (Niedersächsisches Landesarchiv/ Hauptstaatsarchiv Hannover, Hann. 152, Acc. 68/94, 5, auch Hann. 151, Nr. 183).
Cf. a document held in the Lower Saxony State Archive. In response to a newspaper article published in the Dresdner Zetiung on May 5, 1933, reporting on a »dissolution of the modern section of the Dresdner Stadtgallerie« and a »deterrent art exhibition«, Court Treasurer Hartmann issued the memo: »1) Dr. Lambert, prospective Chairman of the Museum commission, discussed the deterrent measures also communicated by other museums and also suggested implementing similar measures in Provinzialmuseum, presenting the Abstract Cabinet as a counterexample to the present-day approach. 2) Original reply to Prof. Dorner, Prov. Mus. on the observations for the Museum für Kunst etc. The Museum Commission plans to hold a meeting in the course of the month. D.L.D. sgd. Hartmann.« This document displays the following response from Dorner: »Original Dorner to Hartmann, May 9, 1933, upon return of the report, after consultation with Hartmann an adequate inscription has been incorporated into the Expressionist and Abstract Cabinet. Sgd. Dorner.« (Lower Saxony State Archive/ Central State Archive Hanover, Hann. 152, Acc. 68/94, 5, and Hann. 151, no. 183).
10 Cf. Katenhusen, Ines: »Ein Museumsdirektor auf und zwischen den Stühlen. Alexander Dorner (1893–1957) in Hannover«. in: Peters, Olaf; Heftrig, Ruth; Schellewald, Barbara (Eds.): Kunstgeschichte im »Dritten Reich«. Theorien, Methoden, Praktiken. Berlin 2008, p.156–170.
11 N. dat. Äußerung Alexander Dorners, Busch-Reisinger Museum/Harvard University Museums, Alexander Dorner Papers, Folder 226–239.
Undated statement from Alexander Dorner, Busch-Reisinger Museum/Harvard University Museums, Alexander Dorner Papers, Folder 226–239.
12 Bode, Ursula: »Ihr Geschenk an Hannover. Lydia Dorner und das abstrakte Kabinett«. Hannoversche Allgemeine Zeitung, June 22-3, 1968.
13 Sophie Küppers-Lissitzky an Harald Seiler, Niedersächsisches Landesumseum Hannover, 22.7.1968, Sprengel Museum Hannover, Alexander Dorner-Papiere, Nachlass Harald Seiler.
Sophie Küppers-Lissitzky to Harald Seiler, Niedersächsisches Landesmuseum Hannover, July 22, 1968, Sprengel Museum Hannover, Alexander Dorner-Papiere, bequest of Harald Seiler.
14 Cf. Gough, Maria: Constructivism Disoriented. El Lissitzky's Dresden and Hannover Demonstrationsräume. in: Perloff, Nancy; Reed, Brian (Eds.): Situating El Lissitzky. Vitebsk, Berlin, Moscow. Los Angeles 2003, p.77–128.

Kai-Uwe Hemken

Podien staatlicher Selbstdarstellung:
Die internationale Presse-Ausstellung 1928 in Köln

Die Internationale Presse-Ausstellung (Pressa), die im Mai 1928 auf
dem neu errichteten Messegelände in Köln eröffnet wurde, war in ihrer
Themenstellung ein ungewöhnliches Projekt, sollte doch ein ideelles und
nicht materielles Gut ausgestellt werden. So bestand noch bis in den
Sommer 1928 in der Öffentlichkeit große Skepsis, ob das Pressewesen
überhaupt ausstellbar sei. Dagegen waren sich die Veranstalter schon
in der frühesten Planungsphase darüber einig, dass gerade in der Vermittlung und Präsentation ideeller kultureller Werte die Chance lag, eine
außergewöhnliche Ausstellung zu verwirklichen, wie der damalige
Oberbürgermeister der Stadt Köln, Konrad Adenauer, bereits 1926 bei
einer Rede anlässlich der Gründungsversammlung des Komitees der
Internationalen Presse-Ausstellung ausrief.

Bereits seit Beginn der Vorbereitungen im Jahre 1926 beabsichtigten die
Veranstalter der Pressa, aus dieser zunächst kommunalen Ausstellung
ein Unternehmen von internationalem Rang zu machen. Man versicherte sich
daher der Unterstützung der Reichsregierung, der Ministerien des Reichs
und der Länder. Es wurden neben der deutschen Druckindustrie auch die
europäischen und außereuropäischen Nationen eingeladen, in Köln ihre
Leistungen auf dem Gebiet der Presse in »geschlossenen Sondergruppen«
zu präsentieren. Die Stadt Köln versuchte, mit dem internationalen Charakter
der Pressa ihr kommunales Ausstellungsprojekt aus der Vielzahl ähnlicher
Projekte herauszuheben, denn neben Köln veranstalteten u. a. die Städte
Dresden, Hamburg, Bremen und Halle sowie Leipzig, München und Berlin
regelmäßig Messen und (Fach-)Ausstellungen, die den wirtschaftlichen
Aufschwung ihrer Kommunen und Regionen unterstützten.

Grundsätzlich wurde die Pressa in zwei Bereiche gegliedert: in die deutschen
und die ausländischen Abteilungen. Während die ausländischen Sektionen
im sogenannten Staatenhaus geschlossen untergebracht wurden, entfal-
teten sich die deutschen Abteilungen in großem Umfang. Ihnen standen
mehrere Gebäude zur Verfügung, sodass, sehr breit gefächert, die Bereiche
»Tageszeitung«, »Zeitschrift«, »technische Einrichtungen und Hilfsmittel«,
»Verbandswesen der Presse«, die deutsche Presse im Ausland, »Presse
und Verkehr« sowie »Presse und Kunst«, »Buchgewerbe und Grafik« und
letztlich »Papierwesen«, »Werbewesen«, »Fotografie und Kinematografie«
ausgestellt werden konnten.

The state's self-portraits on a pedestal:
The International Press Exhibition 1928 in Cologne

*In its thematic focus the International Press Exhibition (Pressa), which
opened on the newly constructed trade fair grounds in Cologne in May 1928,
was a rather peculiar project; its aim was after all to exhibit something that
is a matter of ideas and has no material substance. This led to a great deal
of scepticism among the general public during the summer of 1928 as to
whether the press as an entity could even be exhibited. Even in the earliest
stages of planning the show's organizers had, by contrast agreed that
conveying and presenting of ideal, cultural values would present an opportunity to realize an extraordinary exhibition, as the then Mayor of the City
of Cologne, Konrad Adenauer, proclaimed in a speech held at the founding
assembly of the International Press Exhibition committee in 1926.*

*From the very beginning of preparations in 1926, Pressa's organizers
intended to use the coming collaborative exhibition to launch an enterprise
of international standing. For in this way one was guaranteed support from
the government, its ministries and the individual states. In addition to the
German press, they also invited the press from Europe and the rest of the
world to come to Cologne and present their achievements in the area of print
media in »special enclosed groups«. Giving the joint exhibition project
a decidedly international flare was the city of Cologne's attempt to outrank
the host of similar projects around at the time, for it had cities such as
Dresden, Hamburg, Bremen and Halle as well as Leipzig, Munich and Berlin
to compete with. And all of them regularly hosted trade fairs and (trade)
exhibitions which were driven by the financial upswing underway in these
municipalities and regions.*

*In principle Pressa would have been divided into two areas: the German
section and the international section, but while the international contributions were exhibited behind closed doors in the so-called Staatenhaus,
the German section developed into a spectacle of large proportions. It was
allocated several buildings, providing plenty of room to exhibit a broad range
of themes from the world of the press, including »dailies«, »magazines«,
»technical equipment and resources«, »press associations«, »the German
press abroad«, »the press and transport« as well as »the press and art«,
»the book trade« and finally »the paper industry«, »advertising« and
»photography and cinematography«.*

3.1   3.2   3.3

Die geplante umfassende Schau des internationalen und besonders des deutschen Pressewesens erforderte eine Vergrößerung der bis 1926 bestehenden Messeanlage, die als Austragungsort der Pressa gedacht war. Der Stadtbaudirektor Alfred Abel wurde beauftragt, das etwa 500.000 m² große Gelände am Rheinufer, inklusive der bereits vorhandenen Baulichkeiten, für die Pressa umzugestalten. Darüber hinaus wurden benachbarte Bauten, wie die ehemalige Kürassierkaserne, in die Planungen einbezogen.

Die Schauräume der verschiedenen Nationen und besonders der deutschen Abteilungen zeigten sich geradezu weihevoll. Sowohl in der Kollektivausstellung der Reichsregierung als auch in den Räumen der Länderregierungen sowie der deutschen Privatwirtschaft, d. h. der Druckindustrie und ihrer Fachverbände, wurden in endlosen Reihen und in streng geometrischer Anordnung die Wände mit Druckerzeugnissen, die »hinter Glas« oder auf großen Tafeln präsentiert wurden, behängt. Daneben versuchte man, durch eine Inszenierung von Licht und Material wie Glas oder verchromtes Metall, den Schauräumen eine exklusive Atmosphäre zu verleihen. ›3.1 Eine geometrisch-gleichförmige Anordnung der Exponate, monochrome Wandgestaltungen, schwarze Tischvitrinen, schlichte typografische Elemente und Schriftzüge gaben den Ausstellungsräumen eine würdevolle Gesamterscheinung, die jedes Exponat zu einem Artefakt werden ließ. ›3.2 Schautafeln unterbrachen mit vereinzelten Schriftzügen und schematisierten Darstellungen diese strenge Inszenierung, ohne aber dabei den Gesamteindruck zu stören.

Diese Tafeln hatten belehrenden Charakter und provozierten zwischen Objekt und Rezipienten eine hierarchische Struktur; denn in den Räumen der Reichsregierung sollte der Status der Amtsgrafik, gemeint waren Gesetzestexte, Hoheitszeichen usw., versinnbildlicht werden. ›3.3 Hier trat der Staat als Lehrmeister auf, der die Grundprinzipien der Staatsordnung vermitteln wollte. Insgesamt hatte man sich offenbar an modernen Museumsgestaltungen, z. B. in Dresden, Halle, Essen und Hannover, sowie an der noch jungen, formenreduzierten Schaufenstergestaltung orientiert. Der Formenelementarismus und die Anwendung von Industriematerialien wurden zu Chiffren einer industrienahen Lebensform.

Plans for this extensive display of international and in particular German print media called for the expansion of Pressa's intended venue, Cologne's trade fair site pre-1926. The city's planning director Alfred Abel was commissioned to redesign the approximately 500,000 sqm site on the banks of the River Rhine specially for the occasion. The intention was to incorporate the trade fair's extant structures into Abel's plans as well as neighbouring buildings such as the former cuirassier barracks.

The exhibition spaces for the various nations involved (the German sections of course more than others) had quite a solemn appearance. Both in the collective exhibition by the government and in the exhibition spaces allocated to the various German states and Germany's private sector, ergo the print industry and its respective trade associations, the walls were bedecked with endless rows of printed material, arranged in a strict geometric pattern and presented »behind glass« or mounted on large panels. In addition, a targeted orchestration of light and material (using glass or chromed metal, for example) constituted an attempt to lend these spaces something of an exclusive atmosphere. ›3.1 With the geometrical/uniform arrangement of the exhibits, the monochrome walls, the black table showcases and the modest typography and lettering, the spaces assumed a rather stately appearance that transformed each exhibit into an artefact. ›3.2 This strict mise-en-scène was interrupted by information panels featuring sporadic text and diagrams, though these were implemented in such a way as not to affect the overall impression.

They had an educational feel to them and prompted a hierarchical arrangement between object and recipient; for in the rooms filled with exhibits from the Republic's own government, the aim was to symbolize the status of official graphic elements, meaning legal texts, the national emblem etc. ›3.3 The state presented itself as the master teacher, and this lesson was on fundamental principles of state order. On the whole it was abundantly clear that the organizers had oriented themselves on modern museum design as seen in Dresden, Halle, Essen and Hanover, as well as the emergent, rather reduced design á la mode in window dressing at the time. Elementarism in terms of shape and form and the use of industrial materials became ciphers for an industry-oriented way of life.

3.4–3.6 *in: Ribalta, Jorge (Ed.): Public Photographic Spaces: Exhibitions of Propaganda, from Pressa to The Family of Man, 1928-55. Barcelona 2009, p.62-63.*
© *Russian Archiv*

Das Grundmuster der Flächenaufteilung in den deutschen Hallen war ein rein geometrisches Formenvokabular ohne Abwechslungen, das sich auf Gestaltungsmodi, wie die axiale und symmetrische Anordnung sowie die Rondell-, Kreis- und Zickzack-Anordnung, stützte. Hier bestimmte vor allem das Gebot einer möglichst ökonomischen Ausnutzung und demokratischen Verteilung der vorhandenen Fläche die Gestaltung, sodass dem Besucher allerdings auch keine Höhepunkte geboten wurden.

Die Präsentation in den deutschen Abteilungen lenkte die Aufmerksamkeit des Besuchers verstärkt auf das Endprodukt und weniger auf die Produktionsweise. Dabei resultierte die nüchterne Ausstellungsästhetik aus einem Selbstverständnis, das die Lebensprinzipien einer modernen Industriegesellschaft bejahte.

Einen für die Geschichte des Ausstellungsdesigns wegweisenden Beitrag für die Pressa lieferte der sowjetische Pavillon, der von dem Konstruktivisten El Lissitzky gestaltet wurde. Im Dezember 1927 wurde er zum künstlerischen Leiter des Sowjet-Pavillons auf der Pressa berufen. Es waren insgesamt 20 verschiedene Abteilungen geplant, die eine außergewöhnlich große Gruppe von Künstlern unter der Leitung Lissitzkys erstellte. Die Gestaltung des sowjetischen Pavillons erwuchs zu einer raumgreifenden, monumentalen Propaganda, die in einem umfassenden Konzept Typografie, Fotografie und Architektur zu einem ästhetischen und bisweilen pathetischen Schauspiel zusammenführte. Schrittweise wurden dem Besucher auf ca. 1.000 m² Grundfläche die Geschichte und Funktion des Pressewesens in der Sowjetunion nahegebracht. So hatte Lissitzky den gesamten Raum in einzelne, überschaubare Abschnitte gegliedert, ohne jedoch auf eine monumentale ästhetische Gesamtinszenierung zu verzichten. Verglichen zum Beispiel mit den Ausstellungshallen der deutschen Abteilungen war der sowjetische Pavillon von einer aufgelockerten Anordnung der Objekte, Stände und Installationen gekennzeichnet. Große Freiräume wechselten mit dicht gedrängt aufgestellten Objekten, sodass sich ein abwechslungsreiches Schauspiel von Installationen bot.

Lissitzky empfing den Ausstellungsbesucher im Eingangsraum mit sechs überdimensionalen Förderbändern und einem übergroßen Sowjetstern, deren imposante Wirkung durch eine große Freifläche noch gesteigert wurde. Die sechs riesigen Förderbänder, die sogenannten »Transmissionsriemen«, präsentierten Zeitschriften, Hefte und Flugblätter aus der sowjetischen Presse.

The basic pattern used to sub-divide the exhibition space in the German rooms was a purely geometric formula without variations, based upon certain composition modes, such as axial and symmetric arrangements or circular and zigzag ones. These design concepts were determined above all by the precept prescribing that the space available be used as economically as possible and be divided up democratically, so that visitors would not be drawn to one particular highlight.

In the German section, the visitor's attention was more clearly directed to the end product with less emphasis on the production methods behind it, whereby the sober exhibition aesthetics resulted from the self-conception that affirmed the lifestyle principles within a modern industrial society.

A pavilion designed by constructivist El Lissitzky, the Soviet Union's contribution to Pressa, would prove to be pioneering in the history of exhibition design. Lissitzky had been appointed creative director of the Soviet pavilion for Pressa in December 1927 and his plans soon came to include a total of 20 different sections, which led to the formation of an exceptionally large group of artists all working under Lissitzky's direction. The Soviet pavilion's design grew into an expansive, monumental piece of propaganda, which combined typography, photography and architecture along with a clear aesthetic and at times a somewhat melodramatic spectacle to form one comprehensive exhibition concept. Over a surface area of approx. 1,000 sqm visitors were gradually brought closer to the history and function of the press in the Soviet Union. To this end, Lissitzky had divided the entire space into straightforward, individual sections, without however causing detriment to the overall spatial effect, monumental and aesthetic as it was. When compared, for example, with the exhibition spaces dedicated to the German print media, the Soviet pavilion stood out for its less regimented arrangement of the objects, stands and installations. Large open spaces were interspersed with densely packed groups of objects, offering a multifarious pageant of installations.

Visitors to Lissitzky's exhibition space were greeted by six colossal conveyer belts and an oversized Soviet Star, their imposing effect enhanced even further by the large amount of free space surrounding them. The six giant »conveyer belts«, the so-called »transmission belts« held magazines, books and flyers from the Soviet press and were driven by motors providing a rotating exposition of the achievements of the Soviet print media.

3.4

3.5

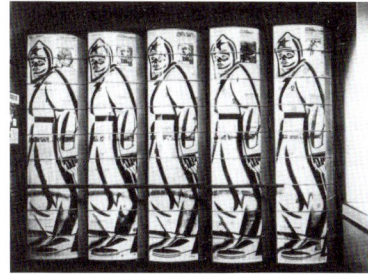
3.6

Diese Förderbänder wurden durch Motoren bewegt und zeigten am laufenden Band die Leistungen des sowjetischen Druckgewerbes. Der mehrere Meter hohe Sowjetstern, der »Große Stern«, verkündete in Leuchtschrift die Parolen der sowjetischen Gesellschaft. Er sollte die Grundprinzipien der Sowjetverfassung veranschaulichen. ›3.4

Nach der Einstimmung im Eingangsbereich des Pavillons passierte der Besucher die Förderbänder, Schautafeln sowie Landkarten und gelangte zu einem überdimensionalen »Photographischen Fries« (3,5 x 24 m), der u. a. eine »filmartige« Zusammenfassung der gesamten Ausstellung lieferte. Der Fotofries war neben den Förderbändern und dem Sowjetstern ein zentrales Exponat des Pavillons. Zeigte Lissitzky hier doch die neue Form und Gestalt der Propaganda-Presse und des sogenannten »Massenbuches«, das allein mit Bildern bzw. Fotografien gestaltet wurde. ›3.5
Die Montage und Überblendung von verschiedenen Fotos und deren Perspektiven erzeugten einen filmartigen Ablauf, der dem avantgardistischen Sowjetfilm beispielsweise eines Dsiga Werthoff nahe stand. Die filmartige Dramaturgie der Fotomontagen entsprach Lissitzkys Forderungen an eine neue, sozialistische Buchform.

Viele Ausstellungsstücke waren Anspielungen auf Maschinen und maschinenähnliche Apparaturen der Industrieproduktion. ›3.6 Die »Bewegungen« und die Geräuschkulisse der Motoren verliehen dem Pavillon den Charakter einer Maschinenhalle. Der Raum wurde durch die Gestaltung zu einer überdimensionalen Produktionsstätte. Lissitzky hatte ein Gesamtkunstwerk inszeniert, das die Industrialisierungspolitik der Sowjetunion zur Schau tragen sollte. Er legte bei seiner Symbolsprache, die er für die Pressa auf Grundlage des künstlerischen Programms der Gruppe OKTJABR entwickelte, auf die Vermittlung eines gesamten Ideengutes, auf die Präsentation einer Lebensform und Ideologie größten Wert. Die Einrichtungen im Sowjet-Pavillon gaben somit nicht nur Detailinformationen, sondern es wurde beständig das Detail als Bestandteil eines großen Komplexes verständlich gemacht.

In neon lights the »Great Star«, mounted several meters above the belts, heralded the paroles of Soviet society, a visual representation of the basic principles of the constitution of the Soviet Union. ›3.4

After the tone had been set in the pavilion's entrance area, the visitors passed by the conveyer belts, the information boards and the maps, finding their way to an enormous »photographic frieze« (3.5 x 24 m), which among other things provided a »film-like« summary of the entire exhibition. Alongside the conveyer belts and the Soviet Star, the photo frieze was one of the pavilion's main exhibits. After all, this was Lissitzky's way of presenting the new face of propaganda press and the so-called »books for the masses«, its design comprising solely of images, or rather photographs. ›3.5 *The montage and over-blend of different photographs and their angles made for a film-like sequence which was not far removed from avantgardist Soviet cinema of the time, such as films by Dsiga Werthoff. The photo montage's film-like dramatics also conformed to Lissitzky's requirements for a new socialist take on the book.*

Many of the pieces featured in the exhibition were allusions to the machines and machine-like gadgetry found in industrial production. ›3.6 *The »movements« and the background noise from the motors transported the pavilion's visitors to a factory plant floor, while the design transformed the space into a colossal manufacturing plant. Lissitzky had produced an artistic synthesis that put the Soviet Union's policy of industrialisation on display for the world to see. In Lissitzky's symbolic vocabulary, which he developed specifically for Pressa based on the program put forward by the OKTJABR art group, he placed a great deal of emphasis on the conveying an integral idea, on the presentation of a way of life, an ideology. Thus the installations in the Soviet pavilion not only provided its visitors with detailed information, but also made consistently clear that detail is merely a component of a larger complex entity.*

>>> author p.211

Kai-Uwe Hemken
Die Abteilung des Deutschen Werkbundes auf der
»Exposition de la Société des Artistes Décorateurs« 1930 in Paris

»Da haben Sie uns ja einen schönen Blechladen (!) geschickt!«[1], posaunte der deutsche Botschafter Hoesch in Paris, als er der dortigen Ausstellungs- eröffnung der »Société des artistes décorateurs« 1930 beiwohnte. Sein Erschrecken galt der deutschen Abteilung, die Walter Gropius unter reich- licher Verwendung von Metall, Glas und einem neuen Wandverkleidungs- material namens Trolit eingerichtet hatte. Gegen Ende 1929 erhielt Gropius seitens des Deutschen Werkbundes den Auftrag, der offiziellen Einladung des französischen Verbandes für Kunstgewerbe, der »Société des artistes décorateurs«, zu folgen und die Beteiligung Deutschlands an der für das Jahr 1930 geplanten Ausstellung in Paris auszurichten.

Die Ausstellung, die vom 14. Mai bis 13. Juli 1930 in den Räumen des Grand Palais in Paris stattfand, war jedoch keineswegs international ausgerichtet, sondern lud allein Deutschland zur Teilnahme ein. Gropius konnte ehemalige Mitstreiter am Bauhaus in Dessau wie Oskar Schlemmer, Herbert Bayer, Marcel Breuer und László Moholy-Nagy für eine Mitarbeit gewinnen.

Die Ausstellung der deutschen Sektion, die in einem Gebäudeteil des Grand Palais untergebracht war, bestand aus insgesamt fünf Ausstellungsab- schnitten. Gropius aber schien bemüht zu sein, die vorhandene Ausstel- lungsfläche möglichst sinnvoll zu gliedern und darüber hinaus die von ihm programmatisch bekämpfte historistische Architektur optisch nicht in Erscheinung treten zu lassen. Gropius ließ den Ausstellungsrundgang nicht mit einer Foyersituation beginnen, sondern konfrontierte den Besucher zunächst mit einem Schwimmbecken, das dieser rechts liegen zu lassen hatte, um in den eigentlichen Empfangsraum zu gelangen. Den Kern des Raumes 1 bildete der Gemeinschaftsraum eines Wohnhochhauses, beste- hend aus einer Bar und weiteren Sitzgelegenheiten, an denen sich seitlich Sitznischen anschlossen. Über diesen Nischen erhob sich in der zweiten Ebene eine Bibliothek.

Bereits im Durchgang zu Raum 2 wurde der Besucher mit Produkten der industriellen Serienherstellung zum Thema »Licht und Beleuchtung« konfrontiert. Montierte und durch Trennflächen separierte Lampen wurden mit Fotoreihungen verbunden. Das Serienprodukt »Beleuchtungsgegen- stand« war auch Thema des von Moholy-Nagy gestalteten Raumes 2, der allerdings zu einem nicht geringen Teil auch Exponate zum Thema »Theater« zeigte.

The Deutscher Werkbund section at the 1930
»Exposition de la Société des Artistes Décorateurs« in Paris

»Well, they've certainly sent us a nice tin can (!),[1] proclaimed German ambassador Hoesch at the inauguration of the 1930 »Société des artistes décorateurs« exhibition in Paris. It was German section of the exhibition that had been the cause for his dismay; designed by Walter Gropius it was made predominantly from metal, glass and a new wall-paneling material called Trolit. Towards the end of 1929, Gropius was commissioned by the Deutscher Werkbund to take up the invitation sent by the French society of decorator-artists, »Société des artistes décorateurs«, and coordinate Germany's contribution to the show to be held in 1930.

But the exhibition, which took place in Paris' Grand Palais between May 14 and July 13, 1930, transpired to be anything but international in its orientation, Germany being the only other nation invited to attend. Gropius was succeed- ing in persuading former colleagues from his time at Bauhaus in Dessau to join the project, including Oskar Schlemmer, Herbert Bayer, Marcel Breuer and László Moholy-Nagy.

Germany's share in the exhibition was housed in its own section of the Grand Palais and consisted of five exhibition segments. However, Gropius seemed to have taken great care to divide up the space provided in the most sensible way possible and, furthermore, to prevent the space's historical architecture from providing a visual distraction, a battle that he executed in the most programmatic way. Gropius did not want the visitor to begin their tour of the show in a foyer setting but confronted them first with a swimming pool, at which point they had to turn off to the left to find their way into the actual reception room. A replica of a common room as could be found in a high-rise residential building formed the focal point of room 1; the room housed a bar and other places to seat, with other seating alcoves adjacent to it and a library towering above them on the second floor.

Even in their transition from room 1 to room 2, the visitor was confronted products of industrial, mass-production all from the field of »light and lighting«. Mounted on the walls and separated by dividing elements, the luminaires were linked to one another by means of photo sequences. »Lighting objects« as serial products constituted the main focus of room 2, designed by Moholy-Nagy, which in no small part also featured exhibits from the world of theater.

3.1

3.2

Im Zentrum befand sich ein Filmprojektionsraum mit Sitzgelegenheiten. Daran schlossen sich Vitrinen mit dem Modell des Totaltheaters Gropius', mit Bühnenmodellen Moholys und dessen kinetischem »Lichtrequisit« an. Auffallend waren die drei Theaterfigurinen Oskar Schlemmers, von denen die mittlere sich nach Augenzeugenberichten sogar gedreht haben soll. Eine auf Eck gestellte Vitrinen- und Fototafel-Stellwand, die wiederum Serienprodukte zeigte, lenkte den Besucher zum Idealtyp eines standardisierten Postamtes von Vorhoelzer, das dem Katalogverkauf diente.

Eine gebogene Glaswand führte den Besucher zu Raum 3, das heißt, er wurde auf eine metallene Rampenkonstruktion, das sogenannte Tezett-System, gelenkt, das ihm nun die Möglichkeit eröffnete, nicht nur den Gemeinschaftsraum, sondern auch die von Marcel Breuer eingerichteten »Wohnzellen« des Raumes 3 aus der Vogelperspektive zu betrachten. ›3.2

Der von Herbert Bayer gestaltete Raum 4 wurde von einer überdimensionalen Vitrine beherrscht, während an den Wänden entlang des Raumes Stoffe, Serienmöbel sowie weitere Produkte gezeigt wurden, die nach dem Prinzip der Typisierung und Standardisierung entworfen worden waren.

Im letzten, ebenfalls von Herbert Bayer eingerichteten Raum wurde die Architektur des Neuen Bauens thematisiert. Großformatige Fototafeln wurden an Drähten und in drei Ebenen entlang einer Wand aufgehängt, die zentrale Beispiele dieses Baustils zeigten. Dazu wurden zwei Architekturmodelle präsentiert: Das Scheibenhochhaus (1928) von Ludwig Mies van der Rohe sowie das Gebäude des Bauhauses in Dessau (1926) von Walter Gropius. Bayer ordnete zudem in zwei gegenüberliegenden Ecken des Raumes Stühle der Serienproduktion an, das heißt, er montierte die Stahl- und Buchenholzstühle übereinander an die Eckwände, um das Serielle und die Leichtigkeit dieser Möbel zu betonen. ›3.3

Wie Herbert Bayer nachträglich resümiert, muss die Pariser Ausstellung in der Geschichte des modernen Ausstellungsdesigns für die Bauhäusler ein wichtiges Ereignis dargestellt haben, zeigte diese Ausstellung doch erstmals eine Art Vokabular des modernen Ausstellungsdesigns: Lichtregie, Denotation und Konnotation, Sukzession, Schließung und Öffnung, Materialästhetik, Fülle und Kargheit, Wechsel der Betrachterperspektive, Raumgliederung, Rhythmik.

At the center there was a projection room with spaces for visitors to sit and observe. This was adjoined by a number of showcases containing models of Gropius' »total theater«, stage models by Moholy herself, and kinetic »light props« to accompany them. The three theater figurines made by Oskar Schlemmer were particularly striking; according to reports from visitors, one of the three even rotated. Another display made up of showcases and photo boards was placed in the corner, again displaying a series of mass-produced items, and directed the visitor's gaze toward the model of a stereotype post office worker created by Vorhoelzer for catalog sale.

A curved glass wall then led visitors on to room 3, ushering them onto a metal ramp structure, the so-called Tezett System, and affording them a bird's-eye view not only of the common room but of room 3 too, filled with »living cells« designed by Marcel Breuer. ›3.2

Room 4, which had been conceived by Herbert Bayer, was dominated by a colossal showcase, while the room's walls displayed fabric, mass-produced furniture and other products that had been designed in accordance with the principles of typification and standardization.

In the last room, its creator (also Herbert Bayer) took the architecture of the New Building movement as his theme. On one of the walls, large-format photo boards were hung using wire, arranged on three different levels, and exhibited key exemplars of this architectural style. In addition two architectural models were presented to the public: Ludwig Mies van der Rohe's high-rise (1928) and Walter Gropius' Bauhaus building in Dessau (1926). Bayer also created arrangements of mass-produced chairs in two opposite corners of the room, ergo he mounted a number of metal and beech wood chairs on the walls one above the other, and in doing so emphasized the object's seriality as well as their precarious lightness. ›3.3

As Herbert Bayer commented in retrospect, the Paris exhibition must have represented a major event in the history of modern exhibition design for the Bauhaus members, after all this was the first to display a kind of lexicon of modern exhibition design: lighting design, denotation and connotation, succession, closing and opening, material aesthetics, fullness and scantiness, offering the visitor alternative perspectives, division of the space, rhythm.

3.3

Die Bestrebungen der Avantgarde lassen sich geradezu als Strategien mit folgenden Zielen bezeichnen: Intensivierung der Betrachtung, Information statt Persuasion, Erleichterung der Rezeption bei gleichzeitiger Eindeutigkeit der Aussage, Vermeidung von visueller Monumentalität und Entsprechung eines neuen Raumgefühls, Dynamisierung des vorgegebenen Volumens der Ausstellungsräume.

Gropius nutzte das zu seiner Zeit entwickelte Vokabular des Ausstellungsdesigns, um die Ideale einer Weltanschauung auf verschiedene Ebenen zu transportieren. Dabei war er stets dem Primat der Aufklärung und der Vermeidung des Monumentalen verpflichtet. Die Sukzessivität der Informationen, der Wechsel der Betrachterperspektive, das Spiel von Transparenz und Geschlossenheit, die Unabhängigkeit der Ausstellungsinstallation von der vorgegebenen Architektur waren Mittel zur Intensivierung der Wahrnehmung, zur sachlichen Vermittlung von Informationen und zur Vermeidung des Monumentalen. Monumentalität entsprach nicht Gropius' demokratischem Anliegen, das auf die Ideale einer Lebensform zielte, die selbstverantwortlich eine Befreiung von den Zwängen prekärer Lebensverhältnisse, eine Erneuerung von Körper und Geist in Einklang mit der Natur und eine Entsprechung veränderter sozialer Bedürfnisse im Sinn hatte.

Dem Vorwort des Kataloges ist zu entnehmen, dass Gropius hier offenbar das Diktum der Funktionalität aufgegeben hatte und dem Standarderzeugnis nicht mehr die Rolle eines Objektes des massenhaften Gebrauchs zubilligte, sondern nun als Zeichen wertschätzte. Schönheit erfülle sich nicht mehr bloß in der ökonomischen wie funktionalen Formgebung, sondern vielmehr in der symbolisch vollzogenen Synthese von Kunst und Technik. Diese Synthese sei die Vorbotin eines Zustandes der prophezeiten Verschmelzung von Realität und Utopie. In seinen Exponaten schien sich eine komplette Weltinterpretation inklusive Wertemodell zu spiegeln, die sich durch ihre Eigenschaft als Gebrauchsartikel einer massenhaften Verbreitung erfreuen konnte. Hier scheint das Ausstellungsdesign eine Sinnebene hervorzurufen, die dem Massenprodukt scheinbar von vornherein zugeeignet wurde und nun neben dem Aspekt der Funktionalität an das Tageslicht befördert wird: der utopische Gehalt. ›3.4

The avant-garde's arduous attempts can only be described as strategies working toward the following objectives: to intensify our consideration of what we see, to inform rather than persuade, to facilitate perception simultaneously maintaining the unambiguousness of the message, to avoid visual monumenality and to parallel a new feel for the space, to inject dynamism into the given dimensions of exhibition spaces.

Gropius used this vocabulary, which had been developed during his own time, to convey the ideals of an ideology on a range of levels. Whereby, he was always bound to the primacy of the enlightenment and the avoidance of the monumental. The successive nature of the information, the changes in the visitors' perceptive, the interplay between transparence and obscurity, the independence of the installation from the architecture of the exhibition space; these were all ways of intensifying perception, of conveying information in an objective way and of avoiding monumentality. For monumentality was by no means in agreement with Gropius' democratic principles, which looked to the ideals of an autonomous way of life that entailed a liberation from the constraints of precarious living conditions, a renewal of the body and mind in harmony with nature, and a correlation to modified social needs.

As can be taken from the catalog's foreword, Gropius had obviously renounced the dictum of functionality, and furthermore no longer assigned the standardized commodity product the given role of an object made for mass use, but rather valued it as a symbol. The criteria of aesthetic beauty can no longer be fulfilled by a design that does nothing more than pander to prerequisites of economics and functionality, but can only be achieved by a design that achieves the synthesis of art and technology, complete only in a symbolically sense. This synthesis is the precursor for a state of characterized by the prophetic amalgamation of reality and utopia. A complete interpretation of the world, even inclusive of value systems, appears to be reflected in his exhibits, which thanks to their nature as everyday items were able to enjoy large-scale distribution. Here, the exhibition design appears to evoke a level of meaning that, as it would seem, was dedicated to the mass product from the very beginning and is now brought into the spotlight alongside the aspect of functionality: the utopian content. ›3.4

So war die Ausstellung von Gropius keinesfalls nur eine herkömmliche Warenmesse mit Produkten von deutschen Fließbändern. Vielmehr zeigte sich hier eine visionäre Zukunftsperspektive, die die moderne, aufgeklärte Industriegesellschaft im Blickfeld hatte.

Doch der reine und naive Blick auf die Utopie mag sich nach etwa zehn Jahren moderner Gestaltung nicht mehr so recht einstellen, musste doch der ungebrochene Wille zur gesellschaftlichen Modernität zumindest mit all seinen Konsequenzen bedacht werden. Fließbandarbeit bringt nicht von vornherein die Erfüllung menschlichen Lebens; technischer Fortschritt birgt nicht für alle das Staunen über die Innovationsleistung. Diese verblasst in dem Moment, in dem sich die Konsequenzen offenbaren.

Die Pariser Werkbund-Ausstellung aber war für Gropius ein zu begrüßendes Forum zur rekapitulierenden Inszenierung seiner Ideen und Weltanschauung. In diesem Sinne besaß sie monografischen Charakter. Geschickt war dieser Schachzug umso mehr, da sein künstlerischer Werdegang engstens mit der Geschichte des Werkbundes und der des Bauhauses verknüpft war. Die Ausstellung im Grand Palais war ein Balanceakt, bei dem es folgende Positionen zu vereinen galt: Gropius als individuellen Protagonisten der Moderne, die Darlegung des Programms des Dessauer Bauhauses, dem Gropius bis 1928 vorstand, die Repräsentation des Deutschen Werkbundes als Vertreter moderner Gestaltung in Deutschland und schließlich die Dokumentation deutscher Industrieproduktion.

In this way Gropius's exhibition was much more than a conventional product trade fair displaying articles produced on Germany's assembly lines. On the contrary, the exhibition presented a visionary perspective of the future looking toward a modern, enlightened industrial society.

After around ten years of modern design, his pure and somewhat naïve utopian perspective may no longer appear quite as fitting as it did then, but this iron will for social modernity should at the very least be regarded together with all its consequences. Work on an assembly line may not constitute life fulfillment a priori; technological progression is not able to trigger amazement at its innovative achievements in all of us. This fades as soon as the consequences become apparent.

But the Werkbund exhibition in Paris did provide Gropius with an open forum, a blank canvas to recapitulate and present his ideas and ideology. In this sense, it actually had a monographic quality to it. This move by Gropius was all the more sophisticated given that his artistic career was inextricably linked with the history of the Deutscher Werkbund and of course Bauhaus. The exhibition in the Grand Palais was a balancing act, whereby he was required to unify the following positions: to present Gropius the individual as a protagonist of Modernism, to present the Bauhaus program in Dessau, which Gropius chaired until 1928, to embody the Deutscher Werkbund as the representative of modern design in Germany and finally, to document German industrial production.

>>> author p.211

1 Cf. Sievert, Johannes: Aus meinem Leben. Unveröffentlichtes Typoskript, Berlin 1966, p.324. Politisches Archiv des Auswärtigen Amtes, Bonn.

salle 5
composition de la salle
herbert bayer

linoléum
deutsche linoléum werke a.g. bietigheim.
dessous en linoléum cellotex
deutscher cellotex-vertrieb g.m.b.h. posdam

appareils d'éclairage
zeiss ikon a.g. berlin

revêtement mural en couleurs
verznique wernststten münchen

agrandissements photographiques
ideoperra. berlin.

3.4

121

Kai-Uwe Hemken

Lehrbuch der Welt:

Die Internationale Hygiene-Ausstellung (IHA) 1930 in Dresden

Am 16. Mai 1930 wurde in Dresden auf dem Ausstellungsgelände des Volksparks Großer Garten die Internationale Hygiene-Ausstellung (IHA) eröffnet.[1] Sie bildete den Endpunkt der Veranstaltungsreihe »Jahresschau deutscher Arbeit«, die seit 1922 alljährlich von der Stadt Dresden veranstaltet worden war. Der konkrete Anlass, eine Ausstellung zum Thema »Hygiene« zu organisieren, war die Eröffnung des ersten deutschen Hygiene-Museums in Dresden.

Die Tradition Dresdens in der Pflege des Hygienewesens reicht bis ins letzte Drittel des 19. Jahrhunderts zurück und geht maßgeblich auf die Initiative des in Dresden ansässigen Industriellen Karl August Lingner (»Odolfabrikant«) zurück. Nachdem bereits 1903 eine Wanderausstellung und 1911 die 1. Internationale Hygiene-Ausstellung in Dresden mit großer Resonanz veranstaltet worden waren, reifte die Idee eines National-Hygiene-Museums. Als sich 1926 in Düsseldorf mit der Ausstellung »Gesundheitspflege, soziale Fürsorge und Leibesübungen« (GeSoLei) eine große Konkurrenz ankündigte, wurden die Museumspläne in Dresden vorangetrieben.

Die Hygiene-Ausstellung von 1930, Teil der »Jahresschauen deutscher Arbeit«, besaß den Rang einer international ausgerichteten Veranstaltung. Die Hygiene war ein Themenbereich mit einem gesamtkulturellen Charakter, der – fernab von konkurrierenden Interessen auf politischem oder wirtschaftlichem Gebiet – auf einen friedlichen Wettstreit zugunsten einer »übernationalen« Humanität hoffen ließ. Doch der Wettstreit der Nationen wurde auch auf dieser »Kulturschau« fortgesetzt, jedoch mit der Argumentation, dem Frieden der Welt und damit dem Wohle der Menschheit zu dienen.

Die Veranstalter der IHA scheuten keine Mittel, eine repräsentative und komplexe architektonische Ausstellungsanlage zu errichten. Zu diesem Zwecke wurde ein Generalbebauungsplan entwickelt, für dessen Konzeption der Dresdener Stadtbaurat Dr. Ing. Paul Wolf verantwortlich zeichnete. In Zusammenarbeit mit zahlreichen namhaften Architekten entstand auf diese Weise eine regelrechte »Ausstellungsstadt«, deren architektonischen Höhepunkt ohne Zweifel das 1930 eingeweihte Hygiene-Museum bildete.

Textbook for the World:

The 1930 International Hygiene Exhibition in Dresden

On May 16, 1930 the International Hygiene Exhibition opened its doors to the public in the exhibition grounds of Dresden's Grosser Garten Park1 and marking the end of the »Annual Show of German Labor«, a series of events that the city of Dresden had hosted every year since 1922. The idea behind creating a hygiene exhibition was in fact the inauguration of Germany's first museum with a focus on hygiene.

The hygiene industry has something of a tradition in Dresden, one that dates back to the late 19th century and can be attributed in great measure to the initiatives of the Dresden-based industrialist Karl August Lingener (manufacturer of Odol oral hygiene products). Following the realization of a traveling exhibition as early as 1903 and the 1st International Hygiene Exhibition in Dresden in 1911, the idea for a National Hygiene Museum was gradually evolved. In 1926, the trade fair on »Sanitation, Social Welfare and Physical Education« held in Düsseldorf emerged as a major rival, and in so doing spurred Dresden's plans for the museum.

The 1930 International Hygiene Exhibition, part of the so-called »Annual Show of German Labor«, occupied the upper echelons of the internationally oriented exhibition. Hygiene was a subject that in its character spanned all areas of culture, which (far from the conflicting interests within the political or economical arena) gave hope for a peaceful competition in favour of a »trans-national« humanity. Yet rivalries between nations did not cease for the sake of this »culture show«, but continued under the guise of serving world peace and the good of humanity.

The exhibition's hosts spared no resources in the construction of a representative and architecturally-complex exhibition venue. A general construction plan was developed to this end, the man in charge being Dresden's city planning officer, Dr. Paul Wolf. He collaborated with several prestigious architects, the result: an »exhibition city« in the true sense of the word; in this context, the Hygiene Museum (it was inaugurated in 1930) was doubtlessly the project's major highlight.

3.1

Der Architekt Wilhelm Kreis hatte das Hygiene-Museum streng achsensymmetrisch konzipiert und für die Fassadengestaltung eine neoklassizistische Formensprache gewählt. ›3.1 Das Hygiene-Museum war nur ein Teil des groß angelegten Ausstellungsgeländes, auf dem bereits in den Vorjahren zahlreiche Bauten errichtet worden waren, wozu u. a. der alte Ausstellungspalast (1914), das Georg-Arnold-Bad (1926) und die sogenannte Ilgen-Kampfbahn (1923) als Stadion gehörten.

Die Gebäude, in denen die Staaten ihre Ausstellungsobjekte präsentierten, waren letztlich schlichte Messehallen, die den Eindruck von Produktionsstätten erweckten. Die Eingänge der jeweiligen Sektionen wurden durch eine Glaswand gekennzeichnet. Die monotone Reihung dieser Eingänge gab keinen Aufschluss über das jeweilige Ausmaß der Ausstellungsfläche. Jedoch standen den Staaten höchst unterschiedliche Flächen zur Präsentation zur Verfügung. So hatte die Sowjetunion mit 1.000 m² den größten Raum gemietet, während Spanien 300 m², die Tschechoslowakei 600 m², die Türkei 250 m² und andere Staaten ca. 100 m² belegten.

Architect Wilhelm Kreis devised the Hygiene Museum according to the strict rules of axial symmetry and chose a neo-classical style for the façade. ›3.1 The Hygiene Museum was only one part of the rambling exhibition grounds where several other buildings had been erected in previous years, including the old exhibition palace (1914), the Georg Arnold public baths (1926) and the so-called Ilgen Kampfbahn stadium (1923).

The buildings created to host the work of the various exhibiting nations were ultimately simple exhibition halls, giving the impression of a production hall. The entrances to the respective sections were simply denoted by a glass wall. The monotone sequence of these entrances gave no indication of the dimensions of the respective exhibition spaces but the participating nations had in fact all been allocated areas that differed considerably in their size, such that the Soviet Union had rented the largest space at 1,000 m², while Spain (300 m²), Czechoslovakia (600 m²), Turkey (250 m²) and various other states (approx. 100 m²) had much less space to work with.

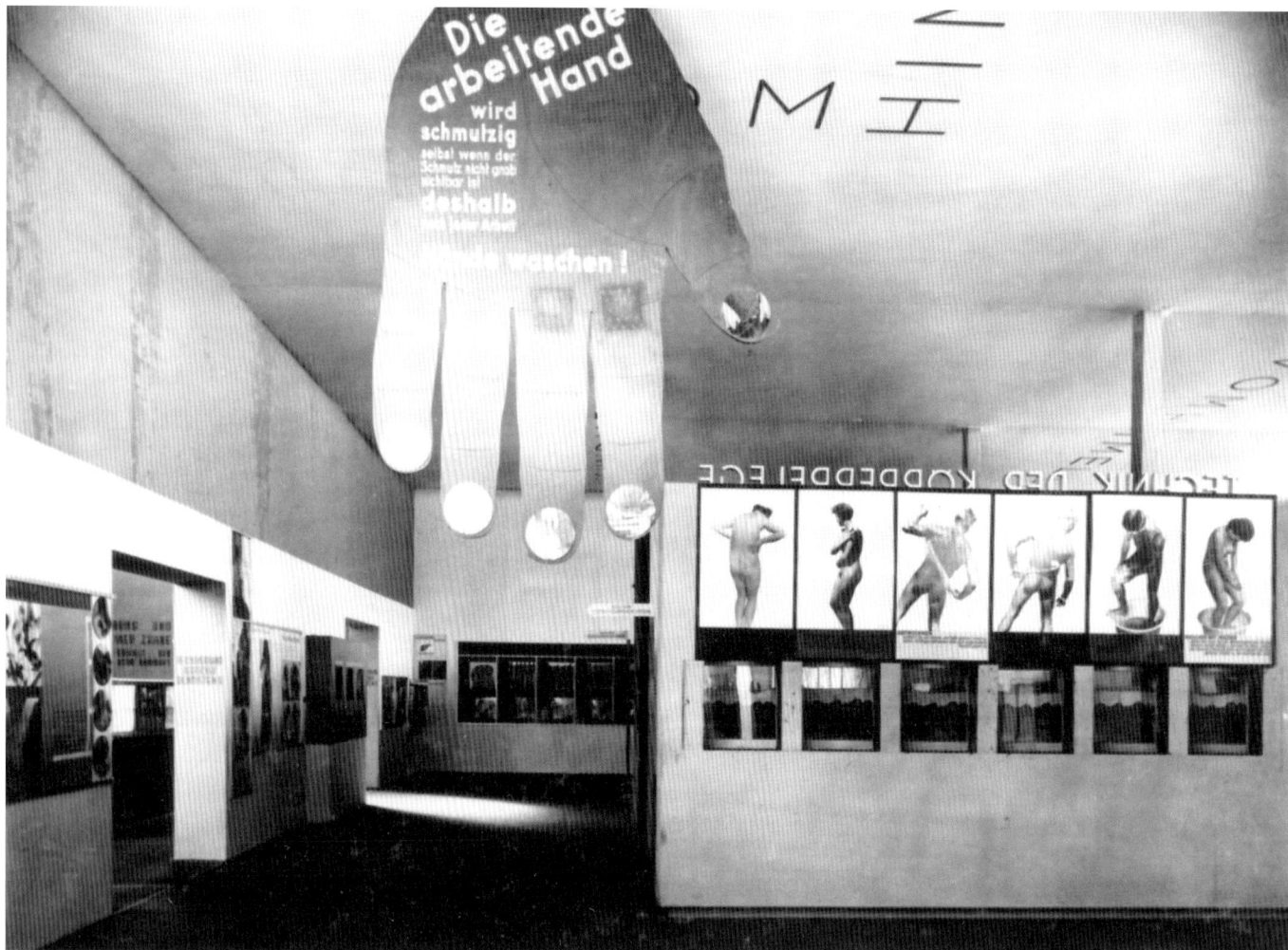

3.2

Es lässt sich allein schon an dem immensen architektonischen Aufwand erkennen, dass der Stadt Dresden als Veranstalterin der IHA daran gelegen war, ihre Hygiene-Ausstellung zu einem bedeutenden Unternehmen nicht nur in der Geschichte des Hygienewesens, sondern auch im Ausstellungsbetrieb Deutschlands werden zu lassen. Die Veranstalter der IHA waren bestrebt, ausstellungstechnisch, d. h. besonders architektonisch, neue Maßstäbe zu setzen; denn die zahlreichen Ausstellungsbauten suggerierten, dass in Dresden das eigentliche Zentrum des Hygienewesens in Deutschland beheimatet war.

Die Internationale Hygiene-Ausstellung diente offenbar nur dazu, diesem Bestreben die entsprechende internationale Publizität zu verleihen; denn der Eröffnung des Hygiene-Museums als bauliches Glanzstück der Ausstellung wurde die IHA im Grunde lediglich anbeigegeben. Die Ausstellung wurde daher als ein überregionales Unternehmen inszeniert, das daraufhin seitens der deutschen Veranstalter zu einem Podium der Selbstdarstellung wurde, doch sich gleichzeitig als Möglichkeit für die ausländischen Teilnehmer darbot, die Errungenschaften des eigenen Landes zur Schau zu stellen. Dabei wurden durch die Originalität der Ausstellungsästhetik mancher ausländischer Teilnehmer die Leistungen der deutschen Aussteller bisweilen in den Schatten gestellt.

Zwischen Humanität und Wirtschaft: Das verstärkte Interesse für die allgemeine Volkshygiene und Hygiene-Forschung in Deutschland Ende des 19. Jahrhunderts und zu Beginn des 20. Jahrhunderts war eine Folgeerscheinung der zunehmenden Industrialisierung. Der Zuzug der Landbevölkerung in die Industriestädte brachte schwerwiegende soziale Probleme mit sich, die das Wohnen, die Hygiene und allgemein städteplanerische Fragestellungen betrafen. Hygiene-Ausstellungen waren ein Mittel, den urbanen Problemen zu begegnen. Besonders die Industrie war an einer Verbesserung der »Volksgesundheit« interessiert. Schlechte Lebensqualität bedingte soziale Spannungen und eine Verringerung der Arbeitskapazitäten. Die Volksgesundheit wurde also zu einem Kapitalfaktor. Auch Lingners Engagement für die Volkshygiene ist auf seine Stellung als »Odolfabrikant« in der Dresdner Industrie zurückzuführen.

The enormous expenditure assigned to the architecture alone was indicative that as the exhibition's host, the City of Dresden was intent upon making its hygiene exhibition an enterprise of great importance not only in the history of the hygiene industry but Germany's exhibition industry too. Those organizing the International Hygiene Exhibition had endeavoured to set new standards in exhibition practices, especially in exhibition architecture; for the numerous exhibition constructions functioned as implications of Dresden's status as the real home of the hygiene industry in Germany.

The International Hygiene Exhibition was quite clearly nothing more than a means of gaining international publicity for this endeavour; for it was for all intents and purposes nothing more than an ancillary to the inauguration of the Hygiene Museum as the exhibition's architectural pièce de résistance. The exhibition was therefore positioned as a trans-regional enterprise, which subsequently became a platform for self-display for the German hosts yet also offered foreign participants the opportunity to present their own country's achievements. That said, the German exhibitors' achievements were at times overshadowed by the originality of the exhibition aesthetics as seen in the displays of some of the international exhibitors.

Between humanity and economy. The heightened interest in the general hygiene of the populace as well as increased research into hygiene as was witnessed around the turn of the 20th century was an after-effect of the increasing industrialisation of the day. The migration from rural areas to the cities also brought grave social problems in its wake, with serious consequences for housing, hygiene and general issues surrounding urban planning. Hygiene exhibitions served as a means to confront such urban problems. The industrial sector in particular had a vested interest in improving the »people's health«. A poor quality of life made for social tensions and lowered labor resources, such that the people's health had become an important impact on business success. Even Lingner's commitment to the people's health and hygiene can be attributed to his position within the Dresden industrial world as the »Odol manufacturer«.

3.3

Da die Volksbelehrung das Hauptanliegen der Dresdner Hygiene-Ausstellung war, prägten erklärlicherweise vornehmlich Schautafeln, Diagramme, großformatige Karten und Statistiken die Schauräume des neu errichteten Hygiene-Museums sowie die Räume der benachbarten Hallen. Dabei wurden alle Register der Ausstellungsdidaktik gezogen. Die deutsche Industrie, die sich in Harmonie mit den Teilnehmern öffentlicher Institutionen auf der Ausstellung präsentierte, zeigte in den ihr zugedachten Sälen Apparaturen und Instrumentarien aus dem Bereich der Hygiene und des Krankenhauswesens. Zu diesem Zweck hatte Architekt Wolf das Muster-Krankenhaus errichtet, das diese Schauräume beherbergte. >3.2

Im Hygiene-Museum sowie in den angrenzenden Hallen waren Installationen, wie z. B. große Schautafeln, statistisches Material, Filme oder Apparaturen, die betätigt werden konnten, zu sehen. Insgesamt wurde darauf Wert gelegt, dass die bildhafte Darstellung Vorrang vor dem Text gewann. Darüber hinaus wurde bei der Vermittlung von Informationen darauf geachtet, dass ausgehend von allgemeinen Hinweisen auch spezielle Aussagen zur Hygiene getroffen wurden. Zudem war man stolz darauf, optische Höhepunkte, wie z. B. die Einbeziehung der Decke in die Gestaltung, präsentieren zu können. Die didaktischen Mittel zielten aber keineswegs darauf ab, den Besuch der Ausstellung zu einem sinnlichen Erlebnis werden zu lassen. Vielmehr galt es, die Darstellungsmethoden zu vereinfachen, um die gewünschten Informationen eindringlich zu übermitteln. Letztlich sollte sich der Besucher auf intellektuelle Weise die Regeln und Lehren der Hygiene aneignen. >3.3

Auch Japan, Großbritannien und Frankreich waren gleichermaßen wie Österreich, Chile, die Niederlande oder die Türkei bemüht, die Leistungen und die Weltgeltung ihrer Arbeit auf dem Hygienesektor darzulegen. Das Motto dieser Abteilungen war ebenso die Volksbelehrung. Das Hygienewesen wurde als ein Mittel zur Sicherung der »Arbeitskraft« gesehen, wodurch sich die Hygienewissenschaft letztlich auch in ihrer gesellschaftlichen Relevanz zu legitimieren suchte.

The main objective of the Dresden exhibition was to educate the people, and so the exhibition rooms of the newly-built Hygiene Museum and those in the neighbouring halls were understandably characterized predominantly by display panels, diagrams, large-format charts and statistics. They certainly pulled out all the stops in terms of exhibition didactics. Germany's private industrial sector, which exhibited in harmonious apposition with representatives from public institutions, used the exhibition rooms allocated to them – housed in the model hospital erected by architect Wolf – to display apparatuses and instruments from the hygiene and hospital industries. >3.2

The Museum and neighbouring halls also presented a series of installations, such as large display panels, statistical material, films and apparatuses that were to use the modern term »interactive«. On the whole a great deal of value was placed on giving visual depictions priority over textual commentary. Furthermore, when conveying information to the public, the organizers made sure that more general advice was used as a basis for making more specific points relating to hygiene. They were also proud to be able to present optical highlights such as the inclusion of the ceiling in the room's design. But such didactic means were certainly not geared towards turning the exhibition into a sensory experience for its visitors. It was rather a matter of simplifying the representational methods in order to convey the desired information emphatically. After all, the aim was that the visitors left with a new-found knowledge of hygiene imparted by these teachings and guidelines. >3.3

Japan, the United Kingdom and France and similarly Austria, Chile, the Netherlands or Turkey went to great deal of effort to present their achievements and highlight the global significance of their work in the hygiene sector. These sections were equally shaped by their objective to educate the public. The hygiene industry was considered a way of safeguarding the »workforce«, whereby hygiene science ultimately sought to legitimize its relevance within society.

Es scheint, als ob sich allein die Sowjetunion von dieser ausschließlich ökonomisch ausgerichteten Hygiene-Volksbildung distanzierte, denn das Hygienewesen wurde zu einem zentralen Faktor in der Formierung einer neuen Gesellschaft überhöht. El Lissitzky, der für die Gestaltung des Pavillons verantwortlich war, erfüllte mit einer propagandistischen Schau der sowjetischen »Hygieneleistungen« diese Aufgabe.

Wie zur gleichen Zeit auf der Internationalen Pelz-Fachausstellung (IPA) in Leipzig führte er auch in Dresden die Auswirkungen der Planwirtschaft glorifizierend vor Augen. Zu diesem Zwecke inszenierte er ein kompliziertes Gesamtschauspiel von Fotomontagen, Reliefs, Objekten und einzelnen Rauminstallationen: Räumliche Strukturierung, Steuerung des Ausstellungsbesuchs, Fotomontagen, typografische Objekte, großformatig-skulpturale Installationen u. a. setzten neue Maßstäbe des Ausstellungsdesigns. Es gelang Lissitzky, neue, innovative Mittel der didaktisch-erläuternden sowie ideologisch-suggestiven Inszenierung unabhängig von örtlichen Gegebenheiten und verschiedenen Themenstellungen zum Zweck staatlicher Selbstdarstellung zu entwickeln. ›3.4

It seems as though the Soviet Union were alone in distancing itself from this notion of »educating the people« on hygiene exclusively in light of economic factors, for the hygiene industry was elevated to become a key factor in the formulation of a new society. El Lissitzky, who was responsible for designing the Soviet pavilion, fulfilled this task by means of a propagandist show of the Soviet Union's »achievements in hygiene«.

As could also be seen in the exhibition design at the simultaneous »International Fur Trade Exhibition« in Leipzig, he brought the effects of the controlled economy well and truly home in a glorifying display. To do so he created a complex, cumulative spectacle of photo montages, reliefs, objects and individual spatial installations. Among other elements, spatial structuring, navigation of the route through the exhibition, typographic objects and large-format, sculptural installations went towards setting new standards in exhibition design. Lissitzky succeeded in the development of new innovative means of orchestrating exhibitions in both a didactically-explanatory and ideologically-suggestive way for the purpose of the self-representation of the state, irrespective of the local conditions and distinct subject areas. ›3.4

>>> author p.211

1 Die Ausstellung ging bis zum 28. September 1930. In leicht veränderter Form wurde sie ein Jahr später an gleicher Stelle wiederholt.

The exhibition ran until September 28, 1930 and was repeated one year later in the same location though slightly altered in its form.

Kai-Uwe Hemken

»Entartete Kunst«, München 1937: Ideologische Diffamierung der
modernen Kunst durch den Nationalsozialismus

Eine ideologische Diffamierungsausstellung richteten die Nationalsozialisten
im Jahre 1937 im Archäologischen Institut des Münchner Hofgartens ein.
650 Gemälde, Skulpturen, Grafiken und Bücher von etwa 118 Künstlern der
Klassischen Moderne wurden den Beständen von 32 deutschen Museen
entrissen, um die moderne Kunst insgesamt an den demagogischen
Pranger zu stellen. Als »entartet« galten jene modernen Kunstrichtungen
und Einzelkünstler, deren Werke vornehmlich formalästhetisch wie motivisch
nicht dem rassistisch geprägten und ideologisch ausgerichteten Kunstbegriff bzw. den Kunstvorstellungen der Nationalsozialisten entsprachen.
Hierzu zählten u. a. Surrealismus, Kubismus, Fauvismus, Konstruktivismus,
De-Stijl-Kunst, Bauhaus-Künstler und Expressionismus.

Bereits Wochen zuvor wurden vergleichbare Hetzausstellungen zur modernen
Kunst in verschiedenen Regionen Deutschlands gewissermaßen als Test-
versionen veranstaltet, bis schließlich die Großausstellung in München
eröffnet und danach als Wanderausstellung in verschiedenen Städten
Deutschlands, darunter Berlin, Düsseldorf, Frankfurt/M. und Halle, gezeigt
wurde. Ca. zwei Millionen Besucher konnte die Ausstellung verbuchen,
während das Pendant, die »Große Deutsche Kunstausstellung« im Haus
der Deutschen Kunst in München (1937), bestückt mit ca. 600 nationalsozialistischen künstlerischen Hervorbringungen, 420.000 Besucher
bilanzieren konnte.

So chaotisch die Ausstellung in ihrer Erscheinung auch sein mochte, sie
hatte doch eine systematische Anlage: Der Präsident der Reichskammer
der bildenden Künste, Adolf Ziegler, wurde von Propagandaminister Joseph
Goebbels beauftragt, eine Schau zur Diffamierung der modernen Kunst seit
1910 zusammenzustellen. Ziegler scharte einige Gleichgesinnte, die bereits
zuvor durch rechtsradikale Äußerungen zur modernen Kunst an die Öffentlichkeit getreten waren, um sich, bereiste zehn Tage lang Deutschland und
ließ alle eilig konfiszierten Kunstwerke moderner Prägung nach München
transportieren. Diese Aktion war Teil einer groß angelegten nationalsozialistischen Säuberungswelle, die die kulturellen wie künstlerischen Einrichtungen (Museen, Akademien), Verwaltungsinstanzen zu Kunst und Kultur,
das gesamte Bildungssystem auf dem Felde der Kunst, die Gesetzgebung
und eine Vielzahl von Künstlerpersönlichkeiten betraf.

*»Degenerate Art«, Munich 1937: National Socialism's Ideological
Defamation of Modern Art*

*In 1937, the Nazis chose the Institute of Archeology in Munich's Hofgarten
as the venue for an exhibition of ideological, cultural defamation. A total of
650 paintings, sculptures, graphic works and books by around 118 artists
representing Classical Modernism had been wrested from 32 German
museums in order to put modern art as a whole in the demagogic docks.
The term »degenerate« was used to describe those modern art establish-
ments and individual artists whose works – principally in formal aesthetic
terms such as their use of motifs – failed to correspond to the Nazi's definition
and conception of art, which was of course hugely ideologically oriented
and tainted by racism. Some artistic movements to be categorized as such
included Surrealism, Cubism, Fauvism, Constructivism, De Stijl, Bauhaus
and Expressionism.*

*Weeks before the main event, the Nazis began holding comparable agitator
and propaganda exhibitions on modern art in various regions throughout
Germany, intended as something of a test run. The main exhibition finally
opened its doors in Munich and then made its way around Germany as a
traveling exhibition, visiting Berlin, Düsseldorf, Frankfurt/Main and Halle,
to name but a few. »Degenerate Art« attracted approximately two million
visitors, while its counterpart, the »Great German Art Exhibition« in Munich's
Haus der Kunst (1937), a show of around 600 Nazi works of art, counted just
420,000.*

*As chaotic as the exhibition may have been in its appearance, it was in fact
highly systematic in its arrangement. After all, propaganda minister Joseph
Goebbels had charged Adolf Ziegler as President of the Reich Chamber
for Fine Arts with the task of compiling an exhibition to defame post-1916
modern art. Ziegler brought together a number of like-minded individuals
who had already expressed their radical opinions regarding modern art in the
public arena and spent ten days traveling the length and breadth of Germany,
hastily confiscating artworks from German museums and sending them
back to Munich. This act constitutes just one element of a large-scale purge
conducted by the Nazis against Germany's cultural and artistic establish-
ments (museums and academies), administrative bodies in charge of art
and culture, the field of art within the education system, the legal system,
and a large number of prominent individuals in the art world.*

3.1

3.2

Auf zwei Ebenen wurden zahlreiche Räume nebst eingezogenen Stell-
wänden mit Kunstwerken bestückt. Der Besucher wurde mit einer Überfülle
an Exponaten konfrontiert, die flächendeckend über alle verfügbaren
Hängeflächen verteilt wurden. Die einzige ersichtliche Regie war die rein
quantitativ-ökonomische Hängung. Alle Wände wurden überdies mit groß-
und kleinformatigen Schriftzügen und Hinweisschildern der besonderen Art
versehen: Der Besucher wurde darüber informiert, wie hoch der Ankaufs-
preis des jeweiligen Werks war, wobei verschwiegen wurde, dass es sich bei
dem horrend hohen Preis um das Ergebnis von Inflationszeiten handelte.
Ein Hinweis, dass die Kunstwerke von den Steuergeldern der Bevölkerung
bezahlt worden waren, fehlte nicht. Darüber hinaus fanden sich graffitiähn-
liche, handgemalte Schriftzüge auf den umgebenden Wandflächen, die eine
weitere Disqualifizierung der modernen Kunst darstellten. Die Museums-
direktoren, Kunstwissenschaftler und -kritiker, die sich als Förderer der
modernen Kunst verdient gemacht hatten, wurden gleichermaßen diffamiert,
indem man Textpassagen ihrer Schriften zusammenhangslos hinzufügte
und sie auf diesem Wege der Lächerlichkeit preisgab. >3.1

Der expositionelle Grundtenor war, eine Auratisierung der Kunstwerke
beinahe zwanghaft zu vermeiden. Überdies wurde durch die Hängung und
textliche Kommentierung der Kunstbetrachter entmündigt, da eine individuelle Einschätzung dezidiert verhindert wurde. Stets wurden ideologische
Umdeutungen der Motive vorgenommen, Realität bzw. Realitätswiedergabe
gezielt mit Fiktion verwechselt, De-Kontextualisierungen vorgenommen
und immer wieder aufs Neue Polaritäten in der Polemik aufgebaut, die
immerfort eine medizinische Diagnose der modernen Kunstentwicklung
nachzeichnen wollte. >3.2

Aufschlussreich ist in diesem Zusammenhang der Katalog, der die Grund-
struktur der Abteilungen widerspiegelt und entsprechende Argumentationen
liefert. Gruppe 1: Unter einer Glorifizierung des Handwerks wurde das
scheinbare motorische Nichtkönnen der modernen Künstler disqualifiziert.
Gruppe 2: Unter Hinweis auf Glaubensgemeinschaften prangerte man
die (angebliche) Verletzung religiöser Gefühle an. Gruppe 3: Kunstwerke
wurden als Indizien für eine aus nationalsozialistischer Sicht politische
Entgleisung (Anarchie, Kommunismus) gewertet. Gruppe 4: In dieser
Gruppe zeigte sich eine Nuancierung des Politischen, indem man eine
politische Instabilität der Bevölkerung – bewirkt durch moderne Kunst –
entdeckt haben wollte.

*Spread over two levels, artworks filled the numerous rooms and covered
the partition walls that had been newly installed there. Visitors were
confronted with a glut of exhibits covering all available surfaces. The only
apparent order here was a purely quantitative-economic approach to
hanging the works. Furthermore, each and every wall was covered with
large and small-format text panels and signs informing visitors of the
purchase price of each work, though they were not told that these
horrendously high prices were in fact so awfully high due to economic
inflation. Naturally the organizers did not fail to also deploy signs saying
that the artworks had been paid for using taxpayer's money. Moreover,
the surrounding walls were covered in hand-painted, graffiti-like lettering,
serving to further denigrate Modernist art. Those museum directors,
art scholars and critics who as friends of such art had also earned a place
in the exhibition were defamed in equal measure, passages from their
texts inserted incoherently into the exhibition, exposing them to public
ridicule. >3.1*

*The exhibition's basic thrust – almost taken to the point of paranoia –
was to avoid a mystification of the artworks at all costs. Furthermore,
the works were hung and the text commentaries inserted so as to
undermine the beholder's capacity for personal judgment, for the
presentation decidedly impeded an individual appraisal of the works.
Ideological reinterpretations of the themes in the works were present
throughout; reality or the representation of reality was confounded
with fiction, works were subjected to decontextualization, and polarities
were repeatedly constructed forming part of their polemic, which
continuously aimed to offer a psycho-medical diagnosis of the
development of modern art. >3.2*

*The exhibition catalogue also proves rather enlightening in this respect,
for it reflects the basic layout of the sections and indicates congruous lines
of argument. Group 1: In the context of a glorification of craftsmanship,
they highlighted an apparent incompetence in the motor skills of modern
artists. Group 2: An adulation of religious communities was denounced
as an apparent slur against the religious beliefs of the people. Group 3:
Here, artworks were displayed, which from a National Socialist standpoint
were classified as evidence of a political derailment (anarchy, communism).
Group 4: This group presented a differentiation of the political, whereby
the Nazis purported to have discovered political instability among the
population – effectuated by modern art.*

3.3 in: Berlinische Galerie (Ed.): Stationen der Moderne. Die bedeutenden Kunstausstellungen des 20. Jahrhunderts in Deutschland. Berlin 1988, p.295, fig. 9/13. © Reinhard Henze, Halle

Gruppe 5: Das Interesse der modernen Kunst für Randgruppen der Gesellschaft (Prostituierte, Arme, Verbrecher etc.) wurde als Beweis für das Außenseitertum der Künstler gewertet. Gruppe 6: Die moderne Kunst wurde als rassenideologische Gefahr gedeutet, wenn man sich für die Südseeindianer motivisch interessierte. Gruppe 7: In dieser Objektgruppe findet sich eine Akzentuierung des Randgruppenthemas, wenn man der modernen Kunst vorwarf, sich geistig und körperlich Kranken zu widmen. Gruppe 8: Die Nationalsozialisten stellten hier alle Künstler an den Pranger, die dem jüdischen Glauben zugehörig waren oder der jüdischen Kultur nahe standen und sich dieser motivisch annahmen. Gruppe 9: Erneut wurde das Thema »Kunst und Krankheit« in diffamierender Weise aufgegriffen.

Das Argumentationsmuster, das sich durch den Katalog und auch die Ausstellung in ihrer formalen wie inhaltlichen Konzeption zeigt, wird im Vorwort erkennbar: Getragen von einer hohen Intellektuellenfeindlichkeit wird eine Drohkulisse skizziert, die Deutschlands unmittelbare Zukunft einem Untergangsszenario anglich. In der Folge konnten sich die Nationalsozialisten als Retter und Heilsbringer inszenieren. Die deutsche Bevölkerung wurde als Inhaber einer souveränen Urteilskraft beschworen, im gleichen Atemzug jedoch – wie es die nationalsozialistische Diktatur vorsah und verwirklichte – in vollem Umfang entmündigt. Insgesamt wurde eine Verschwörungstheorie propagiert, die bestimmten Bevölkerungskreisen der Politik, Wirtschaft, Kultur und Religionszugehörigkeit eine Unterjochung Deutschlands unterstellte.

Die Reaktionen des Publikums wurden nur vereinzelt in Augenzeugenberichten festgehalten und ergeben ein widersprüchliches Bild, wenn man Peter Günthers Erinnerungen folgt: »Die folgenden Räume waren ähnlich verwirrend. Bilder waren sehr nahe zusammengehängt, manche übereinander, andere sogar über den Türrahmen. Die starken Farben der Gemälde, die dazwischentretenden Texte, die großen Wandtafeln mit Zitaten aus Hitlers und Goebbels Reden ergaben chaotische Impressionen. Ein Gefühl von Klaustrophobie beschlich mich. Die drängende, sich belustigende Masse Mensch, ihren Unmut über die Kunstwerke proklamierend, mutete wie eine Bühnenaufführung an, die darauf abzielte, eine Atmosphäre von Aggressivität und Wut zu fördern. Wieder und wieder lasen sich die Leute die Verkaufspreise laut vor und lachten, schüttelten die Köpfe oder verlangten ›ihr‹ Geld zurück« (S. 41). ›3.3

Group 5: Modern art's interest in marginalized members of society (prostitutes, the poor, criminals etc.) was deemed evidence of the artists' status as outsiders. Group 6: Modern art was subjected to interpretation as a danger to Nazi racial ideology, the featured works' motifs displaying an interest in natives of the South Pacific for example. Group 7: This group of objects further emphasized the marginalized-groups theme and accused modern art of a consecration of the mentally and physically ill. Group 8: Here, the organizers decried all artists who belonged to the Jewish faith or had connections to Jewish culture and embraced this in their works. Group 9: This group once again highlighted the theme »Art and illness« in a defamatory way.

The pattern of argumentation running through the catalogue and the exhibition itself relating to both the content and formal attributes is made clearly apparent in the foreword: Borne of a great hostility towards intellectuals, the writer adopts a threatening position, approximates Germany's immediate future with a doomsday scenario, allowing the Nazi's to present themselves as saviors and redeemers of the Fatherland. The German people were testified as possessors of a sovereign power of judgment, yet – as the Nazi dictatorship planned and ultimately implemented – completely disempowered in the same breath. A conspiracy theory had been spread throughout the entire population, insinuating that Germany was living under the yoke of certain groups within their society – political, economical, cultural and religious.

Only a few, isolated eye-witness accounts provide use with a documentation of the public's response to the exhibition, and even these prove somewhat contradictory. Based upon Peter Günther's recollections: »The subsequent rooms were just as confounding. The pictures were hung very close together, some overlapping, others were even hung over the doorframes. The strong colors in the paintings, the texts between the works, the large wall panels with quotes from speeches by Hitler and Goebbels; all resulted in a chaotic impression. I was overcome by a feeling of claustrophobia. The thronging mass of people making fun of the works, proclaiming their displeasure at the artworks, it all looked like a staged performance, aiming to promote an atmosphere of aggressiveness and rage. Over and over, the people read the sales prices aloud and laughed, shaking their heads or demanding ›their‹ money back« (p. 41). ›3.3

3.3

Die suggestiv-aggressive Inszenierung schien ihr Ziel erreicht zu haben, laut den Beobachtungen Günthers. Ein zweiter Besuch der Ausstellung seitens des Augenzeugen lässt hoffen, dass sich nach einer ersten Negativ-euphorie eine allmähliche Distanzierung der Kunstöffentlichkeit einstellte: »Allerdings erinnere ich mich, dass bei einem erneuten Besuch von ›Entartete Kunst‹ eine eigenartige Änderung eingetreten war. Die Besucher waren leise, als ob sie einer ›richtigen‹ Ausstellung beiwohnten. Nur wenige gab es, die etwas gedämpft sprachen, und es schien, als ob einige diese Werke bereits vorher gesehen hatten, sie sogar mochten. Diese standen längere Zeit vor einem Werk als andere Besucher, obwohl sie kaum etwas sagten, nicht einmal zu denen, die sie begleiteten. Ich habe noch von einer Frau, die vor einigen graphischen Werken im Erdgeschoß stand, ein geflüs-tertes ›Sind die nicht wunderbar?‹ im Ohr. Darauf ging sie schnell weg.«

Eine propagandistische Gegenveranstaltung stellte die gleichzeitig im Haus der Kunst in München eingerichtete »Große Deutsche Kunst-ausstellung« dar.

This passively aggressive orchestration of the exhibition seemed to have the desired effect, if we are to go by Günther's account at any rate. A second eye-witness account gives us some hope that following this initial adverse euphoria, a gradual dissociation took place among the art public: »However, I recall that upon a second visit to ›Degenerate Art‹ a peculiar change had taken place. The visitors were quiet, as though they were visiting a ›real‹ exhibition. There were only a few who spoke to one another in low tones, and it seemed as though some of them had seen the works before, that they even liked them. They would stand in front of work a little longer than other visitors, although they barely said a word, not even to the people they had come with. I can still hear a ›Aren't they wonderful?‹ whispered by a woman standing before a graphic work on the ground floor. After which she hurried on.«

The »Great German Art Exhibition« represented a propagandist counter-part to the exhibition and was held simultaneously in the Haus der Kunst in Munich.

>>> author p.211

Kai-Uwe Hemken

Gestaltung höherer Ordnung:
Die Ausstellung »Die gute Form« 1949 in Basel

»Form aus Funktion und Schönheit« lautet jene Generalformel, mit der der Schweizer Designer und Künstler Max Bill 1948 einen Sturm der Entrüstung heraufbeschwor. Längst war die Bauhaus-Generation und -Nachfolge einem regelrechten Dogmatismus verfallen, der die Funktion als alleinigen Richtwert eines zeitgemäßen Produktdesigns gelten ließ. Der ehemalige Bauhaus-Schüler und Mitbegründer der Gruppe »abstraction-creation« konnte seine »empörenden« Thesen auf Einladung des Schweizer Werkbunds der Fachöffentlichkeit vorstellen und erntete trotz vehementer Ablehnung ein Interesse der Gastgeber, das zu einer Beauftragung führte: Bill wurde eingeladen, seine Thesen zu konkretisieren, indem er eine Ausstellung zum Thema konzipieren und realisieren sollte.

Mit »Die gute Form« wurde nicht nur das Konzept, sondern auch die Ausstellung betitelt, die im Mai 1949 als Sonderschau auf der Mustermesse in Basel stattfand.[1] Hiernach sollte die Sonderschau alljährlich stattfinden und erfuhr in späterer Zeit lediglich eine Veränderung des Titels.

Der vorhandene Raum – eine Industriehalle ohne dekorative Hinzufügungen – wurde durch eine filigrane, hölzerne Lattenkonstruktion, die zwischen Boden und Decke eingespannt wurde, in leichter, geschwungener Formation gegliedert. Bill befestigte – auf beiden Seiten der Konstruktion – insgesamt 80 mit Texten und Fotos bedruckte Tafeln derart, dass auf Augenhöhe ein umlaufendes Band entstand. Zwischen den Lattenkonstruktionen wurden Sockel mit Designobjekten aus der Alltagswelt gewissermaßen als Vorzeigebeispiele für eine gelungene Formgebung platziert. > 3.1

Als Vorgänger solcherlei Gestaltungsprinzipien können die Ausstellungsgestaltungen von Friedrich Kiesler auf der Internationalen Ausstellung neuer Theatertechnik 1924 in Wien, von El Lissitzky auf der Werkbund-Ausstellung »Film und Foto« 1929 in Stuttgart oder von Hannes Meyer und Herbert Bayer im Rahmen von Bauhaus- bzw. Werkbund-Ausstellungen gesehen werden. Nicht unerwähnt dürfen eine Reihe von Umbauten in Museen gegen Ende der 1920er Jahre, etwa in Köln, bleiben, die ein modernes Präsentationsdesign wählten: Das Gestaltungsprinzip der genannten Ausstellungen basierte auf formreduzierten, transparenten und temporären Konstruktionen.

Design of the highest order:
The 1949 exhibition »Die gute Form« in Basel

»Form from function and beauty« was the idea championed by Swiss designer and artist Max Bill in 1948; it would go on to invoke a wave of outcry. The Bauhaus generation and its successors had long since lapsed into absolute dogmatism, accepting function as the sole benchmark in contemporary product design. Upon invitation from the Swiss Werkbund, former Bauhaus students and co-founders of the »abstraction-creation« group were afforded the opportunity to present their »outrageous« theories to the design community and despite vehement opposition managed to win the interest of the host, which in turn led to a commission. Subsequently, Bill was invited to substantiate his theory by conceiving and realizing an exhibition on the topic.

»Die gute Form« (Good Form) was not only the title of the concept but of the exhibition, too; it took place as a special event within the Mustermesse Basel in May 1949.[1] Hereafter, this special exhibition was to become an annual occurrence, the only change to be made in subsequent years being the title.

Filigree wooden slats were suspended between the floor and ceiling, lending the exhibition space – a former factory hall completely devoid of any decorative elements – a light and curved feel in its arrangement. Both sides of the structure were covered with a total of 80 panels, which had been printed with texts and photos, creating an eye-level band snaking through the room. Pedestals displaying everyday design objects were positioned in among the lath constructions, as showcase of successful design, as it were. > 3.1

Exhibition design concepts created by Friedrich Kiesler for the 1924 »Internationalen Ausstellung neuer Theatertechnik« (International exhibition of new theater technology) in Vienna, by El Lissitzky at the 1929 Werkbund exhibition »Film und Foto« (Film and photography) in Stuttgart or by Hannes and Herbert Bayer in various Bauhaus and Werkbund exhibitions over the years can all be considered precursors to the design principles implemented in »Die gute Form«. Electing for a modern presentation design, there is a series of installations in museums, in Cologne for example, completed toward the end of the 1920s that should not be overlooked in terms of its influence – the design principle seen here based upon temporary structures that were transparent and reduced in their form.

Die einzelnen Tafeln zeigten jeweils drei Beispiele einer gelungenen Formgebung mit einer Fotografie und einem kurzen erläuternden Text. Der Rapportstil, der sich nach immer gleichem Schema über alle Tafeln zog, lief Gefahr, den Besucher zu ermüden, wenn nicht einzelne Beispiele auch als Original präsentiert worden wären. › 3.2 Diese fachspezifische Ausstellung bot nachträglich und willentlich den propagandistischen Inszenierungen des Nationalsozialismus Paroli und formulierte eine Sprache der Sachlichkeit, die den Betrachter als emanzipierten Besucher einlud, die vorgetragenen Argumente abzuwägen.

Die genannten gestalterischen Aspekte, die an Sachlichkeit und Aufklärung orientiert waren, ließen schließlich die Ausstellung zu einer Neuauflage des Gesamtkunstwerkes erwachsen, in welchem unweigerlich die verschiedensten alten wie neuen »Medien« wie Architektur, Typografie, Fotografie und Plastik (Kinetik) zusammenflossen. Bill konnte sich hier auf die Leistungen des Bauhauses in Dessau berufen: In komplex angelegten Untersuchungen experimentierten die Bauhäusler Joost Schmidt und Heinz Loew beispielsweise mit der Mechanisierung und Typisierung von Raumgestaltungen, um diese dann zur Serienreife zu führen. Fragen des Raumbegriffs, von Licht und Schatten oder der menschlichen Wahrnehmung standen im Vordergrund der Arbeit in der »Plastischen Werkstatt« (1927–1930). Schließlich unterschieden Schmidt und Loew drei Typen von Ausstellungen: die Verkaufsausstellung, die Spezialausstellung und die Prestigeausstellung. Stets ging es zunächst rein pragmatisch um die Funktions- und Auftraggebung, dabei jedoch beachtend, dass man keinesfalls werbestrategische Animationsdienste leisten, sondern lediglich informieren wollte: Aufklärung statt Überredung war das Motto. Abweichungen von dieser Planung wurden jedoch bei der Prestigeausstellung erlaubt. Atmosphäre und Symbole, also inszenatorische und suggestive Mittel, wurden eingesetzt, und man enthob sich nur dort einer selbst auferlegten puren Informationspflicht.

So wurde am Bauhaus der Grundstein für eine sachbezogene Informationsvermittlung, für die »Visuelle Kommunikation«, wie sie seit der HfG Ulm genannt werden sollte, und für neue künstlerische Anwendungsbereiche, wie sie die Reklame und das Ausstellungsdesign darstellen, gelegt. Bill aktualisierte die formalästhetische Grundlegung des Ausstellungsdesigns durch das Bauhaus, indem er das Konzept der »Guten Form« auf die Ausstellung übertrug. Bei aller Sachlichkeit der Informationsübermittlung wird in der radikalen Formreduzierung, der räumlichen Komposition der Lattenkonstruktionen und Objekte und nicht zuletzt dem Layout der Schautafeln eine ästhetische Dimension offenkundig, die über das rein Funktionale hinausgeht.

Each of the individual panels displayed three examples of successful design with a photograph and a short explanatory text for each. Were it not for the individual design exhibits in their original form, the standardized, repetitive format used for display the panels alone would have run the risk of jading the visitor. › 3.2 This sector-specific exhibition deliberately and retroactively pitted itself against the propagandist arrangements preferred during the Third Reich and formulated a language of objectivity, which invited the beholder – the emancipated visitor – to weigh up the arguments presented to them.

The creative aspects mentioned, with their focus on objectivity and enlightenment, ultimately transformed the exhibition into a remake of the artistic synthesis whereby a blend of old and new media from across the creative spectrum including architecture, typography, photography and (kinetic) sculpture inevitably emerged. Here, Bill was able to invoke the achievements of Bauhaus in Dessau: in a series of complex studies Bauhaus artists Joost Schmidt and Heinz Loew for example, experimented with the mechanisation and categorization of interior designs, the aim being to prepare them for mass production. Questions regarding the concept of space, light and shadow and human perception were at the forefront of work carried out in the »Plastische Werkstatt« (1927–1930). Ultimately, Schmidt and Loew distinguished between three types of exhibition: the sales exhibition, the special exhibition and the prestige exhibition. At first it was always a purely pragmatic matter of the commission and the prescribed function, whereby close attention was paid that the aim was under no circumstances to function as an animate promotional strategy but rather simply to inform: the motto being »enlightenment, not persuasion«. However, deviations from this premise were permitted in the case of the prestige exhibition, where certain atmospheres and symbols, ergo means of orchestration and suggestion, were implemented and only here was one relieved of a self-imposed yet nonetheless compulsory duty to inform.

Thus, it was at Bauhaus that the ground stone was laid for a pertinent presentation of information – or for »visual communication« as it should be referred to since the emergence of Ulm School of Design – and for new artistic areas of application, as depicted in advertising and exhibition design. Bill used Bauhaus to bring the formerly aesthetic foundations of exhibition design up to date in that he translated the concept of »Gute Form« into the exhibition itself. For all the objectivity of this way of conveying information, the radical reduction in form, the spatial composition of the slatted structures and objects, and not least the arrangement of the display panels all succeed in evincing an aesthetic dimension that goes beyond the purely functional.

3.2

Mit seiner Ausstellung »Die gute Form« wähnte sich Bill in der Tradition des Bauhauses, zugleich jedoch nahm er einen elementaren Streitpunkt der Bauhaus-Rezeption vorweg, der zu Beginn der 1950er Jahre über einen längeren Zeitraum diskutiert wurde: die Glorifizierung des Kubisch-Geometrischen im Kontext des Bauhauses und die Ausblendung des Ästhetischen. Dieses Dogma, das den Gestalter als rein dienende Kraft des Funktionalen degradiert und eine orthodoxe Auslegung des Bauhauses darstellt, kann anhand der Schriften Gropius' unter dem Hinweis der sogenannten Wesensforschung des Objektes widerlegt werden. Bill begnügt sich nicht mit einer diesbezüglichen Beweisführung, sondern formuliert eine aktualisierte Version moderner Produktgestalt.

Das Ausstellungsdesign erweist sich als Ergebnis von Erkenntnissen der Technik und Wissenschaft und den Bedürfnissen menschlicher Sozialität und Ästhetik. So zeigt sich der Designer im Sinne Bills als Künstler und Erzieher der Gesellschaft, dessen Produkt – so auch das Ausstellungsdesign – nicht dekorativen Zwecken folgt, sondern auf eine intuitive Erziehung der Gesellschaft abzielt. Der Gebrauchswert des Produktes beziehungsweise der Ausstellung misst sich an den vieldimensionalen Bedürfnissen des Menschen.

With »Die gute Form« Bill did indeed consider himself as working in the lineage of Bauhaus. However, he had at the same time anticipated a fundamental controversy at the heart of the Bauhaus' reception of the exhibition, which would be subject to debate over an extended period during the early 1950s. For he clearly saw the glorification of the cubic-geometric in the Bauhaus context and the back seat accorded the aesthetic. Gropius' writings referencing the so-called »study of essentials« in objects have the potential to prove this to be a faulty dogma that degrades the designer to the status of being purely ancillary to the function and presents an orthodox interpretation of Bauhaus. Bill was likewise not content with this line of reasoning and so formulated his own updated version of Modernist product design.

The exhibition design was intended to be the sum of scientific knowledge and technology, of the human need for community, and aesthetics. Thus in the »Bill« sense, the designer proves to be an artist and an educator of society, whose product (including exhibition design) does not fulfil a decorative function but is geared toward an intuitive education of society. The practical value of the product or the exhibition is measured against the multifarious needs of humans.

Bill nahm implizit Bezug auf eine elementare Disposition des Ausstellungs-designs in der modernen demokratischen Gesellschaft: Die Bedeutung von Informationen und die Form ihrer Vermittlung hatten Bill und zuvor das Bauhaus erkannt und zum Gegenstand der künstlerischen Gestaltungen wie theoretisch-analytischen Untersuchungen am Bauhaus erhoben. So wurde versucht, zwangsläufigen, systemimmanenten Entwicklungen von Kapitalismus und Marktwirtschaft, wie der schleichenden Autonomi-sierung einzelner gesellschaftlicher Sphären, entgegenzuwirken. Nach Mies van der Rohe, selbst Ausstellungsgestalter, sollten hier Ausstellungen die notwendige Vernetzungsarbeit leisten, wie er 1928 – nicht ohne romantisch-idealistische Ereiferung – formulierte: »Auf diesem Wege begegnet Wirtschaft und Technik den entscheidenden Kräften des geistigen und kulturellen Lebens. Wir stehen mitten in einer Wandlung, einer Wandlung, die die Welt ändern wird. Diese Wandlung aufzuzeigen und sie zu fördern, wird die Aufgabe der kommenden Ausstellungen sein. [...] Nur wenn das zentrale Problem der Zeit – die Intensivierung des Lebens – Inhalt der Ausstellungen wird, finden sie Sinn und Rechtfertigung. Sie müssen Demonstrationen führender Kräfte sein und zu einer Revolutionierung des Denkens führen.«[2]

Dass bei dieser hochkarätigen Aufgabe der Gestaltung von Ausstellungen, also dem Ausstellungsdesign, eine nicht weniger bedeutsame Rolle zuteil wird, versteht sich von selbst. Das im Grunde abstrakte Gesellschaftssys-tem der Demokratie mit seinem hierarchischen Netzwerk von Institutionen, Gremien und Verwaltungseinrichtungen ist geradezu abhängig von Informa-tionsübermittlungen. Gleichermaßen können Demokratie und Verwaltung nur funktionieren, wenn auch die Betroffenen, die Bevölkerung, die Klavia-tur der Gremien zu spielen weiß.

Die Ausstellungen als Demonstrationsräume, wie sie anfänglich die Avant-gardisten einrichten wollten, sollten der Überbrückung der Gegenwart auf dem Weg in die Zukunft dienen. Diese Orte, die informierenden Ausstellun-gen von Max Bill in der Tradition des Bauhauses, waren Spielräume, Experimentierfelder der Moderne zur Spiegelung und Visualisierung der eigenen Utopie und gleichzeitig Instrumente zu deren Realisierung.

>>> author p.211

1 Die Ausstellung wurde vom 7.–17. Mai 1949 als Sonderschau auf der Mustermesse Basel gezeigt. Zeitgleich (14. Mai–3. Juli) war die Schau auf der ersten Ausstellung des Deutschen Werkbunds in Köln nach dessen Begründung zu sehen. Später wurde die Ausstellung in verschiedenen Städten im In- und Ausland präsentiert. 2 Mies van der Rohe: Ausstellungen, in: Das Neue Frankfurt. 1930, no. 6, p.296.

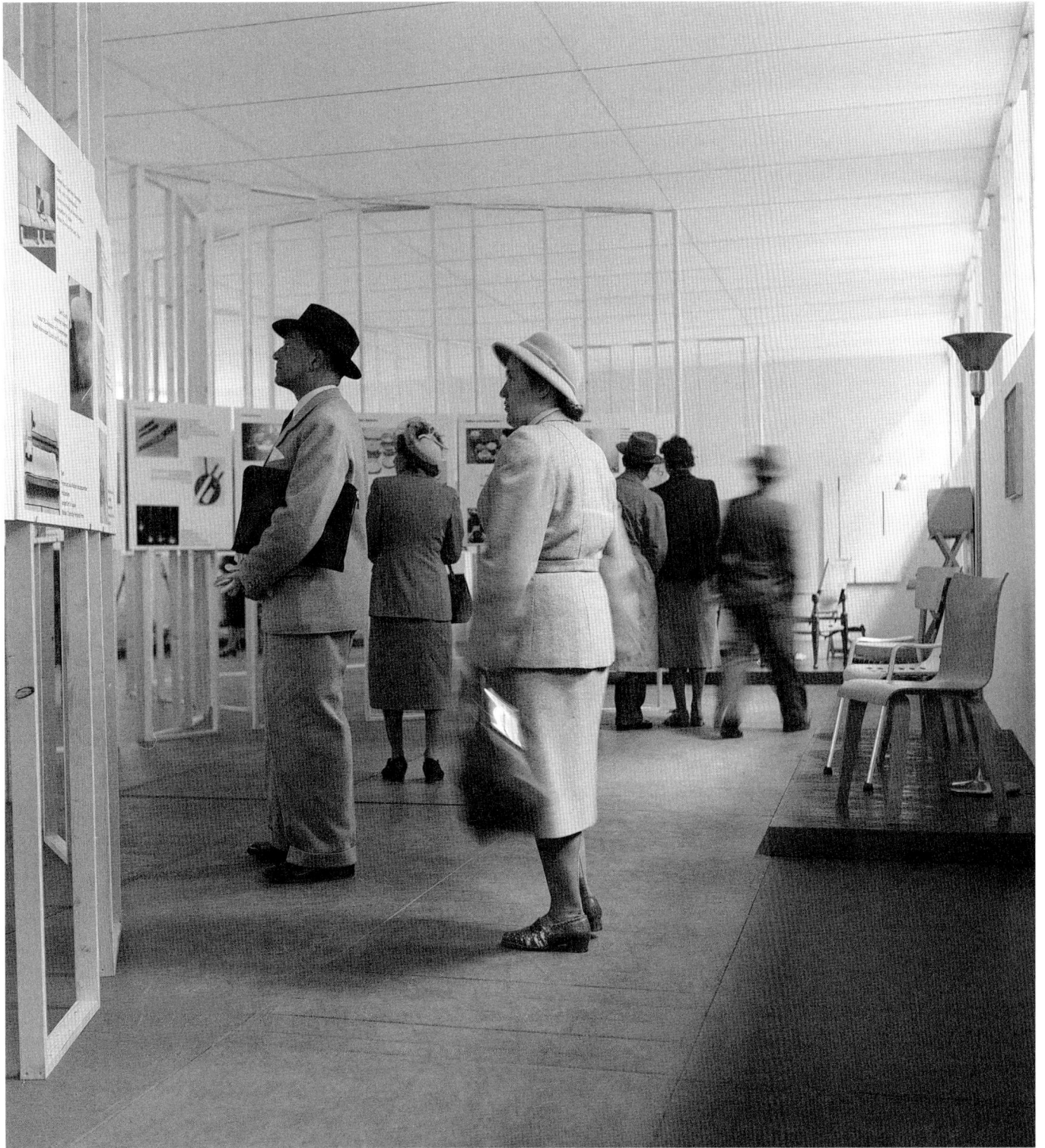

3.3

documenta. Kunst des XX. Jahrhunderts.
Internationale Ausstellung

Simon Großpietsch

»Ja, dann lässt sich's machen.«[1]

»documenta«, Kunst des 20. Jahrhunderts, Internationale Ausstellung

Jedes große Ereignis scheint aus einem Mythos zu entstehen –
oder vielmehr: einer nachträglichen Verklärung unterworfen zu sein.

Die Geschichte eines außergewöhnlichen Ausstellungserfolgs ließe sich
wie folgt erzählen: Als ein kleiner, lebhafter Maler und Akademieprofessor,
über den unter den Nationalsozialisten Berufsverbot verhängt worden war,
mit seinen Studenten im Oktober 1954 an einem nach wie vor ruinösen
Museum in Nordhessen vorbeiging, soll er seine Schüler gefragt haben,
welche Maße wohl das Haus haben könnte, das einst das erste Museum
auf dem europäischen Festland gewesen war. Nach einigen Grübeleien und
Versuchen, das Gebäude abzuschreiten, wurde ein Ergebnis gefunden.
So begab es sich, dass der Professor nachdenklich die Machbarkeit seines
kühnen Unterfangens bekundete.

So weit der Mythos. Acht Monate später, am 15. Juli 1955, öffnete die
documenta für 65 Tage ihre Pforten. Die Ausstellung mit 670 Werken von
148 Künstler(innen) aus sechs Ländern versammelte zeitgenössische
Kunst, als ein festes Museum für moderne Kunst in Deutschland undenk-
bar schien. Professor Arnold Bode initiierte das Museum auf Zeit, das als
einmalige Ausstellung geplant war.[2]

In der Stadt Kassel, welche im Oktober 1943 durch britische Angriffe über
80% ihrer Bausubstanz verlor, stockte der Wiederaufbau. Das »Wirtschafts-
wunder« der 1950er Jahre blieb in Nordhessen weitestgehend aus und die
Arbeitslosenquote war hoch. Einst im Zentrum des Landes gelegen, war
Kassel nun eine Stadt am Zonenrandgebiet geworden. Ökonomische wie
kulturelle Defizite zwangen die Stadtväter zum Handeln, sodass staatliche
Finanzmittel zur Ausrichtung der Bundesgartenschau 1955 genutzt wurden.
Eine überschaubare, integrierte Ausstellung plastischer Kunst sollte die
Floralmesse begleiten.[3]

Lange vor diesen Bemühungen seitens der Stadt hatte Bode die Idee einer
Ausstellung[4], welche nach der diktatorischen Zeit der Nationalsozialisten
die Kunst der 1920er Jahre zeigen und einen Überblick der (europäischen)
Kunstentwicklung seit Ende des 19. Jahrhunderts bieten sollte.[5] »Was tun
in dem zerstörten Kassel? So am ›Untergang‹ mußten wir neu beginnen!«[6],
so Bode in einem Interview 1977.

»Yes, then it can be done.«[1]

»documenta«, 20th century art, International Exhibition

*All major occurrences seem to have their foundations in myth – or rather,
they are subject to post hoc glorification.*

*The story of an extraordinarily successful exhibition would go something like
this: In October 1954, accompanied by a group of his students, a small yet
cheerful painter-and-professor who had been banned from exercising his
profession during the Third Reich was walking past a museum in northern
Hessen. It still stood in its war-damaged state and he turned to his flock and
asked them how big they thought the building, which was once the first museum in mainland Europe, could be. After a few musings and some attempts
to pace out the building, they arrived at the correct answer. And so it came
to pass that the professor provided his students with a thought-provoking
demonstration of the feasibility of this seemingly bold endeavor.*

*So at any rate the myth would have it. Eight months later, on July 15, 1955,
documenta opened its doors for 65 days. With 670 works by 148 artists
from six countries the exhibition presented an array of contemporary art
at a time when a permanent museum dedicated to modern art would have
been unthinkable in Germany. The Temporary Museum had been initiated
by Professor Arnold Bode and had been planned as a one-off exhibition.[2]*

*At the time, reconstruction work in the City of Kassel, which had over 80%
of its buildings destroyed in an air raid by British forces in October 1943,
had ground to a halt. The »economic miracle« of the 1950s had for the most
part eluded northern Hessen and the rate of unemployment in the area was
high. Once located at the very heart of the country, Kassel now found itself in
the area bordering the Soviet zone. Both economic and cultural deficiencies
meant the city fathers had no choice but to act, and so, they pumped state
resources into the direction of the Bundesgartenschau 1955. The horticul-
ture show was also to be accompanied by an extensive, integrated exhibition
of sculptural art.[3]*

*Long before these efforts from the state, Bode had come up with an idea for
an exhibition,[4] which following years of Nazi dictatorship would once again
present art from the 1920s as well as offering an overview of (European) art
development from the end of the 19th century onwards.[5] »What can we do
with a destroyed Kassel? Just at the point of ›extinction‹, we have to start
again!«[6] said Bode in an interview in 1977.*

3.1

3.2

Aus einer inneren Notwendigkeit heraus empfahl sich die Stadt mit Provinz-charakter und ihren zerstörten Häusern und Ruinen nicht nur aus der Tatsache heraus, dass Arnold Bode dort 1900 geboren wurde. Es war ferner die Gestaltungsfreiheit mit der vernichteten, jedoch geschichtsträchtigen Bausubstanz wie der des Museum Fridericianum, mit der sich Kassel anbot.

Getragen wurde die documenta seitens der Stadt von Oberbürgermeister Lauritz Lauritzen. Für die konkrete Durchführung war die Gesellschaft »Abendländische Kunst des 20. Jahrhunderts e.V.« verantwortlich, ein von Bode gegründeter Verein, der es ermöglichte, Subventionen von Bund und Land zu erhalten – wobei »abendländisch« als »europäisch« zu lesen ist, wie Harald Kimpel zurecht feststellt.[7] Bode gewann den Kunsthistoriker Werner Haftmann sowie Alfred Hentzen, Kurt Martin und Hans Mettel für den Arbeitsausschuss der documenta.

Im unter der Leitung von Simon Louis du Ry erbauten, 1779 vollendeten Museum Fridericianum entfaltete sich die documenta 1955 als eine Art Wiedergutmachungsgeste gegenüber jener Künstlergeneration, welche Jahre zuvor aus deutschen Museen zwangsweise verbannt worden war. Bereits in der Rotunde, am zentralen Treppenaufgang, wurde dieser Eindruck mit »Die Kniende«, 1911 von Wilhelm Lehmbruck, deutlich. Jene Plastik wurde zentral positioniert. Ab 1937 war sie in der Wander-ausstellung »Entartete Kunst« als »Beleg für die Minderwertigkeit der modernen Kunst zu dienen gezwungen.«[8] Damit einhergehend sollte eine neue, zuvor aus dem Bewusstsein verbannte Kunst gesichtet und den Kunstbetrachtern vertraut gemacht werden, um einem Nachholbedarf gegenüber dem Rezipienten und den ihm unbekannten Werken gerecht zu werden.

Vorgelagert, im Entree des Hauses, eröffneten sich dem Besucher – neben einem historischen Vorspann aus collagierten Tafelbildern der Kunstgeschichte – Portraitfotografien der ausgestellten Künstler(innen), die großflächig auf den Eingangswänden verteilt wurden. › 3.3

It was an inner necessity and not only the fact that Arnold Bode was born there in 1900 that presented this city with its provincial character, destroyed houses and post-war ruins as a good location to hold such a venture. An additional selling point for Kassel was the blank canvas provided by its completed obliterated yet historically charged cityscape, the former Museum Fridericianum being a prime example.

Lord Mayor Lauritz Lauritzen was responsible for supporting documenta on behalf of the state. However, the actual driving force behind the event was the »Society of the Occidental Art of the 20th Century«, an association founded by Bode himself enabling the project to receive grants from the state and the federal government, whereby »Occidental« is to be read as »European«, as correctly ascertained by Harald Kimpel.[7] Art historian Werner Haftmann, Alfred Hentzen, Kurt Martin and Hans Mettel were some of the experts Bode succeeded in persuading to join documenta's working committee.

In Museum Fridericianum, built under the direction of Simon Louis du Ry and completed in 1779, documenta 1955 emerged as a kind of compensation, a good-will gesture, for that generation of artists that had been banished from German museums years before. Visitors were made unambiguously aware of this intention before they even entered the exhibition, for positioned directly in the centre of the patio at the foot of the central staircase stood Wilhelm Lehmbruck's 1911 sculpture »Die Kniende« (Kneeling Woman), which as of 1937 had been forced to serve as part of the traveling exhibition »Degenerate Art« as a testament to the inferiority of modern art.[8] The aim here was to trigger a consideration of a »new« art that had previously been banned from the public conscience and to familiarize the beholder with it, in the process fulfilling a need created by this backlog on behalf of the recipient (the public) and the works that were unknown to them.

Upon entering the building, at the very beginning of the exhibition, visitors were greeted by portrait photographs of all exhibiting artists, spread across the walls of the foyer and accompanied by a historical prefix – a collage of panel paintings drawn from throughout art history. › 3.3

Eine Vielzahl der ausgestellten Werke war den Hauptströmungen des Jahrhunderts – Futurismus, Expressionismus und Surrealismus – entnommen. Neben u. a. Umberto Boccioni mit »Der Lärm der Straße dringt ins Haus«, 1911, Piet Mondrian, Joan Mirò, Paula Modersohn-Becker, Wassily Kandinsky und Hans Mettel zeigte die documenta eine Auswahl von Skulpturen und Plastiken in unmittelbaren, substantiellen Kontexten: u. a. von Julio Gonzales, Henry Moore, Hans Wimmer, Alberto Viani und Hans Arp.

Im Obergeschoss des Hauses sind zudem fotografisch neue Richtungen der Architektur untergebracht worden. Nicht zuletzt machte ein cineastisches Filmprogramm die documenta 1955 zu einer über eine reine Kunstausstellung hinausgehenden, hochkarätigen Veranstaltung ihrer Zeit.

Die Präsentation der Werke trug die Handschrift Arnold Bodes. Während Werner Haftmann weitestgehend den theoretischen Überbau ermöglichte, schuf Bode eine raumgreifende, präzise Intervention in den provisorischen Räumen des Hauses. Die Werke wurden inszenatorisch angeordnet und fanden unter dem Zwang der Improvisation jene visuelle Entfaltung, welche Bode als Akademieprofessor in der Theorie bereits kannte.[9] Die Kunst reagierte im Raum und der Raum reagierte auf die Kunst: Die teils grob gemauerten, partiell verrußten Backsteinwände wurden statt mit einer aufwendigen Verputzung mit weißer Farbe versehen, sodass diese ihre grobe Struktur nicht verlieren würden. › 3.3 In den großen Hallen der Seitenflügel installierte Bode ein Trägersystem, welches den Präsentationsraum zwar gliederte, ihn sich jedoch gleichzeitig in voller Gänze entfalten ließ. Einbauten des behelfsmäßigen Gebäudes, wie eingezogene Betonpfeiler, blieben unbehandelt. »Nirgendwo [ist] vertuscht [worden], was dem Bau im Weltkrieg angetan wurde.«[10] Um diesen Eindruck zu unterstreichen, sind einige Gemälde auf filigranen Metallgestängen mit Abstand vor den Wänden präsentiert worden. Die Lichtregulierung strukturierte die Vorhänge aus einem – mittlerweile legendären – Material, den sogenannten »göppinger plastics«, welches in seinen langen Kunststoffbahnen darüber hinaus den starren Strukturen der Wände entgegenwirkte.

The majority of works on display had been taken from the main artistic movements of the century – Futurism, Expressionism and Surrealism. In addition to Umberto Boccioni's 1911 La strada entra nella casa (The Street Enters the House) and works by Piet Mondrian, Joan Mirò, Paula Modersohn-Becker, Wassily Kandinsky and Hans Mettel to name a few, documenta presented a selection of sculptures in immediate, substantive contexts, such as works by Julio Gonzales, Henry Moore, Hans Wimmer, Alberto Viani and Hans Arp.

The building's upper floor also housed a collection of photographs depicting the century's new trends in architecture. It was not least with the inclusion of a film program, that in 1955 made documenta an art event of the highest caliber for its time, one that went beyond the perimeters of a mere art exhibition.

The presentation clearly bore the hallmark of Arnold Bode, for while the theoretical framework was predominantly the work of Werner Haftmann, it was Bode who was responsible for creating an extensive yet detailed intervention in the building's make-shift exhibition spaces. The works were highly orchestrated in their arrangement and under the constraints forced upon them by the improvisatory conditions displayed that visual development that Bode was already familiar with as a professor, at least in theory.[9] The art was a response to the space and the space was a response to the art: Rather than undergo timely and costly plastering works, the brick walls (some of which were exposed, others still scorched) were given nothing more than a lick of white paint, so as not to lose the effect of their raw, coarse construction. › 3.3 Bode also opted for a hanging system in the larger halls within the building's wings, which while dividing the room into sections did not detract from the overall impression of the space. Original features of the building desperately in need of renovation such as concrete pillars were left untouched, too. »We have made no attempt to hide the traces of what the War inflicted upon this building.«[10] So as to enhance this impression, a number of paintings were hung from filigree metal rods at a distance from the walls. Lighting was used to give structure to these curtains made of a now-legendary material, so-called »Göppinger plastic«; these long swaths of fabric also served to counteract the walls' stark surfaces.

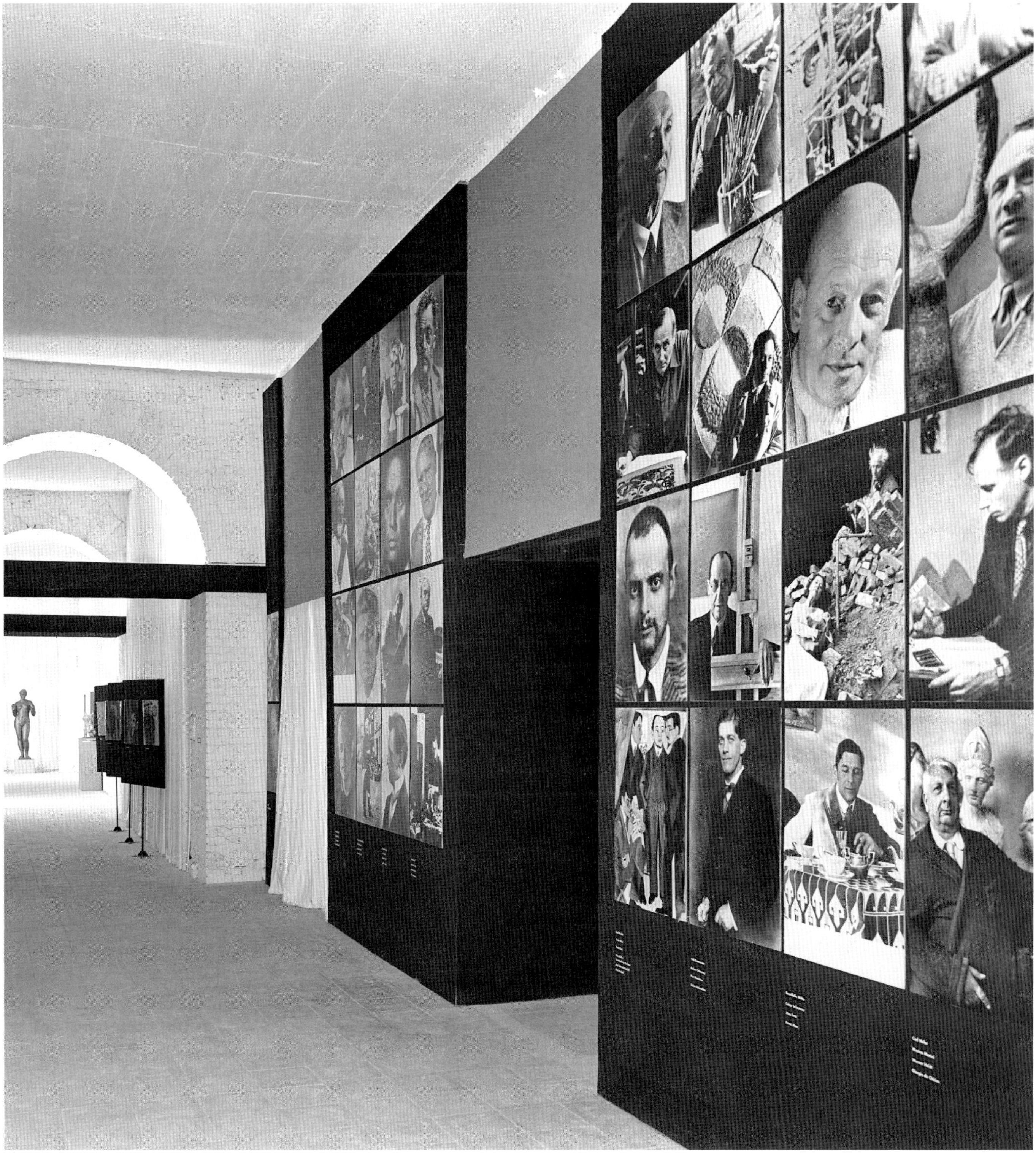

3.3

Diese allgemeinen kreativen Grundzüge der Ausstellung genossen große überregionale Aufmerksamkeit. Durch die unmittelbare Lage am Bundesgartenschaugelände wurde die documenta 1955 ein unerwarteter Erfolg.

Vieles der documenta 1955 wurde nachträglich mystifiziert. Es gibt nur noch wenige Zeitzeugen und die Versuche, an die Präsentation und Atmosphäre anzuknüpfen, sind im Laufe der über 56-jährigen Ausstellungsgeschichte so oft unternommen worden, wie sie zumeist gescheitert sind.[11] Die documenta 1955 bleibt einmalig und ebnete einen unvorhergesehenen Weg zu einer Weltkunstausstellung mit über 750.000 zahlenden Besuchern im Jahr 2007. Und das, obwohl Kassel seinen Provinzcharakter nie wirklich ablegen konnte. Aber vielleicht ist gerade dies einer der großen, fortbestehenden Erfolge dieser Ausstellung.

These general creative features brought the exhibition a great deal of national attention, while its immediate proximity to the Bundesgartenschau grounds made documenta 1955 an unexpected success.

Many elements of documenta 1955 have been mystified in subsequent years. There are only a handful of contemporary witnesses left and over the course of the exhibition's 56-year history there have been so many attempts to draw upon the unique presentation techniques and atmosphere of documenta 1955, the majority of them failing to live up to their model.[10] Documenta 1955 remains a one-off and paved the way for an international art exhibition with over 750,000 paying visitors over half a century later in 2007. All of this has been achieved despite Kassel's inability to ever shake off its provincial image. But perhaps it is precisely this that is one of the greatest sustaining successes of this exhibition.

>>> author p.212

1 Cf. Kimpel, Harald: Documenta. Mythos und Wirklichkeit. Köln 1997, p.86.
2 Aus diesem Grund erscheint es als unangebracht, von »documenta 1« zu sprechen. Eine numerische Zählung wie diese wurde erst ab 1959 zur »documenta 2« verwendet.
It is for this reason that it appeared somewhat inappropriate to speak of »documenta 1«. Such a numeric denotation was only used as of 1959 with »documenta 2«

3 Cf. Kimpel, Harald: Documenta. Mythos und Wirklichkeit. Köln 1997, p.14.
4 Die von Heiner Georgsdorf veröffentlichten Notizen Bodes lassen die Rekonstruktion zu, dass dieser die Idee einer umfassenden, internationalen Ausstellung zeitgenössischer Kunst bereits im November 1947 der Hessischen Sezession vorstellte.
Bode's notes, which were published by Heiner Georgsdorf, allow us to reconstruct

that he presented the idea of staging a comprehensive international exhibition of contemporary art to the Hessische Sezession
in: Georgsdorf, Heiner (Ed.): Arnold Bode - Schriften und Gespräche. Berlin 2007.
5 Jedoch ohne Preise und Pavillons, wie sie aus Venedig bekannt waren.
But without awards and pavilions, such as those known from Venice.

6 »Ich mußte aus Kassel etwas machen, um nicht unterzugehen – Interview mit Prof. Arnold Bode«.
»I have to make something of Kassel, or it'll be the end of me – interview with Prof. Arnold Bode.«, in: Kunst und Medien. Materialien zur documenta 6, Kassel 1977, p.139.
7 Cf. Kimpel, Harald: Documenta - die Überschau. Fünf Jahrzehnte Weltkunstausstellung in Stichwörtern. Köln 2002, p.17.

8 Ibid., p.21.
9 Cf. Ibid., p.25.
10 Ibid., p.26.
11 So sah sich zum Beispiel Roger M. Buergel 2007 ambitioniert, Vorhänge und Wandsysteme zu modifizieren und referentiell in die documenta 12 zu übertragen.
Roger M. Buergel, for example, was inspired to create a modified version of the curtains and wall system and implement them referentially at documenta 12 in 2007.

3.4

Janina Poesch
Poème électronique von Le Corbusier

Auf der Weltausstellung 1958 in Brüssel stellt der Philips-Pavillon das erste Gesamterlebnis aus Architektur, Projektion, Licht und Musik dar.

»Das Mysterium des Philips-Pavillons beginnt in der Sekunde, in der ein junger Mann am Regiepult der Kommandozentrale auf einen unscheinbaren Knopf drückt und sich der hohe, asymmetrisch geformte Raum verwandelt: leuchtendes Rot flammt auf, ein zugleich zischendes und klirrendes Geräusch wird hörbar und wieder abgelöst von seltsamem Heulen und Pfeifen, das von allen Wänden gleichermaßen auszugehen scheint. Und während der Besucher urplötzlich von tosendem Lärm umgeben ist, setzen überdimensionale Bilderfolgen ein. Ein lodernder Feuerball wird sichtbar, inmitten von einem Gewirr sich ständig in Form und Tönung verändernder Farbflecken. Teils umgeben, teils überdeckt tauchen bizarr geformte Lebewesen auf und Ungeheuer wachsen ins Riesenhafte – in sekundenschnellem Bildwechsel erlebt der Besucher das Werden der Welt und ihm offenbart sich das unergründliche Formenspiel der Natur. All dies wird von sphärenhaften Klängen und makabren Geräuschen untermalt, von Geräuschen, die bald dem Schrei eines hungrigen Raubtieres, bald dem Zwitschern eines dahin flatternden kleinen Vogels, bald dem Klappern eines Holzinstrumentes ähnlich sind – alles in einer einzigen Minute, der ersten jener acht, in die Le Corbusier seine Erzählung von der Entwicklung der Menschheit ebenso geschickt wie mutig zwängte [...].«

Jene bildhaften Worte stammen aus der Mitarbeiterzeitung »Wir bei Philips« und beschrieben vor über fünfzig Jahren eindringlich das »Poème électronique« – eine visuelle Darbietung von Le Corbusier, die mit einer Partitur von Edgard Varèse unterlegt wurde. Uraufgeführt wurde die erste multimediale Inszenierung der Neuzeit zur Brüsseler Weltausstellung 1958 im Philips-Pavillon und kann als innovatives Gesamtkunstwerk verstanden werden, das architektonische, visuelle und musikalische Komponenten vereint.

Als Le Corbusier im Winter 1956 den Auftrag erhielt, für Philips einen Pavillon zur Weltausstellung zu entwerfen, faszinierte ihn nicht nur die Aufgabe an sich, sondern vielmehr die Idee, seine kulturellen und politischen Intentionen einem breit gefächerten Publikum aus aller Welt zugänglich zu machen. Somit schlug er dem damaligen künstlerischen Direktor sogar vor, auch das inhaltliche Konzept des Bauwerks zu gestalten:

Poème électronique by Le Corbusier

The Philips Pavilion at Expo '58 in Brussels was the first to present an overall experience featuring architecture, projection, light and music.

»The enigma of the Philips Pavilion begins the second a young man at the mixing console in the command center hits a nondescript button and the high, asymmetrical space is transformed: a bright red color shoots up, a hissing, and at the same time clinking noise rings out, and is then replaced by a strange howling and whistling that appears to be coming from all the walls in equal measure. And while visitors are suddenly surrounded by a thunderous din, over-sized sequences of images appear. A blazing ball of fire becomes visible, patches of color, which, all a jumble permanently change shape and hue. Bizarrely shaped beings emerge in some cases surrounded, in others covered, and behemoths take on giant dimensions; with the images changing every second, visitors experience the world coming into being and are presented with the unfathomable interplay of nature's shapes. All this is set to ethereal sounds and macabre noises, which soon resemble the cry of a hungry beast of prey, now the twittering of a small bird flitting here and there, and now the clattering of a wooden instrument – all in a single minute, the first of the eight into which Le Corbusier crammed his narrative of the development of mankind as skillfully as he did courageously [...].«

These graphic words are from the Philips staff journal and, dating back over 50 years, forcefully describe the »Poème électronique«, a visual presentation by Le Corbusier set to a musical score by Edgard Varèse. The premiere of the first multi-media performance of the Modern age was in the Philips Pavilion at Expo '58 and can be seen as an innovative gesamtkunstwerk, combining architectural, visual, and musical components.

When, in the winter of 1956, Le Corbusier was awarded the contract to design a pavilion for the World Expo for Philips he was fascinated not only by the assignment itself, but much more by the idea of making his idea of cultural and political intentions accessible to a wide audience from all over the world. To this end he even suggested to the artistic director at the time that he also be responsible for the concept for the contents of the structure:

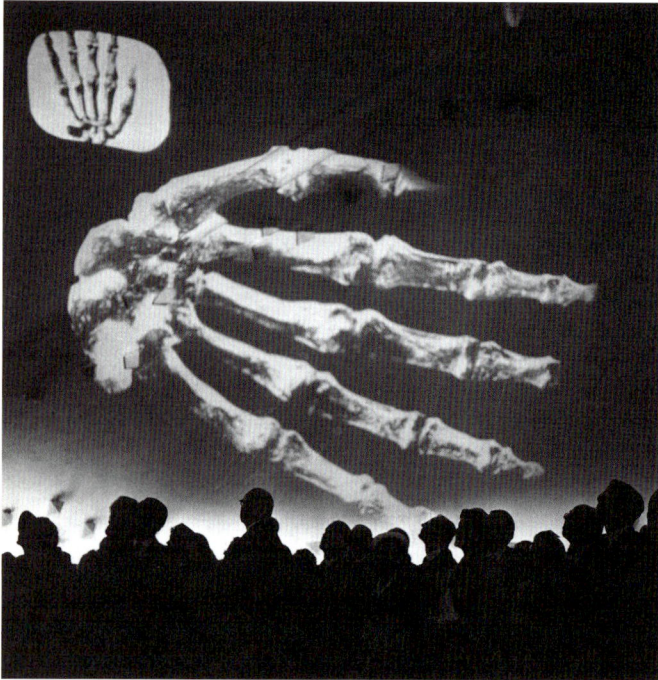

3.2

3.3

Den Besuchern sollte ein musikalisch untermaltes Schauspiel geboten werden, das nicht nur Le Corbusiers Ideologie zeigen sollte, sondern ganz nebenbei auch das, was die Technik auf einigen der wichtigsten Arbeitsgebieten des renommierten Unternehmens – Beleuchtungstechnik, Akustik, Elektronik und Automation – zu leisten vermag.

Erste Gestaltungsideen skizzierte Le Corbusier mit den Worten: »Kontrast zwischen Tag und Nacht und alle Nuancen der Dämmerung. Stimmungen, die 500 Besucher fesseln und ihnen psychophysiologische Eindrücke vermitteln werden: Rot, Schwarz, Gelb, Grün, Blau und Weiß. [...] Eine stereofonische Musik, die eine statische Räumlichkeit erweckt oder Bewegung in ihr. Geräuschmassen, Lärmberge oder Tonsümpfe. Als Kontrast: Geräuschrouten, auf denen der Ton schnell oder langsam, sprungweise oder verbreitet läuft. Ein unbeschreiblicher Lärm, eine der Stille nahe, unendliche Ruhe, die Stille selber.«

Visitors were to be presented with a spectacle set to music that was intended not only to demonstrate Le Corbusier's ideology, but, en passant, what technology was capable of in one of the renowned company's most important fields, lighting, acoustics, electronics, and automation.

Sketching his initial ideas for the design, Le Corbusier wrote: »A contrast between night and day, with all the nuances of twilight. Moods, which captivate 500 visitors and present them with psychological and physiological impressions: red, black, yellow, green, blue, and white. [...] Stereophonic music, which wakens static premises or sets them in motion. Sound masses, mountains of noise, or audio swamps. By way of contrast: sound routes, on which tones travel quickly or slowly, intermittently or diffused. An indescribable noise, infinite calm close to silence, silence itself.«

Seine Grundrissskizzen ähnelten derweil einem Magen, was nicht zuletzt auf Le Corbusiers Bewunderung für die Organisation von Schlachthäusern und Fabriken zurückzuführen ist: »Es sollte so aussehen, als würde man einen Schlachthof betreten. Dann, sobald man drinnen ist, BANG, ein Schlag auf den Kopf, und du bist verloren!« Dabei war es nicht nur das Überraschungsmoment, das ihn zu dieser Form inspirierte, sondern vielmehr das Problem der Besucherführung, die einen getrennten Ein- und Ausgang verlangte, um den Ablauf zwischen den Vorführungen zu optimieren.

Die meiste Zeit verbrachte Le Corbusier anschließend mit der Ausarbeitung des Drehbuchs sowie der Auswahl und Gestaltung der Bilder für das audiovisuelle Schauspiel, das die Evolutionsgeschichte der Menschheit darstellen sollte. Entgegen seiner ursprünglichen Pläne entschied er sich, das »Poème électronique« als Werk ohne Worte wirken zu lassen und umging so sehr elegant das Problem der Verständlichkeit gegenüber einem internationalen Publikum.

Vier verschiedene Komponenten umfassten dabei die optischen Bestandteile des »Elektronischen Gedichts«: zum einen Bild- und Filmprojektionen, welche die Wände des Pavillons bespielten, zum anderen farbige Lichtprojektionen, die darauf abzielten, die Effekte der Bilder zu intensivieren und die Bildabfolge zu strukturieren. Die Farbwechsel wurden von Le Corbusier im Drehbuch sekundengenau geplant und durch den Einsatz verschiedenfarbiger Neonröhren realisiert. Jene befanden sich hinter Balustraden, die sich durch den gesamten Randbereich des Innenraums zogen. Hinzu kamen weitere Farbprojektionen, die einfache geometrische Formen über die Bilder und Filme blendeten. Und zu guter Letzt hingen zwei dreidimensionale Objekte von der Decke, die mit Hilfe von UV-Licht illuminiert wurden: ein weiblicher Akt und ein geometrischer Körper – die Symbole für Geist und Materie.

Das gesamte »Poème électronique« hatte eine Länge von genau 480 Sekunden und bestand aus sieben Bildsequenzen, deren Inhalte – vorwiegend Schwarz-Weiß-Fotografien und -Filme – im schnellen Wechsel aufeinander folgten. Sie zeigten Kunst aus allen Erdteilen, technologische Errungenschaften, Menschen in Armut und Kriegsszenarien mit Atombombenexplosionen, um schließlich mit einer Abfolge aus zahlreichen Abbildungen kleiner Kinder und Beispielen moderner Architektur – natürlich jener von Le Corbusier – die Zukunft einzuleiten. › 3.3

Le Corbusier's sketches for the footprint, meanwhile, resembled a stomach, something that was not least attributable to his admiration for the organization of abattoirs and factories: »It is meant to look as if one is entering an abattoir, because once you're inside, BANG, one hit on the head, and you've lost!« That said, it was not just the surprise effect that inspired him to come up with this shape, but rather the problem of visitor guidance, which called for a separate entrance and exit, to improve the flow between performances.

Le Corbusier subsequently spent most time working on the screenplay and selecting and designing the images for the audiovisual spectacle intended to portray the history of the evolution of mankind. As opposed to his original plans he decided to let the »Poème électronique« achieve its impact without the use of words, thereby elegantly avoiding the problem of comprehension on the part of an international audience.

The visual elements of the »Electronic Poem« embraced four different components: on the one hand images and films projected onto the pavilion walls, and on the other projections of colored light intended to intensify the effect of the images and structure the image sequence. In the screenplay Le Corbusier planned the change in color down to the very last second and achieved it using different-colored neon tubes. These were positioned behind balustrades running along the entire perimeter of the interior. In addition to these there were color projections, which overlaid straightforward geometric shapes on the images and films. And last but not least there were two 3D objects suspended from the ceiling and illuminated by ultraviolet light: a female nude and a geometric body, symbols of the mind and material.

The entire »Poème électronique« lasted exactly 480 seconds and comprised seven sequences of images, the contents of which (primarily black and white photographs and films) alternated quickly between one another. They showed art from all corners of the Earth, technological achievements, people in poverty, as well as war scenarios with nuclear bombs exploding, before finally heralding in the future with numerous illustrations of small children and examples of modern architecture, including, it goes without saying, by Le Corbusier. › 3.3

Das strikte Drehbuch, das den Ablauf im Sekundenraster festhielt, diente auch als Vorlage für Edgard Varèses musikalische Komposition – eine Mischung aus elektronischem Sound, aufgezeichneten Geräuschen und Musikfetzen, die das Publikum in ein Meer von Geräuschen tauchte.

In der räumlichen Inszenierung des Klangs liegt vielleicht der revolutionärste Aspekt des Pavillons: Nicht nur, weil jedes musikalische Element in jeder Ecke des Raums abgespielt werden konnte – hierfür wurden mehr als 350 Lautsprecherboxen an den Wänden des Pavillons installiert –, sondern auch, weil sich die einzelnen Elemente in sogenannten Klangbahnen fortsetzten. So verlief der Ruf »Oh God«, dessen Quelle über der Eingangstür lag, und ein flatterndes Geräusch, das die Techniker »birdies« nannten, in einem horizontalen Kreis, während am Ende des Raumes ein Pfeifton zum Dach des Pavillons hinaufschnellte. Genau in der Mitte des Poèmes kam dann der Moment der Stille zum Einsatz, der den Raum zeitgleich in hartes, weißes Licht tauchte.

Interessant ist, dass es zwischen Le Corbusier und Varèse während ihrer Arbeit anscheinend keinerlei Kooperation zu geben schien: Beide arbeiteten ohne größere Absprachen unabhängig voneinander. Es gab zwar immer wieder Vermutungen über eine Koordination zwischen Bildfolge und Sound, aber keine konkreten Aussagen. So lässt auch der Schluss eine eher unverbindliche Zusammenarbeit vermuten, da die Bilder von Babys kaum zu Düsenjet- oder Sirenengeräuschen passten. > 3.4

Rund zwei Millionen Zuschauer besuchten den Pavillon und tauchten kurzzeitig in eine künstliche Welt aus Licht, Farbe, Rhythmus, Ton und Bild ein. Nicht jeder war begeistert und viele verließen irritiert, teilweise erschrocken und verunsichert, das Gebäude. Mit dem Ende der Ausstellung wurde der Pavillon schließlich zerstört. Und das Bauwerk ging später eher wegen seiner revolutionären Form und Konstruktion in die Annalen der Geschichte ein als für das, was es eigentlich darstellen sollte: die erste immersive, elektronische und weitgehend computergestützte Multimedia-Umgebung!

The strict screenplay, which stipulated the sequence down to the very last second, also served as the basis for Edgard Varèse's musical composition, a mixture of electronic sound, recorded noises and snippets of music, which immersed the spectators in a sea of sounds.

The most revolutionary aspect of the pavilion lies, perhaps, in the spatial orchestration of the sound: Not just because every musical element could be played in every corner of the space, to this end more than 350 loudspeakers were installed on the walls of the pavilion, but also because the individual elements continued in what were known as sound strips. And so the cry »oh God«, which emanated above the entrance door, and a fluttering sound the technicians called »birdies«, progressed in a horizontal circle, while at the end of the space a whistling sound rose up quickly. In exactly the middle of the »poème« a moment of silence was used to immerse the space in harsh white light.

What is interesting is that while they were working together there was seemingly no cooperation whatever between Le Corbusier and Varèse: Without any great coordination both worked independently of each other. Though it was assumed on numerous occasions that the sequence of images and sound had been coordinated, there were no concrete statements to this effect. As such it is safe to conclude that their work together was if anything not binding, as the images of babies scarcely fitted in with the noise of jets or sirens. > 3.4

Around two million people visited the pavilion, where they immersed themselves briefly in an artificial world of light, color, rhythm, sound, and images. Not everyone was enthusiastic and many left the building confused, in some cases alarmed and unsettled. At the end of the exhibition the pavilion was ultimately destroyed, with the structure going into the annals of history more on account of its revolutionary shape and construction than for what it was actually meant to portray: the first electronic and for the most part computer-aided multi-media-environment in which visitors could immerse themselves!

Während sich Edgard Varèse und Le Corbusier auf die gemischt konkrete und vokale Musik sowie die Konzeption der dynamischen Licht- und Bildprojektionen im Inneren konzentrierten, wurde der Philips-Pavillon an sich von Iannis Xenakis entworfen. Der Komponist, Bauingenieur und Architekt arbeitete von 1947 bis 1959 in Le Corbusiers Büro und konnte sich hier bereits als Projektleiter für das Kloster La Tourette in Eveux bei Lyon beweisen. 1955 erregte Xenakis mit dem auf mathematischen Prinzipien beruhenden Stück »Metastasis« bei den Donaueschinger Musiktagen gro-ßes Aufsehen und befasste sich in seinem weiteren Œuvre vorwiegend mit der Idee einer »stochastischen Musik«, deren Strukturen sich als zeitlich-räumliche Bewegungen von Klangmassen beschreiben lassen.

Jene Abstraktionen mathematischer Funktionen kann man auch dem Konzept und der Geometrie des Weltausstellungsgebäudes ablesen, die auf der grafischen Notation der Streicherglissandi zu »Metastasis« beruhen und in zahlreichen hyperbolischen Parabolformen Ausdruck finden. Die gekrümm-ten Schalen der zeltartigen Musik-Raum-Skulptur bestehen dabei aus nur fünf Zentimeter starken, vorgespannten Betonplatten und sorgten 1958 nicht nur in der Fachwelt für großes Aufsehen. › 3.5

Whereas Edgard Varèse and Le Corbusier concentrated on the blend of concrete and vocal music and the concept for the dynamic light and image projections on the inside, the Philips Pavilion itself was actually designed by Iannis Xenakis. From 1947 until 1959 the composer, civil engineer, and architect worked in Le Corbusier's studio and performed sterling work as the head of the project for La Tourette Monastery in Eveux near Lyon. At the 1955 Donaueschingen Music Festival Xenakis caused a sensation with his play »Metastasis«, which was based on mathematical principles, and in his later oeuvre primarily addressed the idea of »stochastic music«, the structure of which can be described as the temporal and spatial movement of sound masses.

These abstract mathematical functions are also to be discerned in the con-cept and geometry of the World Expo building, both of which derive from the notation for the string glissandos in »Metastasis«, and which find expression in numerous hyperbolic parabolic shapes. The curved shells of the tent-like musical and spatial sculpture are made just of five centimeter-thick pre-stressed concrete slabs and in 1958 caused a sensation, not just among experts. › 3.5

>>> author p.212

Redaktionelle Anmerkung: ähnlich erschienen in PLOT#3.
Editorial note: a *similar version was published in PLOT#3.*

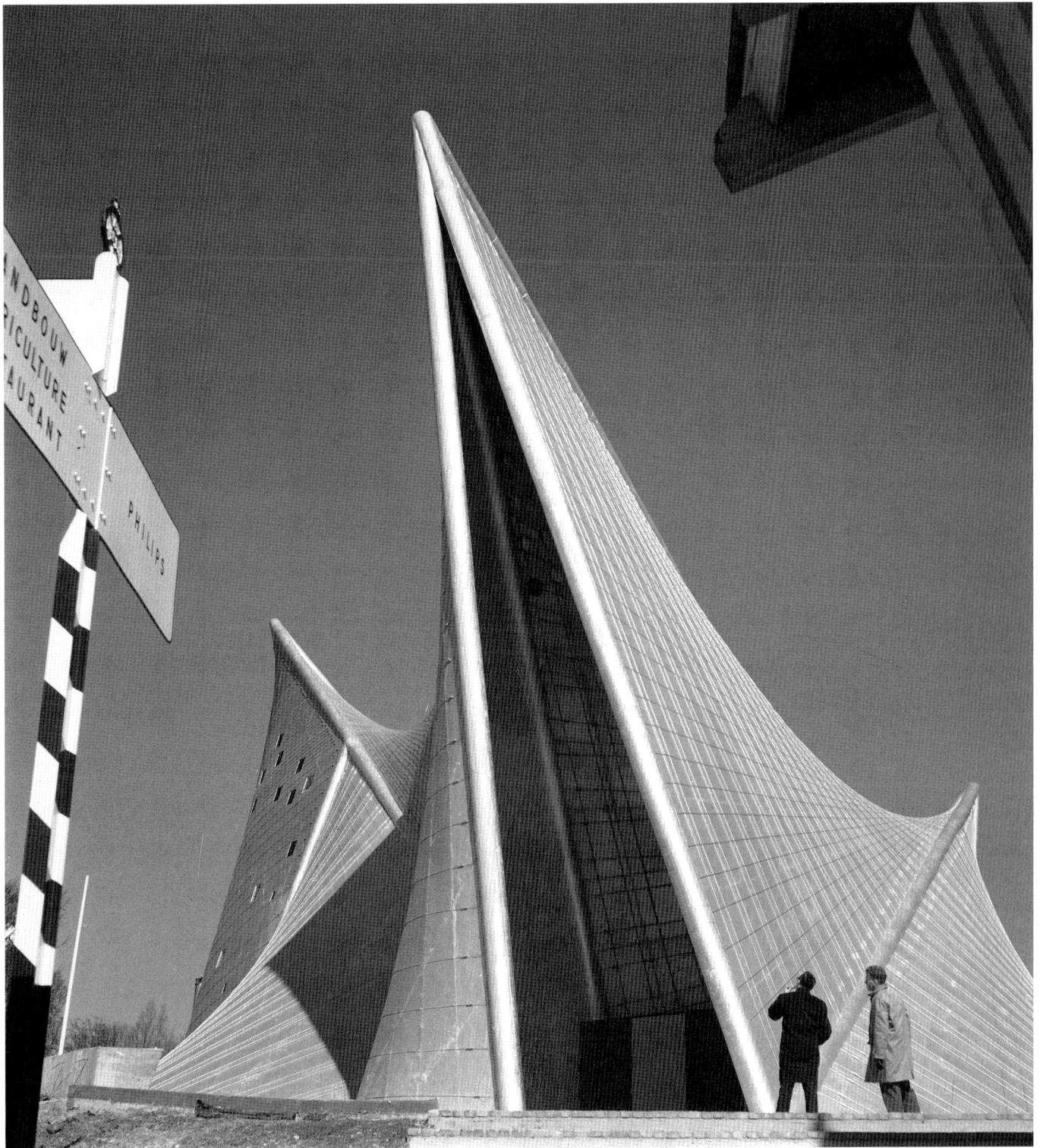

3.5

3.1 *in: Kluser, Bernd; Hegewisch, Katharina (Eds.): Die Kunst der Ausstellung. Eine Dokumentation dreißig exemplarischer Kunstausstellungen dieses Jahrhunderts. Frankfurt am Main, Leipzig 1991, p.162.*
© Ed van der Elsken

3.2 *in: Kluser, Bernd; Hegewisch, Katharina (Eds.): Die Kunst der Ausstellung. Eine Dokumentation dreißig exemplarischer Kunstausstellungen dieses Jahrhunderts. Frankfurt am Main, Leipzig 1991, p.157.*
© Ed van der Elsken

3.3 *in: Kluser, Bernd; Hegewisch, Katharina (Eds.): Die Kunst der Ausstellung. Eine Dokumentation dreißig exemplarischer Kunstausstellungen dieses Jahrhunderts. Frankfurt am Main, Leipzig 1991, p.163.*
© Ed van der Elsken

Kai-Uwe Hemken

Dylaby (Dynamisches Labyrinth) 1962 im Stedelijk Museum Amsterdam

Eine kuriose Ausstellung wurde von Mai bis Juni 1962 im Stedelijk Museum Amsterdam der Öffentlichkeit vorgestellt: Unter der Generalintendanz des Museumsdirektors Willem Sandberg und der künstlerischen Leitung von Jean Tinguely hatten insgesamt sechs Künstler in der namhaften Kunsteinrichtung quasi in Eigenregie eine sehenswerte Kunstpräsentation verwirklicht. Sieben Räume des städtischen Museums wurden nach den konzeptionellen Ansichten des jeweiligen Künstlers eingerichtet, wobei die Ausstellung mehr einem Jahrmarktspektakel ähnelte und weniger ein meditatives, besinnliches Erlebnis versprach.

Der Titel »Dynamisches Labyrinth« (Dylaby) verkündete das von allen Künstlern durch ihr bisheriges Schaffen verbürgte Konzept, eine Kunst zu entwickeln, die der Alltagsästhetik verbunden war und keinem bürgerlichen Kunstideal, das das Kunstwerk als autonom verstand, entsprach. Hier wurde keine Botschaft, keine Aussage vermittelt, sondern es wurde allein die Neugier geweckt und die Erlebnisqualität von Kunst großgeschrieben. Der Ausstellungsbesuch war als ein sukzessives Abschreiten der Räume angelegt, wobei die Anordnung bzw. Zuordnung der Räume keiner programmatischen Sinngebung folgte – sieht man einmal von dem ersten Raum, der als Prolog des Ausstellungskonzeptes diente, ab.

Bereits zu Beginn des Ausstellungsbesuchs wurde der Kunstinteressierte vor die Wahl gestellt, die Ausstellung vermittels zweier direkt benachbarter Zugänge zu betreten. Nach nur wenigen Metern konnte man aber erkennen, dass es nur scheinbar Alternativen waren, denn beide Zugänge mündeten in ein und denselben Raum. Daniel Spoerri hatte in Raum I eine Vielzahl von Einzelinstallationen angeordnet, die sich als ein Labyrinth für überraschende Sinneserfahrungen entpuppten. Der Besucher wandelte durch stockfinstere Raumkompartimente, deren zum Teil surrealistisch anmutende Einbauten einem Erlebnispark ähnelten. Allerorts konnte der Besucher vielerlei haptische Erlebnisse machen, sodass dem Primat des Visuellen, das spätestens seit dem 19. Jahrhundert in der Rangfolge der Sinne und in der Kunst den Vorrang vor den anderen genießt, eine unübersehbare Absage erteilt wurde. Dieses Labyrinth des haptischen Erlebens war der programmatische Auftakt der gesamten Ausstellung und ist auf Spoerris Bühnenexperimente der Jahre zuvor zurückzuführen. Gemeinsam mit Jean Tinguely und Claus Bremer entwickelte Spoerri seit Ende der 1950er Jahre eine Frühform des Happenings, das unter dem Stichwort »dynamisches Theater« den Besucher zum Bühnenakteur erkor und nur wenig später das sogenannte

Dylaby (Dynamisches Labyrint) at the Stedelijk Museum Amsterdam

From May to June 1962, the Stedelijk Museum Amsterdam presented the public with a rather unusual exhibition: Under the baton of museum director Willem Sandberg and the creative direction of Jean Tinguely, a group of six artists took autonomous charge of this prestigious art establishment as a blank canvas and executed a must-see art exhibition. Seven of the state museum's rooms were arranged individually according to concepts created by each of the artists, lending the exhibition an atmosphere that was more alike to a funfair spectacle than the meditative, contemplative experience one may have expected.

The title »Dynamisches Labyrinth« (Dylaby) promulgated the concept as established by these artists in their earlier creative work, namely to develop art that was linked to the aesthetics of the everyday and did not correspond to the bourgeois ideal of art and its understanding of art as autonomous. There was no message, no declaration here, simply an awakening of human curiosity and a somewhat in-your-face expression of the experiential quality of art. A visit to exhibition was set up to resemble a successive pacing off of the rooms, whereby the arrangement or rather order of the rooms – bar the first room, which served as a prologue for the exhibition concept – did not comply with any programmatic reasoning.

Upon arrival at the museum, visitors were faced with the choice of entering the exhibition through one of two portals, positioned directly alongside one another. But after just a few minutes it became clear that this only appeared to be a choice, for both entrances led to one and the same room. In Room I, Daniel Spoerri had arranged a number of individual installations, which transpired as a labyrinth of surprising sensory experiences. Visitors wandered through the pitch-black compartments, whose installations – in parts seemingly surrealistic – lent it a similar feel to an amusement park. The visitors were surrounded with an abundance of objects encouraging them to turn this into a haptic experience such that the artist's rejection of the primacy of the visual, which in artistic terms had enjoyed a supremacy over the other senses since the 19th century, was made unmistakable. This labyrinth of haptic experiences was just the beginning of a pattern that would run through the entire exhibition and was heavily influenced by Spoerri's theater experiments of the previous years. Since the end of the 1950s Spoerri had been working together with Jean Tinguely and Claus Bremer to develop a preliminary form of the »happening«, which dubbed labeled »dynamic theater« turned those in the audience into the protagonists.

3.1   3.2   3.3

»Autotheater« in Antwerpen hervorbrachte, das in einer Ausstellung mit einer Vielzahl von Geräuschen, kinetischen Apparaturen, Objekten und Hell-Dunkel-Choreographien die Sinne des Ausstellungsbesuchers strapazieren sollte. Von zentraler Bedeutung war die Partizipation des Kunstfreundes, der auf das kuratorische Gesamtgebilde Einfluss nehmen und jenseits eines Aufklärungs- und Bildungsbegehrens Erlebnisse und Erfahrungen sammeln konnte.

Per Olof Uitvedt richtete den zweiten Raum ein: Ein komplizierter, d. h. kleinteiliger hölzerner Einbau mit zahlreichen nischenartigen Situationen forderte den Besucher auf, den Ausstellungsraum nicht wie üblich abzuschreiten, sondern diesen mühselig zu erwandern. ›3.1 Eine Vielzahl von zu schließenden und zu öffnenden Türen verwies auf das Prinzip »Aufdecken/Verdecken« und bereitete dem Besucher eine Reihe von Überraschungen.

Spoerri trat im dritten Raum erneut auf den Plan und formulierte eine Institutionen- und Expertenkritik, die auf das Museum und den Kuratorenstatus abzielte. Er stellte das Museum mit seinen Exponaten buchstäblich »auf den Kopf«, indem er eine herkömmliche Kunstausstellung mit an den Wänden hängenden und gesockelten Exponaten insgesamt um 90 Grad drehte, sodass der Besucher verwundert auf einer Wand ging, wenn er den Raum besuchte. ›3.2 Spoerri formulierte mit dieser begehbaren Installation eine deutliche Kritik an der museal-wissenschaftlichen Hängungsrhetorik, die auf der Grundlage eines auf Autonomie setzenden Kunstbegriffs einem Kreis von Experten das Recht zuspricht, Kulturgut der Vergangenheit und Gegenwart als überzeitliche und metaphysische Botschaften bergende Gegenstände zu präsentieren. Der wohlfeile Kunstgenuss – auf diesen Kunstvorstellungen fußend – wurde unversehens auf ein rein Affekte bedienendes Spektakel reduziert.

Der vierte Raum zeigte eine Reihe von Gegenständen der Freizeitgestaltung: Strandkorb, Jukebox, Wasserbassin mit Plastiktieren bevölkern den kleinen Raum und lassen in der musealen Kunstwelt Assoziationen an den vergangenen Strandbesuch entstehen. ›3.3 Theoretische Reflexionen über kulturelle, wirtschaftliche oder politische Entwicklungen der Gesellschaft stellen sich hier wie auch in den anderen Räumen nur mit Mühe ein.

Als Jahrmarktsspektakel lässt sich insbesondere der nachfolgende Raum V von Niki de Saint Phalle bezeichnen. Die Künstlerin hatte einen Raum in zwei Segmente unterteilt, die beide von figural-skulpturalen Formationen beherrscht wurden. Aus verschiedenen Materialien hatte die Künstlerin übergroße Ungeheuer hergestellt, die zum Abschluss freigegeben wurden,

Not long after, this concept was followed by the so-called »auto-theater« in Antwerp, which attacked the exhibition attendees' senses with an onslaught of noises, kinetic gadgetry, objects and switches from light to dark. The participation of the »friend of art« (ergo the visitor) was of central importance, for he had the power to influence the overall curatorial concept while himself gathering experience beyond a desire for enlightenment and education.

The second room was the work of Per Olof Ultvedt: A complicated, that is to say detailed, wooden installation with numerous niche-like settings prevented visitors from traversing the exhibition hall in the usual way but required them to carefully navigate their way through. ›3.1 A series of doors that could be opened and closed referenced the »reveal/conceal« principle and the unwitting visitors were certainly in for a few surprises.

Spoerri made a re-appearance in the third room where he formulated his own institutional critique, geared towards the museum and the status of the curator. He used the exhibits to quite literally turn the museum on its head, rotating a conventional art exhibition with paintings on the walls and sculptures poised upon pedestals by 90 degrees, such that bewildered visitors found themselves walking on a wall. ›3.2 Spoerri used this walk-through installation to voice, or rather display, an unequivocal rebuke of the pseudo-scientific rhetoric of hanging that reigned in museums of the day. On the basis of a conception of art focused its autonomy, this idea assigned a circle of experts the right to present cultural artifacts – from both past and present – as objects containing time-transcending, metaphysical messages. The inexpensive enjoyment of art – based upon such notions of art – had suddenly been reduced to a spectacle whose sole purpose was the manipulation of human emotions.

The fourth room exhibited a series of recreational objects – a beach chair, jukebox, a pool filled with toy animals. These objects crowded the small room and created associations with past trips to the beach within this museum-based art world. ›3.3 Here as in the other rooms, it was only with great difficulty that one was able to draw any kind of theoretical reflections on society's cultural, economic or political developments from the works on show.

The term »funfair spectacle« is particularly fitting as a description of the subsequent room (V) by Niki de Saint Phalle. The artist divided a hall in two, both sections filled with figurative sculptural formations. She used a variety of materials to create colossal monsters, which had seemingly been placed in the firing line. The result: an installation that resembled a shooting range.

3.4 in: Kluser, Bernd; Hegewisch, Katharina (Eds.): Die Kunst der Ausstellung. Eine Dokumentation dreißig exemplarischer Kunstausstellungen dieses Jahrhunderts. Frankfurt am Main, Leipzig 1991, p.161.
© Ed van der Elsken

3.5 in: Kluser, Bernd; Hegewisch, Katharina (Eds.): Die Kunst der Ausstellung. Eine Dokumentation dreißig exemplarischer Kunstausstellungen dieses Jahrhunderts. Frankfurt am Main, Leipzig 1991, p.160.
© Ed van der Elsken

sodass die Anlage einem Schießstand glich. Wie bereits in anderen Aktionen hatte de Saint Phalle die Kunstobjekte mit rötlicher Munition beschossen: ein Affront gegen das Kunstestablishment, das als ästhetische Erfahrung der meditativen Versenkung den Vorzug gab und einem aggressiven Akt der mutwilligen Zerstörung des Kunstwerks, wie er in Raum V vorlag, beileibe nicht zustimmen konnte.

Für den nachfolgenden Raum zeichnete der amerikanische Pop-Art-Künstler Robert Rauschenberg verantwortlich. Rauschenberg, der vornehmlich des Nachts im Stedelik Museum arbeitete, scharte ein Sammelsurium von gebrauchten Alltagsgegenständen um sich. Uhren, Metallbleche, Gummireifen etc. wurden zu großformatigen Konstruktionen zusammengefügt, die wiederum mit einem Metallgitter – offenbar zum Schutz – umrahmt wurden. Denn einige der Installationen waren kinetisch. Ein »asphaltierter« Laufsteg mit weißer Lineatur erinnerte an eine Straße und verwies damit insgesamt auf eine die Moderne beherrschende, d. h. von Zeit und Mobilität geprägte, Lebenseinstellung. ›3.4

Pure Vergnügungslust verkörperte Raum VII, in dem Jean Tinguely eine Vielzahl von Luftballons platziert hatte, die wiederum von zwei großen Ventilatoren in Bewegung gesetzt wurden. ›3.5 Tinguely stimulierte den Spieltrieb des Menschen, den er als kulturanthropologische Größe erkennt und der als Grundlage seines gesamten künstlerischen Schaffens zu nennen ist: Großformatige maschinenartige Gebilde, wie Tinguely sie schuf, suggerieren eine Produktionsstätte, die jedoch letztlich nichts anderes herstellt als ein munteres, zweckfreies und bisweilen poetisches Spiel kinetischer metallener Schrottteile.

Dieser Raum, der den Endpunkt des Ausstellungsbesuchs markierte, führte erneut das Konzept von Dylaby vor Augen. Die Künstler inszenierten ein großes Spektakel unterschiedlichster Art - jenseits von großen Botschaften. Die versammelten Dylaby-Künstler wandten sich allesamt von einem Kunstbegriff ab, der die Sphäre der Kunst als exklusiv deklarierte und es erlaubte, inmitten einer auf Verwertung zielenden Industriegesellschaft durch den Kunstgenuss eine religionsähnliche Erfahrung zu erlangen. Diese auf die Autonomie der Kunst pochende Vorstellung wurde durch Künstler wie Daniel Spoerri, Jean Tinguely, Niki de Saint Phalle (Neue Realisten) oder Robert Rauschenberg (amerikanische Pop Art) verkörpert.

Die Besonderheit dieser Ausstellung lag in der konzeptuellen, praktizierten wie demonstrativen Zurückhaltung des Ausstellungskurators, der lediglich Räume, Technik und Arbeitskraft bereitstellte. Sandberg überließ den

As seen in some of her previous artistic endeavors de Saint Phalle had shot at the art objects with red ammunition in an affront against the art establishment, which favored meditative immersion as an aesthetic experience and would certainly not have condoned such an aggressive act of vandalism against artwork as seen here in Room V.

American Pop Art artist Robert Rauschenberg was in charge of the next room's contents. Rauschenberg, who was rather nocturnal in his working habits and thus often frequented the Stedelijk Museum through the night, surrounded himself with a hodgepodge of used everyday objects. He used clocks, metal sheets, rubber tires and much more to create large-scale constructions, which were then framed using metal mesh in what was clearly a precautionary measure. An »asphalted« runway with white lines was reminiscent of a street and so made reference to an outlook on life that he felt was dominating the modern age, that is to say, one that was shaped by time and mobility. ›3.4

Room VII was the embodiment of the pure desire for pleasure and Jean Tinguely had filled it with balloons, which were then blown around the room by two large fans. ›3.5 This was Tinguely's way of arousing our natural impulse to play, something he recognized as the height of cultural anthropology and can be cited as the basis of his entire artistic and creative work. As Tinguely created them, these large-scale, machine-like shapes connoted a workshop that produces nothing other than a cheery, purposeless and at times poetic game of kinetic, metallic scrap metal.

This room, which marked the end of the visitors' journey through the exhibition, provided another visualization of the fundamental concept behind Dylaby. The artists orchestrated a huge spectacle of the most diverse kind beyond big messages. Together, the Dylaby artists all turned their backs on this conception of art that declared the art sphere exclusive and used the enjoyment of art to facilitate a quasi-religious experience in the midst of an industrial society focused on exploitation. Artists such as Daniel Spoerri, Jean Tinguely, Niki de Saint Phalle (New Realism) and Robert Rauschenberg (American Pop Art) were the embodiment of this idea, insistent upon the autonomy of art.

The really special thing about this exhibition lay in the conceptual restraint (as skilled as it was demonstrative) displayed by the curator who did nothing more than provide the halls and manpower and take care of any technical requirements. Sandberg completely surrendered his professional territory to the artists and was supposedly absent for the rather limited three-week

3.4

3.5

Künstlern sein berufliches Terrain vollständig und soll sich sogar während des nur dreiwöchigen Aufbaus durch die Teilnehmer auf einer Dienstreise befunden haben. Von nicht geringer Bedeutung ist in diesem Zusammenhang die Biografie des Kurators bzw. Direktors Sandberg: Widerstandskämpfer während der Besetzung der Niederlande durch die Nationalsozialisten, Konzepteur und Ausrichter zahlreicher Ausstellungen, deren Themen und Exponate die nachfolgende Kunstentwicklung in nicht geringem Maße beeinflussten. Die Verbindung von Kunst und Kultur bzw. Alltagsgeschehen, die Sandberg in Anlehnung an den amerikanischen Kunsthistoriker Alfred Barr leitete, war nicht nur bei der Dylaby-Ausstellung ein tragendes Element.

Eine Vorgängerrolle nimmt die Ausstellung »This Is Tomorrow«, die 1956 von der Independent Group in der Whitechapel Gallery in London eingerichtet
wurde, ein. Unter dem Leitmotiv, die Zukunft der Gesellschaft in ästhetischen Ausdrucksformen zu entwerfen und entsprechende Visionen in einer Ausstellung zu präsentieren, waren die inhaltlichen Zielvorgaben definiert. Hierbei war die Vorstellung einer technikbejahenden bis technikkritischen Sicht auf eine zukünftige Kultur von zentraler Bedeutung. Diese Heterogenität entsprach der bisherigen Arbeit der Independent Group, handelte es sich doch um keine feste Künstlergruppe, sondern um eine Schar von Künstlern, die sich regelmäßig und aus freien Stücken zusammenfanden, um sich in Diskussionszirkeln verschiedenen aktuellen Fragestellungen der gesellschaftlichen Entwicklung zu widmen und diese in der Regel kontrovers zu diskutieren.

Konzeptionell wurde den beteiligten Künstlern wie Richard Hamilton, Nigel Henderson, Paolozzi, Peter Smithon u. a. von Kuratoren-Seite freie Hand gelassen, sodass die Museumsmitarbeiter zu bloßen Mitarbeitern der Künstler avancierten. Diese wiederum schrieben sich gemäß ihrer eigenen Künstlersatzung die gleichrangige Kooperation von Architekten, Künstlern und Bildhauern auf die Fahnen und verwirklichten dieses hinlänglich bekannte Ideal der modernen Kunstentwicklung mehr oder weniger erfolgreich in der Ausstellung. Auffällig ist eine mit der Dylaby-Ausstellung Jahre später vergleichbare Ästhetik des einfachen Materials sowie dessen gleichermaßen einfache Verarbeitung und verhaltene, individuelle und traditionslose Ikonografie. Dylaby hatte eine Reihe von Nachfolgern verschiedenster konzeptioneller Ausrichtungen, die sich der vorausgehenden Ausstellung affirmativ und kritisch rezipierend stellten.

set-up period off somewhere on a business trip – leaving the artists in charge. In this respect, the curator's, or rather Director Sandberg's, biography is of no small importance: Resistance fighter during the Nazi occupation of the Netherlands, the brain behind and host of numerous exhibitions, whose thematic focuses and exhibits had a great deal of influence on subsequent developments in art. It was not only in the case of Dylaby that the connection between art and culture, or everyday occurrences, as seen in the work of American art historian Alfred Barr, constituted a fundamental element of Sandberg's curatorial work.

The 1956 exhibition »This is tomorrow«, hosted by the Independent Group in the Whitechapel Gallery in London, plays something of a precursory role here. With a central focus on »designing« the future of society using aesthetic forms of expression and presenting the resulting visions in an exhibition, the objectives of »This is tomorrow« were clearly defined from the off. At this, presenting a variety of views on the culture of the future – be they advocatory or critical of the rise of technology – was of central importance and this multifarious nature conformed to trends seen in the Independent Group's previous work. Yet there was no set group of artists but rather a clutch of artists, who met regularly of their own volition. At these meetings they would form discussion groups and address a variety of topical issues surrounding the development of society, which tended to lead to some rather heated debates.

The curator gave the artists such as Richard Hamilton, Nigel Henderson, Paolozzi, Peter Smithson among others free conceptual reign, such that those assisting in the setup of the exhibition went from being the museum's employees to being the artists' staff. They in turn made it their mission to facilitate a coequal cooperation between architects, artists and sculptors in accordance with »rules« laid down by the artists themselves and so, they more or less successfully brought this well-known ideal of modern art development to life in the exhibition. Of particular note is an aesthetic of simple materials, which although it evolved years later is striking in its parallels to the Dylaby exhibition, as is the equally simple working of these materials and the restrained and highly individual iconography used, which displays no adherence to tradition. Dylaby was succeeded by a series of other exhibitions highly diverse in their conceptual orientations, some having taken an affirmative view of the preceding exhibition, others a rather more critical stance.

>>> author p.211

Jürgen Münch
Goethe 2.0 – Hugo Kükelhaus:
Vom »Naturkundlichen Spielwerk« auf der Expo '67
zum »Erfahrungsfeld zur Entfaltung der Sinne«

»Es ist scheußlich, dass die Spielmaschinen so in die Hände von
Barbaren gefallen sind. Man hätte von Anfang an darauf schreiben
müssen: nur für Kinder«, so Fritz Gotthelf, Koordinator für die
inhaltliche Gestaltung des Deutschen Pavillons auf der Expo '67,
am 29. Mai 1967 an Hugo Kükelhaus.

Mit den »Spielmaschinen« war die Auswahl von 12 Geräten aus dem
von Hugo Kükelhaus entwickelten »Naturkundlichen Spielwerk«
gemeint, die in Montreal innerhalb des deutschen Beitrags den
Themenbereich »Erziehung und Bildung« als Spiel- und Aktionsfeld
für Kinder bereichern sollte. Die »Maschinen« standen auf einer Empore
im Deutschen Pavillon: Rotations- und Balancescheibe, Federbrett,
Pendelkugeln, schwingende Seile, Schleifenbahn, ein Fahrrad zum
Antrieb eines Wasserstrudels, ein Klangturm und anderes mehr.
Doch nicht nur Kinder wurden von diesem ungewöhnlichen »Spielplatz«
angezogen und zu Spiel und Bewegung animiert. Auch und gerade
Erwachsene fühlten sich aufgefordert, sich beispielsweise auf dem
Fahrrad abzustrampeln. Die meisten Geräte waren diesem Ansturm
und der Belastung nicht gewachsen und bereits nach kurzer Zeit defekt.

Weltausstellungen waren – und sind es immer noch – in erster Linie
gewaltige »Seh-Landschaften«, die die Besucher fast ausschließlich
visuell beanspruchen. Und so ist es eigentlich nicht verwunderlich, dass
das Spielwerk von Kükelhaus für alle Altersgruppen eine willkommene
Möglichkeit war, die Rolle eines überwiegend passiven Zuschauers
zu verlassen – mit fatalen Folgen für die aufgestellten Geräte.

Allesamt waren es Prototypen, die durch Vermittlung von Otto Hahn in
den Zentralwerkstätten der Max-Planck-Gesellschaft ursprünglich für
Dortmunder Schulen hergestellt wurden, um Schulkindern Naturgesetze
spielerisch näherzubringen. Sie sollten – vor ihrer dauerhaften Installation
dort – erstmals auf der Internationalen Schulausstellung in Dortmund
präsentiert werden.

Goethe 2.0 – Hugo Kükelhaus:
From the »Experience Playground for Physical Laws« at the Expo '67
to the »Field for the Development of the Senses«

»It is awful that the experience-for-yourself stations fell into the hands
of those barbarians the way they did. They should have been labeled
›for children only‹ from the very beginning,« said Fritz Gotthelf, coordinator
of content design for the German pavilion at Expo '67, to Hugo Kükelhaus
on May 29, 1967.

By »experience-for-yourself stations« Gotthelf was referring to the 12
machines selected from the »Experience Playground for Physical Laws«
as developed by Hugo Kükelhaus as a play and activity area for children
to enhance the »education and development« section at Germany's
contribution to Montreal. The »stops« were positioned in a gallery within
the German Pavilion: roundabouts, swings, spring boards, rolling balls,
swinging ropes, loops, a bicycle that drove a water vortex, a bell tower
and more. But it was not just children that gravitated toward this unusual
»playground«, wanting to play around. Perhaps even more so than the children,
adults too felt the urge to get involved, pedaling away on the bicycle for
example. Most of the stops had not been designed to weather this kind of
assault or carry this weight, and so,it did not take long before they were
broken, left unusable.

First and foremost World Expos have always been vast »optical landscapes«,
which attract their visitors almost exclusively by means of visual stimulation.
And is not so surprising that visitors took advantage of Kükelhaus' Experience
Playground as a welcome break from their role as predominantly passive
spectators – though this had disastrous consequences for the equipment.

They were all prototypes that thanks to Otto Hahn's influence were originally
made in the Max Planck Society's main workshops for schools in Dortmund,
intended as a playful way to bring school children closer to nature. Before
being permanently installed here, they were supposed to be exhibited at the
International School Exhibition in Dortmund first.

3.2 Rotationsscheibe
roundabouts
© Stadtarchiv Soest, Nachlass Hugo
Kükelhaus (VG Bild-Kunst, Bonn 2011),
P 56.83

3.3 Dreizeiten-Pendel, Stadtarchiv
Soest, Nachlass Hugo Kükelhaus,
P 56.61
*three time pendulum, Stadtarchiv So-
est, bequest Hugo Kükelhaus, P 56.61*
© Barbara Vogel-Kükelhaus, VG Bild-
Kunst, Bonn 2014

3.4 Rotationsscheibe, Stadtarchiv
Soest, Nachlass Hugo Kükelhaus,
P 56.61
*roundabouts, Stadtarchiv Soest,
bequest Hugo Kükelhaus, P 56.61*
© Barbara Vogel-Kükelhaus, VG Bild-
Kunst, Bonn 2014

3.5 Stroboskop, Stadtarchiv Soest,
Nachlass Hugo Kükelhaus, P 56.61
*stroboscopic, Stadtarchiv Soest,
bequest Hugo Kükelhaus, P 56.61*
© Barbara Vogel-Kükelhaus; VG Bild-
Kunst, Bonn 2014

3.2

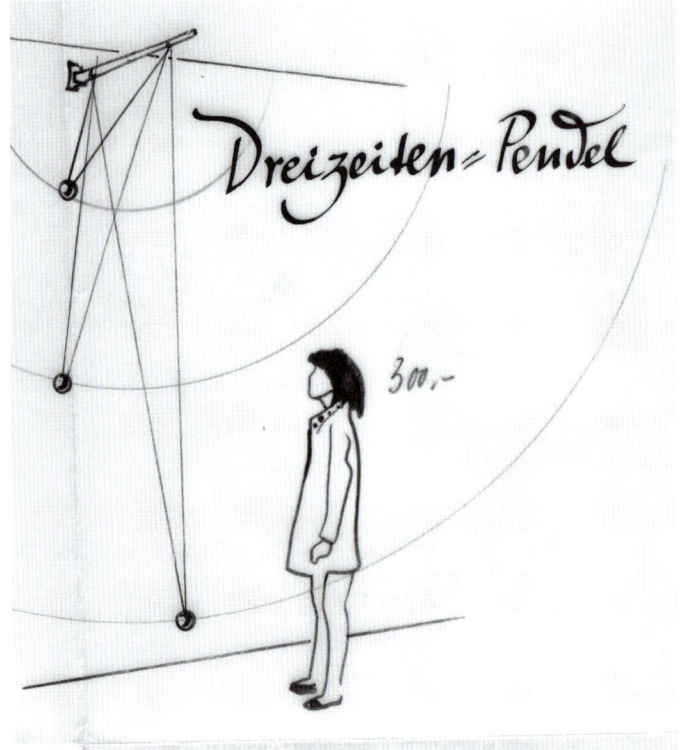

3.3

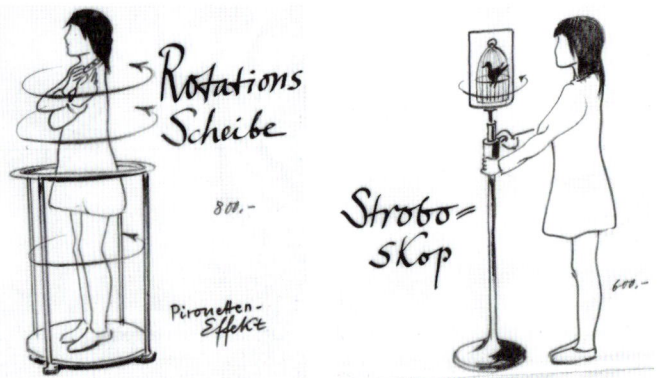

3.4

3.5

Erst im August 1966 war man an Kükelhaus mit der Bitte um einen Beitrag für Montreal herangetreten. Die für den deutschen Pavillon Verantwortlichen waren auf das Spielwerk aufmerksam geworden und erkannten die große Chance, noch etwas Originelles präsentieren zu können, das in dieser Form und Zusammenstellung vollkommen neu war: Geräte, die die Besucher zum aktiven, körperlichen Umgang auffordern, sie zum Spielen, Experimentieren und Entdecken einladen. Kükelhaus war begeistert: »Das wird ganz exquisit – Funktion plus Form. [...] Die Klangtürme werden in Göttingen von Ingenieuren usw. während der Pause betätigt – mit großem Geschick und Vergnügen. Ich habe die (dicken!) Stahlplatten rot, gelb und blau anspritzen lassen, unten dunkel beginnend bis oben hell [...]. Es ist alles so geglückt, daß man sich nur schwer davon losreißen kann.«[1]

Schon sehr lange hatte sich Kükelhaus mit der Bedeutung unmittelbarer Körper- und Sinneserfahrungen als Grundlage menschlicher Bildung beschäftigt. Er vertrat einen humanistischen Bildungsbegriff im klassischen Sinne: Bildung bedeutete für ihn die Ausbildung und Gestaltung aller im Menschen angelegten Fähigkeiten und Begabungen, damit er sich zu einer allseits entwickelten Persönlichkeit entfalten kann. Doch dazu bedarf es nach Kükelhaus einer Umgebung, die vielfältige Anregungen und Erfahrungsmöglichkeiten bietet. »Mit den Sinnen leben« verstand er als Appell für ein aktives, auf vielfältigen Erfahrungen beruhendes Leben und Lernen.

Auf der Suche nach praktischer und methodischer Umsetzung seiner Erkenntnisse führten ihn seine Arbeiten über die sinnliche und körperliche Wahrnehmung zur Entwicklung des »Naturkundlichen Spielwerks«. In der intensiven Auseinandersetzung mit der Gedankenwelt Goethes hatte er dessen Ansatz der Farbenlehre auf weitere Bereiche physikalischer Phänomene übertragen. Es ging ihm darum, wie solche Phänomene durch die Wahrnehmung auf den menschlichen Organismus wirken und nicht um ihre wissenschaftlich-physikalische Beschreibung und Erklärung. Deshalb war das Spielwerk für ihn auch mehr als nur ein neuer Weg in der Physikdidaktik. Es sollte in erster Linie ein Angebot für Kinder sein, an dem sie sich selbst und ihre Umwelt unmittelbar und mit allen Sinnen erfahren können, da sie nach seiner Überzeugung gerade dieses Wechselspiel im Umgang mit den Phänomenen zur Entwicklung des eigenen Organismus benötigen. Knopfdruckexperimente sucht man deshalb bei Hugo Kükelhaus vergebens.

Kükelhaus was first approached with regard to contributing to the Montreal exhibition in August 1966. Those responsible for the German Pavilion had noticed his fields for the senses and saw them as a fantastic opportunity to still present something original, something that in this form and composition was completely unheard of: equipment that prompted visitors to become actively and physically involved and invited them to play, experiment and discover. Kükelhaus was highly enthusiastic about the concept: »It is going to be exquisite – function as well as form. In Göttingen, engineers etc. will come and operate the bell towers in their lunch breaks – with a great deal of skill and enjoyment. I had the (thick!) steel plates spray-painted red, yellow and blue, starting out dark at the bottom and gradually getting lighter until they reach the lightest shade at the top – one blue tower, one yellow and one red. Everything has turned out so well that you can hardly pull yourself away from it.«[1]

Up to this point, Kükelhaus had for quite some time been exploring the significance of immediate physical and sensory experiences as the basis of human education. He was a representative of a humanistic approach to education in the classic meaning of the term: For him education stood for the training and formation of all inherently human abilities and aptitudes, necessary for the establishment of an all-round developed personality. However in order to achieve this Kükelhaus asserted the need for an environment that offered sufficiently diverse sources of stimulation and a range of opportunities to experience. »Live with the senses« was his plea for active living and learning based upon a variety of experiences.

In search of a more practical and methodical way to implement his insights, his work led him – via sensory and physical perception – to develop the »Experience Playground for Physical Laws«. On the basis of a thorough analysis of Goethe's ideas, Kükelhaus applied Goethe's approach to color theory to other physical phenomena. For him it was a question of the effect the perception of such phenomena could potentially have on the human organism, rather than their description and explanation in scientific terms. Therefore, for Kükelhaus the field of experiential sensation was nothing more than a new approach to a didactics based on a hands-on approach. It was initially intended as something for children, whereby they would be able to experience themselves and their surrounding environment directly and with all of their senses, for Kükelhaus was convinced that in dealing with these phenomena it was precisely this kind of interaction was necessary for the development of the individual organism. It is for this reason that any attempt to find a »push-button« experiment in association with Hugo Kükelhaus is a lost cause.

In seinem Beitrag »Über das Erleben von Naturgesetzen im Spiel« für das Handbuch zur Expo '67 schreibt er: »Das hier demonstrierte Prinzip, dessen Entdeckung und Entwicklung auf Goethe zurückgeht, hat zwei spezielle Konsequenzen.

Erstens: Die sogenannte ›Kunsterziehung‹ muß als Teil einer systematischen Schulung der Erlebnisfähigkeit erkannt und gehandhabt werden. Sie endet nicht mit der Ausreifung des Organismus, sondern sie wird fortgesetzt und tritt an die Seite der begrifflichen Verarbeitung des Erlebten, die mit der Pubertät einsetzt.

Zweitens: Sie wird weiter fortgesetzt in den Berufs- und Werkkunstschulen, in den Volkshochschulen und – in den Museen. Denn das Kunsterlebnis ist begründet in einer hohen Differenzierung der Fähigkeit des Organismus, das Leben zu erleben.«

Aufgrund der Erfahrungen in Montreal war Kükelhaus bei der anschließenden Präsentation in Dortmund die ganze Zeit selbst anwesend. Durch die dort erfahrene große Resonanz sah er sich darin bestätigt, dass er auf dem richtigen Weg war, und entwickelte in der Folge das »Naturkundliche Spielwerk« weiter zum »Erfahrungsfeld zur Entfaltung der Sinne«.

Dieses »Erfahrungsfeld« wurde dann seit Mitte der 1970er Jahre als Wanderausstellung an zahlreichen Orten im In- und Ausland gezeigt. Im aktiven Umgang mit ca. 40 Experimentier- und Spielstationen wurde den Besuchern die Möglichkeit geboten, die Gesetzlichkeiten der »äußeren Natur« (z. B. Schwingung, Schwerkraft, Polarität, Farbe) in ihren gegenseitigen Wirkungszusammenhängen mit den physiologischen Gesetzlichkeiten ihrer »inneren Natur« (Sinnesvorgänge, Körperbewegungen) vegetativ unmittelbar zu erfahren. Die Fähigkeit zur Sinneserfahrung wird im Erfahrungsfeld erweitert, sodass man – anders – erleben kann, »[...] wie das Auge sieht – das Ohr hört – die Nase riecht – die Haut fühlt – die Finger tasten – der Fuß (ver)steht – die Hand (be)greift – das Gehirn denkt – die Lunge atmet – das Blut pulst – der Körper schwingt [...]«. Denn, so Kükelhaus weiter: »Nicht das Gehirn denkt, sondern der mit Haut und Gliedern erlebende Mensch!«[2]

In his text »On the experience of nature's laws within play« written for the Expo '67 Handbook he wrote: »The principle demonstrated here, the discovery and development of which can be attributed to Goethe, has two very particular consequences.

Firstly: so-called ›art education‹ must be recognized and handled as a part of a systematic training for the ability to experience. This is not concluded with the maturation of the organism but is pursued and contributes to the conceptual processing of experiences, which sets in at the same time as puberty.

Secondly: This processing takes place once again in vocational schools and schools of applied arts, in community colleges and – in museums. For the experience of art is founded in the great distinction of the organism's capability to experience life.«

In light of his experiences in Montreal, Kükelhaus was at hand on site throughout the subsequent presentation in Dortmund. The great response to the project bore him out and, feeling he was on the right track he went on to further develop the »Experience Playground for Physical Laws« into the »Field for the Development of the Senses«.

Then from the mid-1970s onward, this »Field for the Senses« went on tour as a traveling exhibition visiting numerous locations at home and abroad. In active interaction with the approx. 40 experience and play stations, the visitors were offered an opportunity to experience – in organic proximity – the laws of »external nature« (e.g. oscillation, gravity, polarity, color) in their interrelationships with the physiological laws of their »internal nature« (sensorial processes and bodily movements). The fields serve to extend one's capability to experience with one's senses such that one is able to experience things in a different way, »[...] as eyes see – ears hear – noses smell – skin feels – fingers touch – feet (under)stand – hands grasp – the brain thinks – lungs breath – blood pulses – the body swings - [...]«. For, as Kükelhaus added: »It is not the brain that thinks but the human that experiences with their skin and limbs!«[2]

Strudelzilinder

Bisheriger Einzelpreis
3 500,— DM

3.6

3.7 Hugo Kükelhaus und sein
Strudelgerät auf der Interschul 1967
in Dortmund
*Hugo Kükelhaus and his strudel device
at Interschul 1967 in Dortmund
© Stadtarchiv Soest, Nachlass Hugo
Kükelhaus (VG Bild-Kunst, Bonn 2014),
P 56.83*

»Die gesamte Biologie unseres Lernens ist durch die entdinglichte Form unserer Lebenssituation in Gefahr, an organischer Reizarmut zu verkümmern. Kükelhaus hat mit seinen didaktischen Konzepten den Weg in eine neue Qualität von Lernen gewiesen, ein Lernen, in dem es sinnvoll und selbsterkennend zugeht, das Hunger macht nach eigenständigem Lernen, das der Auslieferung an Ersatz- und Scheinwelten entgegenwirkt«, so Klaus Schneidewind vom Institut für Arbeitslehre der TU Berlin, damals Weggefährte von Kükelhaus.

Mittlerweile gibt es eine Vielzahl stationärer Erfahrungsfeldprojekte weltweit. Darüber hinaus wurde Kükelhaus durch seine pädagogische Vision, die er mit dem »Naturkundlichen Spielwerk« begründete, sowohl zum Wegbereiter für heutige »Mitmachausstellungen«, die Science-Center, als auch der Erweiterung traditioneller Museen durch interaktive Stationen.

»The non-objectified form of our living conditions has put the entire make-up of our learning processes in danger of withering away due to a lack of sensory stimulation. With his didactic concepts, Kükelhaus pointed the way to a new higher quality kind of learning, a kind of learning that makes sense and is self-explanatory, that spurns a hunger for independent knowledge acquisition, that counters the commitment to substitute and illusory worlds,« says Klaus Schneidewind from the Institute for Ergonomics at Berlin's Technical University, one of Kükelhaus' contemporaries.

There are now many stationary experience field projects across the world. Furthermore, his educational vision, established with the work »Experience Playground for Physical Laws«, Kükelhaus not only came to be considered a pioneer for the »hands-on« exhibitions of today, or science centers, but also for the enhancement of traditional museums with the addition of interactive stations.

>>> author p.213

1 Brief Anfang 1967, Nachlass Hugo Kükelhaus, Stadtarchiv Soest. *Letter from 1967, Nachlass Hugo Kükelhaus, Stadtarchiv Soest.*

2 Brief Anfang 1967, Nachlass Hugo Kükelhaus, Stadtarchiv Soest. *Letter from 1967, Nachlass Hugo Kükelhaus, Stadtarchiv Soest.*

Anke te Heesen
»Musée Sentimental de Cologne« von Daniel Spoerri und
Marie-Louise von Plessen

Im März 1979 wurde im Kölnischen Kunstverein die Ausstellung »Le Musée
Sentimental de Cologne – Reliquien & Relikte aus zwei Jahrtausenden –
Köln Incognito« eröffnet. Die Ausstellung wurde von Daniel Spoerri
gemeinsam mit Marie-Louise von Plessen und Spoerris Klasse der
Fachhochschule für Kunst und Gestaltung in Köln kuratiert. Zuvor war
bereits 1977 ein »Musée Sentimental de Paris« anlässlich der Eröffnung
des Centre Pompidou entstanden, später ein »Musée Sentimental de
Prusse« (1981) in Berlin und ein »Musée Sentimental de Bâle« (1989).
Seitdem hat es immer wieder Musées Sentimentaux von Daniel Spoerri
gegeben, zuletzt 2009 in Krems (Niederösterreich), doch das eigentliche
kuratorische und künstlerische Prinzip wurde um 1979 entwickelt und
Spoerri beschreibt das Kölner als »das erste richtige Musée Sentimental«[1].

Eine der wenigen noch existierenden Fotografien der Ausstellung gibt
Einblick in ihre Präsentationsweise und die in ihr dargebotenen Objekte.
Im Vordergrund fallen die monumentalen Gussstücke eines zerstörten
Reiterstandbildes ins Auge, bevor sich der Blick des Betrachters in die
Tiefe des Raumes verliert. ›3.1 Rechts und links sind auf weißen Podesten
einzelne Objekte zu sehen. ›3.4 Neben dem Boden und den länglichen
Podesten erkennt man als dritte Präsentationsweise die klassische
Vitrine, in der Stücke wie die Bleistifte des Schriftstellers Heinrich Böll
zu finden waren. Weitere Vitrinen zeigten einen vom ehemaligen deutschen
Bundeskanzler Konrad Adenauer getragenen Indianerschmuck, seine
Rosenschere, seine Aktentasche und so fort. ›3.2 War das »Musée Sentimental de Paris« in den Bauch eines überdimensionierten, drachenähnlich
geformten Baus – dem »Crocodrome« von Jean Tinguely – integriert,
so wurden die sentimentalen Objekte in Köln zum ersten Mal im gängigen
Kontext des White Cube vorgeführt. Die Objekte – der Ausstellungskatalog
von 1979 führt es als klassischer Objektkatalog vor – stammten aus
zwei Jahrtausenden Kölner Geschichte bis hin zur Gegenwart, waren
kostbar und wertlos und changierten zwischen Hochkunst und trivialem
Kitsch, Feiertag und Alltag, Sakralem und Vulgärem.

*»Musée Sentimental de Cologne« by Daniel Spoerri and
Marie-Louise von Plessen*

*In March 1979, »Le Musée Sentimental de Cologne – Reliquien & Relikte
aus zwei Jahrtausenden – Köln Incognito« opened at Cologne's Kölnischer
Kunstverein; it was an exhibition curated in a collaborative effort between
Daniel Spoerri, Marie-Louise von Plessen and Spoerri's class from the
Fachhochschule für Kunst und Gestaltung in Cologne. As the sequel to the
1977 »Musée Sentimental de Paris« held on the occasion of the opening of
the Centre Pompidou, it was later followed by the 1981 »Musée Sentimental
de Prusse« in Berlin as well as the »Musée Sentimental de Bâle« in 1989;
and this was not to be the last, there have been various musées sentimentaux
by Daniel Spoerri ever since, the most recent example taking place in Krems
(in North Austria) in 2009. However this perennial curatorial and creative
concept was in fact developed around 1979 and the Cologne edition described
by Spoerri himself as the »first real musée sentimental«.[1]*

*One of the few remaining photographs of the exhibition gives an idea of the
particular presentation techniques used and the objects on display there.
The monumental casts, the fragments of a destroyed equestrian statue,
are the first thing to catch your eye, before your gaze becomes lost in the
recesses of the hall. ›3.1 To the left and the right individual exhibits are
poised on white pedestals. ›3.4 In addition to the flooring and the elongated
pedestals one can also discern a third distinctive presentation technique, the
classic display case, used to hold items such as pencils that once belonged
to the famous Cologne-born writer Heinrich Böll. More cases exhibit personal
effects of the former German Chancellor Konrad Adenauer, such as Indian
jewelry, his garden clippers, his briefcase etc. ›3.2 If one considers the
»Musée Sentimental de Paris« as having been integrated into the belly of an
over-sized, dragon-like building – the »Le Crocodrome« by Jean Tinguely,
then the Cologne exhibition can be deemed as the first occasion that such
sentimental objects were presented in the then popular exhibition context
of the white cube. The objects on display here (the 1979 exhibition catalogue
was presented as a classic catalogue of objects) were all artifacts from the
preceding two centuries of Cologne history; they were both precious and
worthless at the same time and were spread between the twin poles
of high art and trivial kitsch objects, between everyday life and special
occasions, between the sacred and the vulgar.*

Diese Gegensätze waren, folgt man Spoerri, zentral: »Ein gutes Beispiel könnte man anhand der ›drei Ursulas‹, wie wir es intern bezeichnen, nennen: Drei Ursulas sind in diesem Museum mit Objekten vertreten. Das eine ist ein bedeutendes Barock-Reliquiar der Heiligen Ursula im Verein mit einer Sammlung von Reliquien-Knochen vom sog. Ursula-Acker, das zweite ist das […] Totenschild der Ursula Maria Columba von Groote, geb. zum Pütz, die angeblich eine Geliebte Casanovas gewesen sein soll, und drittens wäre Ursula Gerdes zu nennen, die erste Mieterin des neu erbauten Eros-Centers in Köln.«[2]

Das Ordnungsprinzip der »drei Ursulas« und anderer ist simpel: Die Objekte wurden im Ausstellungsraum nicht in ihren jeweiligen historischen Kontext eingeordnet, also wie in den damals üblichen historischen Museen (und Ausstellungen) »nach Zeitabschnitten, Gattungen oder nach Territorien«, sondern nach »anekdotischen Gesichtspunkten.«[3] Ihnen war eine alpha-betische Ordnung zugrunde gelegt worden, die eine die Ausstellung durchziehende, abstrakte Struktur bildete. Man berief sich auf das große Aufklärungsprojekt, die Encyclopédie, in der die Wissensbestände der Welt unterschiedslos nebeneinander geordnet erschienen waren.

Interessant sind an dieser Stelle die Ausführungen von Plessens, dass die Objekte so einen sentimentalen Wert in sich tragen können: Sie »leben aus dem subjektiven Gefühl, das der Betrachter gleichsam als Biograph ihnen zukommen lässt – durch Erinnerung an eigene Erlebnisse, Erfah-rungen, Empfindungen, seine Entdeckungen am Objekt.«[4] Es ginge darum, so die Protagonisten, »einen Teppich von Zusammenhängen entstehen«[4] zu lassen. Sentimentalisch, also geleitet von Empfindsamkeit, waren die aus-gewählten Objekte in doppelter Hinsicht: zum einen deshalb, weil die histo-rischen Gegenstände – Reliquien gleich – mit Gefühlen aufgeladen seien und weil »durch die Konfrontation des Gegenstandes mit dem Besucher, der diesen Gegenstand anschaut, seine Einmaligkeit belegt wird durch die ihm anhaftende Anekdote oder das historische Zeugnis eines biographischen Ereignisses.«[5] Zum anderen, weil die Gegenstände dem Besucher Zugänge erlaubten, da er eine der »drei Ursulas« vielleicht persönlich kannte oder da er wusste, wie man einen Nagelknipser – ein weiteres Objekt der Ausstel-lung – bedient. Das Alltagswissen des Besuchers wurde aufgewertet, die Objekte schufen Anknüpfungsmöglichkeiten zwischen der ausgestellten Geschichte und der gelebten Gegenwart.

According to Spoerri, these antagonisms were key to the exhibition concept: »A good example could be taken from the ›three Ursulas‹ as we called them among ourselves: There are three different Ursulas represented by various objects in the museum. One of them is a Baroque reliquary of Saint Ursula, which is of great importance, together with a collection of bones from the so-called »Ursula field«, the second is the […] epitaph of Ursula Maria Columba von Groote, born to Pütz, who is rumored to have been a lover of Casanova, and the third Ursula would be Ursula Gerdes, the first tenant in the newly built Eros-Center in Cologne.«[2]

The principle behind the arrangement of the »three Ursulas« and the other exhibits is simple: The objects were not arranged in relation to their respective historical context, ergo as was practiced in historical museums (and exhi-bitions) typical of the time and thus »according to periods of time, genres or territories«, but based upon their »anecdotal aspects«.[3] Taking the alphabet as their basis, they formed an abstract structure that ran like a red thread through the entire exhibition; the inspiration for this was culled from the Enlightenment's greatest project, the encyclopedia, where the articles com-prising the world's wealth of knowledge appear side by side arranged in accordance with an indiscriminate ordering system.

Von Plessen's remarks on the objects' capacity to be of such sentimental worth are of particular interest here: They »thrive on the subjective feeling that the beholder as a kind of biographer assigns to them by remembering their own experiences, encounters and feelings, their own discoveries within these objects.« For the key figures behind the exhibition it was matter of »creating a fabric of associations«.[4] The objects selected for display were sentimental on two counts: firstly, because like relics these historical objects were charged with emotions and because »by confronting the visitor, who looks at them, the objects' uniqueness is confirmed by means of the anec-dote linked to it or the historical testimony to some biographical occurrence provided by it.«[5] Secondly, the visitors were able to make some kind of direct association, a personal connection to the artifacts; perhaps they knew one of the »three Ursulas« personally or how to use a nail clipper (another object in the exhibition). The visitor's enhanced their everyday knowledge and the objects provided a tangible connection between the history being presented and the living present.

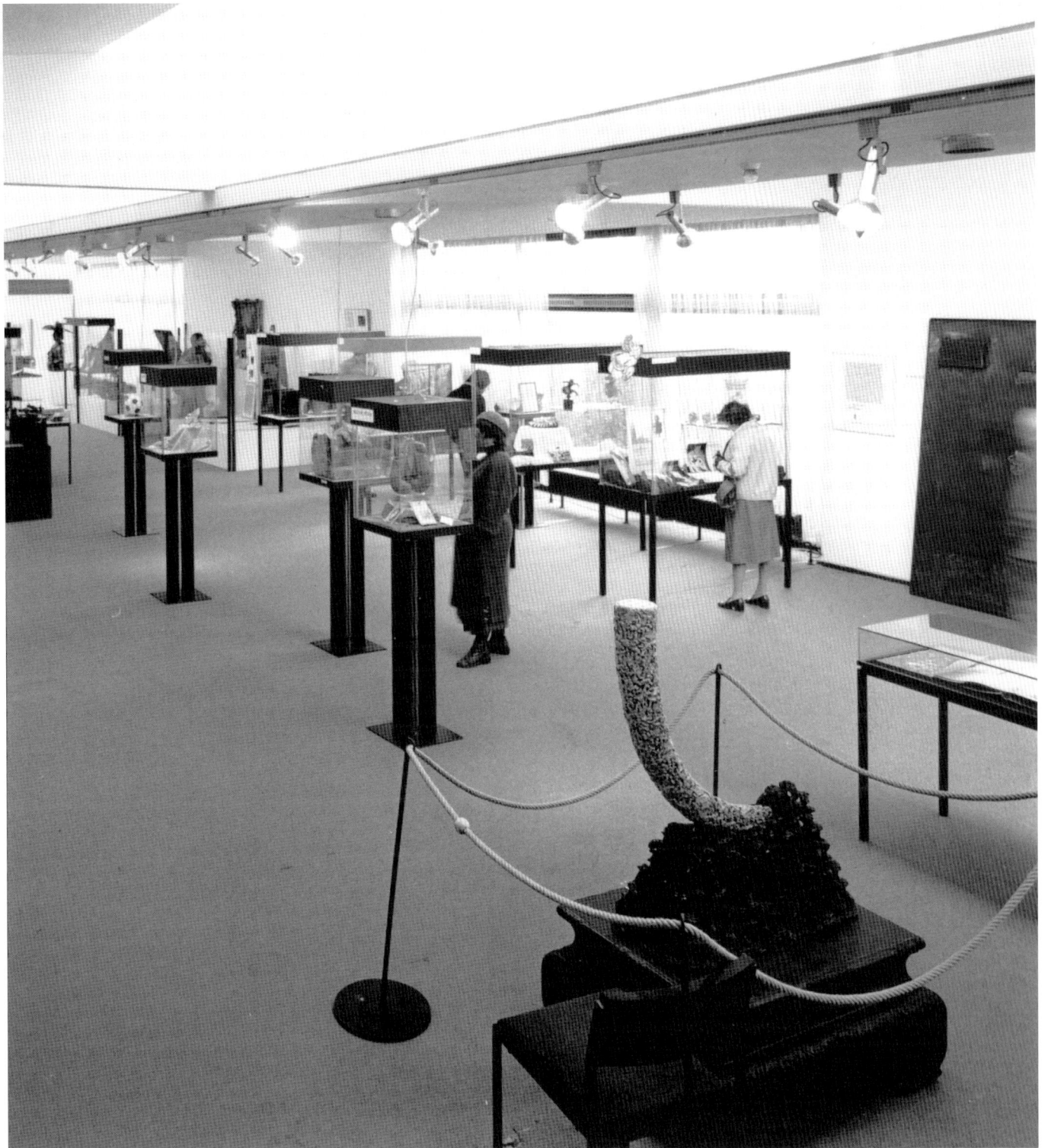

3.3 © Archiv Daniel Spoerri (VG Bild-
Kunst, Bonn 2014), Graphische Sammlung, Schweizerische Nationalbibliothek NB / Friedrich Rosenstiel, Köln

3.3

Über ihre Arbeitsweise mit den Gefühlsobjekten berichtet von Plessen im Frühjahr 1979 in einem Interview mit Walter Grasskamp: Es reize sie, in den Archiven und Depots unbebautes Territorium zu erobern, es sich auf »sehr persönlichem Wege anzueignen, der zwar unwissenschaftlich verfährt, doch sehr nah an der Wissenschaft bleibt.«[6] Dabei hebt sie die Beziehung zu Spoerri hervor: Sie arbeiteten einander direkt in die Hand, »»nur da, wo ich mich dann zu sehr in die Wissenschaftlichkeit verrenne, da hindert er mich dann wieder dran [...]‹ – ›Begrüßen Sie das?‹ – ›Ja, wenn wir zusammenarbeiten schon, auf jeden Fall, ich glaube sogar, daß es eine sehr notwendige Reibung ist und gerade durch diese Reibung etwas entsteht, das eventuell gut sein kann.‹«[7]

Daniel Spoerri war zu diesem Zeitpunkt durch seine Fallenbilder bekannt und hatte in der »Topographie des Zufalls« ein Manifest für die Bedeutung und Definition des Territoriums geliefert: nämlich die zufällig zustande gekommene Zusammenstellung von Dingen auf einer eingegrenzten Fläche und ihre Fixierung. Marie-Louise von Plessen hatte zuvor als promovierte Historikerin zahlreiche Dokumentarfilme gedreht, unter anderem mit Daniel Spoerri.

In den verschiedenen Musées Sentimentaux kommen die Idee des Fallenbildes und das wissenschaftliche Verständnis von Primärquellen, die Form des Objekts und das Wissen um seine Herkunft zusammen. Man kann sagen, dass es das Musée Sentimental ohne Spoerri nicht gegeben hätte, weil seine langjährige Beschäftigung mit der Positionierung von Dingen und ihrer Bedeutung, sein Witz und Humor, der dem Betrachter in den Ding-Konstellationen fluxusartig vermittelt wurde, hervorstachen. Andererseits hätte der Witz der Objekte nicht ohne deren historische Unterfütterung funktioniert, waren doch die Objekte an das Authentizitätsversprechen der Geschichte gekoppelt. Dies macht das Besondere des Musée Sentimental aus. Der zweite hervorzuhebende Aspekt dieser Ausstellung liegt darin, dass dem banalen und wertlosen Objekt ein historischer Wert verliehen und dass es wie Kunst auf einem weißen Podest präsentiert wurde.

In an interview with Walter Grasskamp in early 1979 von Plessen spoke of her methodology in working with these sentimental objects: She enjoyed conquering unchartered territory in the archives and depots, to »appropriate it in a very personal way, which may border on the unscientific yet stays very close to science.«[6] Here she places emphasis on her relationship to Spoerri: They worked together hand in hand, »»he only holds me back when I get carried away with the scientific aspects [...]‹ – ›Do you welcome such intervention?‹ – ›Yes, when we're working together I do. Most definitely. I even believe that such friction is necessary and that it is precisely this friction that results in something that could perhaps turn out really well.‹«[7]

At this time, Daniel Spoerri was already a well-known figure thanks to his pictures of traps and snares; he had also penned a manifesto, the »Anecdoted Typography of Chance«, on the significance and definition of territories; that is the coincidental assembly of things on a contained surface and fixing them there. With a Ph. D. in History, Marie-Louise von Plessen had previously shot a number of documentary films, with Daniel Spoerri among others.

The various musées sentimentaux are combinations of the concept of the trap picture, a scientific understanding of primary sources, the shape of the objects and the knowledge of their origins. One could say that the musée sentimental would never have existed without Daniel Spoerri, for it was his many years spent analyzing the positioning of objects and their meaning, his wit and humor that struck the eye, conveyed above all by configurations of objects similar to those made by the Fluxus artists. On the other hand, the wit surrounding the objects would not have been communicated effectively were it not for their historical underpinning; they were after all bound to history's promise of authenticity. This is what makes the musée sentimental so special. The second aspect of this exhibition that should not be overlooked is the historical value it ascribes to otherwise seemingly banal and worthless objects as well as its presentation of such objects in the same way as art, poised high upon a pedestal.

3.4 ©Archiv Daniel Spoerri (VG Bild-Kunst, Bonn 2014), Graphische Sammlung, Schweizerische Nationalbibliothek NB / Friedrich Rosenstiel, Köln

In der Forschung wurden die Musées Sentimentaux vor allem vor dem Hintergrund der Künstlermuseen betrachtet. Und in der Tat besteht in den alternativen, ironischen Konzeptionen seit den 1960er Jahren eine wesentliche Idee des Musée Sentimental. Doch das Musée Sentimental hat vor allem einen neuen Bedeutungsrahmen für Alltagsobjekte geschaffen, indem es sie aus ihrem Kontext und ihrer Chronologie herauslöste und vor weißem Hintergrund in neuartigen Nachbarschaften zusammenstellte, ohne dabei – und das ist zentral – ihre historische Zeugenschaft zu negieren. Damit wurde für das Museum eine neue Sehkonvention eingeführt: die Nobilitierung eines jedweden Objekts als ein Meisterwerk und seine assoziationsgenerierende Zusammenstellung mit aus anderen Kontexten stammenden Objekten. Diese konfrontierende Gruppierungsweise wurde durch das Musée Sentimental kanonisiert und durch nachfolgende, vor allem kulturgeschichtliche Ausstellungen mehr und mehr zum Darstellungsprinzip erhoben, welches bis heute zu verfolgen ist.

In scholarly terms, the musées sentimentaux are considered above all against the backdrop of the »Künstlermuseen«, museums dedicated to individual artists, which were prolific up to the 1960s. And in fact from the 1960s onwards these alternative, ironic conceptions formed one of the musée sentimental's fundamental ideas. But most importantly the musée sentimental had created a new realm of significance for everyday objects, by releasing them from their historical context and chronology and bringing them together with other artifacts in a new kind of ambiance before a white backdrop, without – and this is a key point –negating the historical testimony they provided. Thereby, a new visual convention for the museum was introduced: the ennoblement of any object as a masterwork and its association-evoking combination with objects from other contexts. The musée sentimental canonized these confrontational groupings, while subsequent, predominantly art-historical exhibitions served to gradually elevate them to the status of a key representational principle – one that holds true to this day.

>>> author p.213

Ähnlich erschienen in: Musée Sentimental 1979. Ein Ausstellungskonzept, hrsg. von Anke te Heesen und Susanne Padberg, Ostfildern 2011.
A similar version was published in: Musée Sentimental 1979. Ein Ausstellungskonzept, published by Anke te Heesen and Susanne Padberg, Ostfildern 2011.

1 Museum Jean Tinguely (Ed.): Anekdotomania. Daniel Spoerri über Daniel Spoerri. Ostfildern-Ruit 2001, p.227.
2 Cf. Spoerri, Daniel: introduction. in: Kölnischer Kunstverein (Ed.): Le Musée Sentimental de Cologne. Entwurf zu einem Lexikon von Reliquien und Relikten aus zwei Jahrtausenden. Cologne 1979, p.8-10, p.10.

3 von Plessen, Marie-Louise: Zum Verhältnis von historischem Museum und Musée Sentimental. in: Kölnischer Kunstverein (Ed.):Le Musée Sentimental de Cologne. Entwurf zu einem Lexikon von Reliquien und Reliktenaus zwei Jahrtausenden. Cologne, 1979, p.15.
4 ibid.

5 von Plessen, Marie-Louise: Autoren-Museum, in: Schwencke, Olaf (Ed.): Museum – Verklärung oder Aufklärung. Kulturpolitisches Kolloquium zum Selbstverständnis der Museen. Rehburg-Loccum 1986, p.164-170, p.166.
6 Grasskamp, Walter: Nichts altert schneller als ein Avantgardist. Fragen

und Antworten aus Interviews mit Daniel Spoerri und Marie-Louise von Plessen. in: Kunstforum International, Bd. 32, Heft 2, 1979, p.81-91, p.91.
7 ibid.

Antonia Wunderlich
Les Immatériaux von Jean-François Lyotard

1985 kuratierte Jean-François Lyotard gemeinsam mit Thierry Chaput im Pariser Centre Pompidou die Ausstellung Les Immatériaux. Er arbeitete also mit einem Medium, das ihm als Philosoph keineswegs vertraut war und nutzte diese Fremdheit, um das Philosophieren selbst zu befragen: »Kann man in Richtung eines großen Publikums philosophieren, ohne das Denken zu verraten?« Man kann, meinte er in einem Interview zur Ausstellung, »indem man vermutet, dass das Publikum für dieselben Fragen sensibel ist wie die Philosophen.« Die Ausstellung sollte ihre Rezipienten in einen Zustand versetzen, der Lyotards Vorstellung davon, wie Philosophieren funktioniert, möglichst nahekam.

Auf der 3.000 m² großen fünften Etage des Centre Pompidou installierte er ein regelrechtes Labyrinth, das den Besuchern eine Vielzahl an Objekten, kurzen Texten, Raumbildern und Wegstrecken vorsetzte. Insgesamt 61 Stationen wurden durch 30 Infrarot-Sendezonen für ein Kopfhörerprogramm und fünf sich durch den gesamten Raum ziehende Wege strukturiert, sodass die Ausstellung aus mehreren ineinander verschränkten semantischen Bündelungen bestand. Die immense körperlich-sinnliche wie intellektuelle Herausforderung, die in dieser Komplexität lag, war ein zentrales Moment von Lyotards Konzeption: Mittels einer Art konstruktiver Überforderung wollte er den Besuchern eine Ahnung ihrer nahen Zukunft in einer digitalisierten, ent- und immaterialisierten Welt vermitteln.

Les Immatériaux sollte spürbar machen, dass das alltägliche Leben sich radikal wandeln würde, und zeigte dies exemplarisch an so disparaten Themen wie Ernährung und Aromen, Mode und Geschlecht, Architektur und Fotografie sowie der Börse und der Autoindustrie.

In den vielen Texten in Katalogen, Pressemitteilungen und Interviews, die parallel zur Ausstellung veröffentlicht wurden und die den Eindruck erwecken, man habe der Sperrigkeit des an Metainformationen bewusst armen Projekts wenigstens irgendwo begegnen wollen, äußert sich Lyotard zu seinen Zielen: Ein alle gesellschaftlichen Bereiche betreffender Umbruch, vor allem in den Fachgebieten Telekommunikation und Informatik, habe große Auswirkungen auf das Denken, das bisher nicht maschinell hätte ersetzt werden können.

Les Immatériaux by Jean-François Lyotard

In 1985, Jean-François Lyotard collaborated with Thierry Chaput to organize his first exhibition, Les Immatériaux, in Paris' Centre Pompidou and so he began to work with a medium that as a philosopher he was by no means familiar with, using this unfamiliarity to question philosophizing itself: »Can one philosophize to a wider audience, without revealing one's thoughts?« In an interview on the exhibition he commented that this was indeed possible, »in that one assumes that the audience is sensitive to the same questions as philosophers are.« The exhibition was intended to put the visitor in a state that corresponded as closely as possible to Lyotard's notion of how philosophizing works.

Over the Centre Pompidou's five floors – 3,000 m² – he installed a labyrinth in the true sense of the word, which presented visitors with a plethora of objects, short texts, stereograms and routes. A total of 61 stations were organized accompanied by an audio program made up of 30 infrared coverage zones and five paths leading through the space such that the exhibition constituted a series of interwoven, semantic »bundles«. The immense physical-sensorial and intellectual challenge created by this complexity was central to Lyotard's concept. By means of a kind of constructive overload, he wanted to give the visitor an idea of how their foreseeable future in a digitalized, dematerialized world could be.

Les Immatériaux was to render the notion that the visitors' everyday lives would soon undergo radical changes palpable, demonstrated with real examples employing such disparate themes as nutrition and scents, fashion and gender, architecture and photography or the stock exchange and the automotive industry.

Lyotard gave his own account of his objectives in this project in the numerous texts featured in catalogues, press releases and interviews accompanying the exhibition, which left the impression that one could have encountered the kind of bulk seen in the project (consciously lacking in meta-information) anywhere: An upheaval in all areas of society, above all in the specialist areas of telecommunications and IT, was having grave effects on thought, which until that point could not have been replaced by machines.

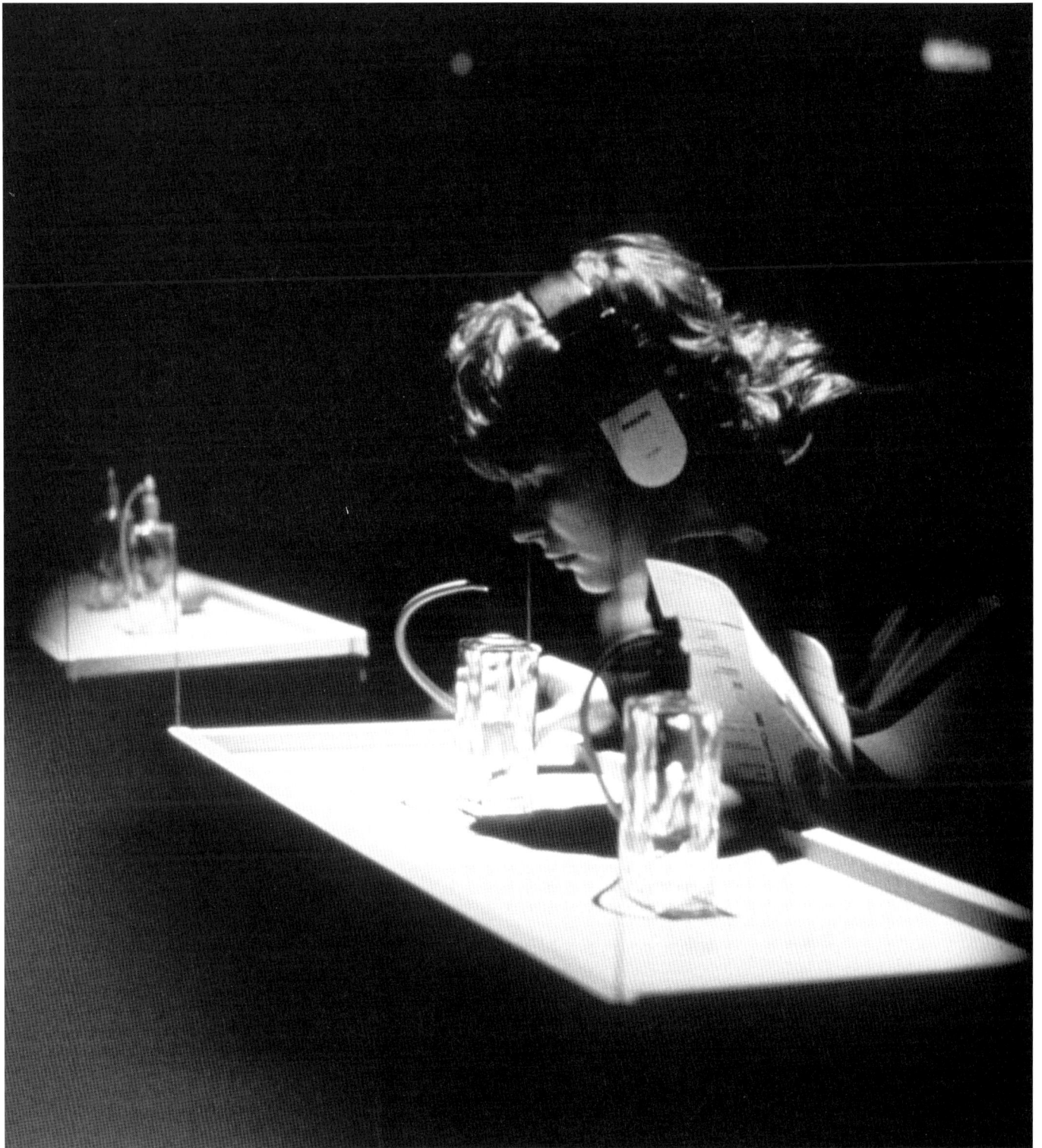

In dem Maße, in dem Technologien Vermögen des Logos übernehmen könnten – durch die Möglichkeiten zur Speicherung und Verarbeitung entmaterialisierter Daten –, relativiere sich grundlegend die »Beziehung des Menschen zum Material, wie [sie] in der Tradition der Moderne festgelegt ist, zum Beispiel durch das cartesische Programm, ›sich zum Herrn und Besitzer der Natur zu machen‹.« Daher waren die neuen Technologien sowohl inhaltlicher Ausgangspunkt für Les Immatériaux als auch zentrales gestalterisches Mittel.

Die Ausstellung funktionierte wie ein großer Datenraum, in dem sich Besucher, Objekte, szenografische Elemente und Klänge in jenem beständigen Austausch miteinander befanden, den Lyotard als Modell der Zukunft diagnostizierte: »Der Besucher spaziert in einem Rhizom herum, in dem kein Wissensfaden aufscheint, sondern generalisierte Interaktionen, Deplatzierungsprozesse, in denen der Mensch nicht mehr ist als ein Interface-Knoten«, schreibt er im Album, einem der drei Katalogteile.

The extent to which given its ability to save and edit immaterial data technology could assume the capacities of the Logos is put into fundamental perspective by »man's relationship to material, as prescribed in the tradition of Modernism, for example by means of the Cartesian program to make ›man lord and master of nature‹.« And so, new technology not only formed the point of departure for Les Immatériaux in terms of its content but also constituted the exhibition's key creative medium.

The exhibition worked like a huge data room, where visitors, objects, scenographic elements and sounds found themselves in the midst of a continuous exchange with one another, an exchange that Lyotard had diagnosed as a model of the future: »The visitor walks around in a rhizome with no apparent logical thread but is rather a series of generalized interactions and processes of displacement, whereby man is nothing more than an interface node,« as Lyotard wrote in Album, one of the catalog's three sections.

3.2

3.3

3.4

Diesem neuen Modell, das Lyotard als Exempel für das Verhältnis von Sprache und Körper oder von Substanz und Struktur anlegte, sollte, so die Grundidee der Ausstellung, auch das Philosophieren Rechnung tragen, das im Zuge dessen einige wesentliche Paradigmen der Moderne – wie etwa den souveränen Subjekt-Autor – aufzugeben habe.

Der multimediale Parcours von Les Immatériaux funktionierte wie eine Art Scharnier zwischen einem neuen Denken und den Besuchern, die einem realen Ort physisch und psychisch ausgesetzt waren. Lyotard nutzte in Zusammenarbeit mit dem Ausstellungsarchitekten Philippe Délis konsequent die medialen Eigenheiten von Ausstellungen – etwa ihre strukturelle Komplexität, bedingt durch eine Vielzahl von Raumbildern und -atmosphären, die prinzipielle semantische Offenheit der Exponate, die körperliche Präsenz der Besucher im Raum – und entwickelte eine für die damalige Zeit einzigartig avancierte Szenografie. › 3.6

According to the idea underlying the exhibition concept, this new model, advanced by Lyotard as an example of the relationship between language and body or between substance and structure, should also be accommodated by philosophizing itself, which in the process has relinquished a number of important paradigms of Modernism, such as the sovereign independent subject/author.

The multi-media trajectory that led through Les Immatériaux functioned as a kind of hinge between the visitor (who had both physically and psychologically been exposed to a real place) and a new kind of thought. In collaboration with exhibition architect Philippe Délis, Lyotard made consistent use of the peculiarities of exhibitions as a medium such as their structural complexity (as determined by a plethora of stereograms and distinct spatial atmospheres), the basic, semantic clarity of the exhibits, the visitor's physical presence in the room, and developed a scenography that was uniquely advanced for its time. › 3.6

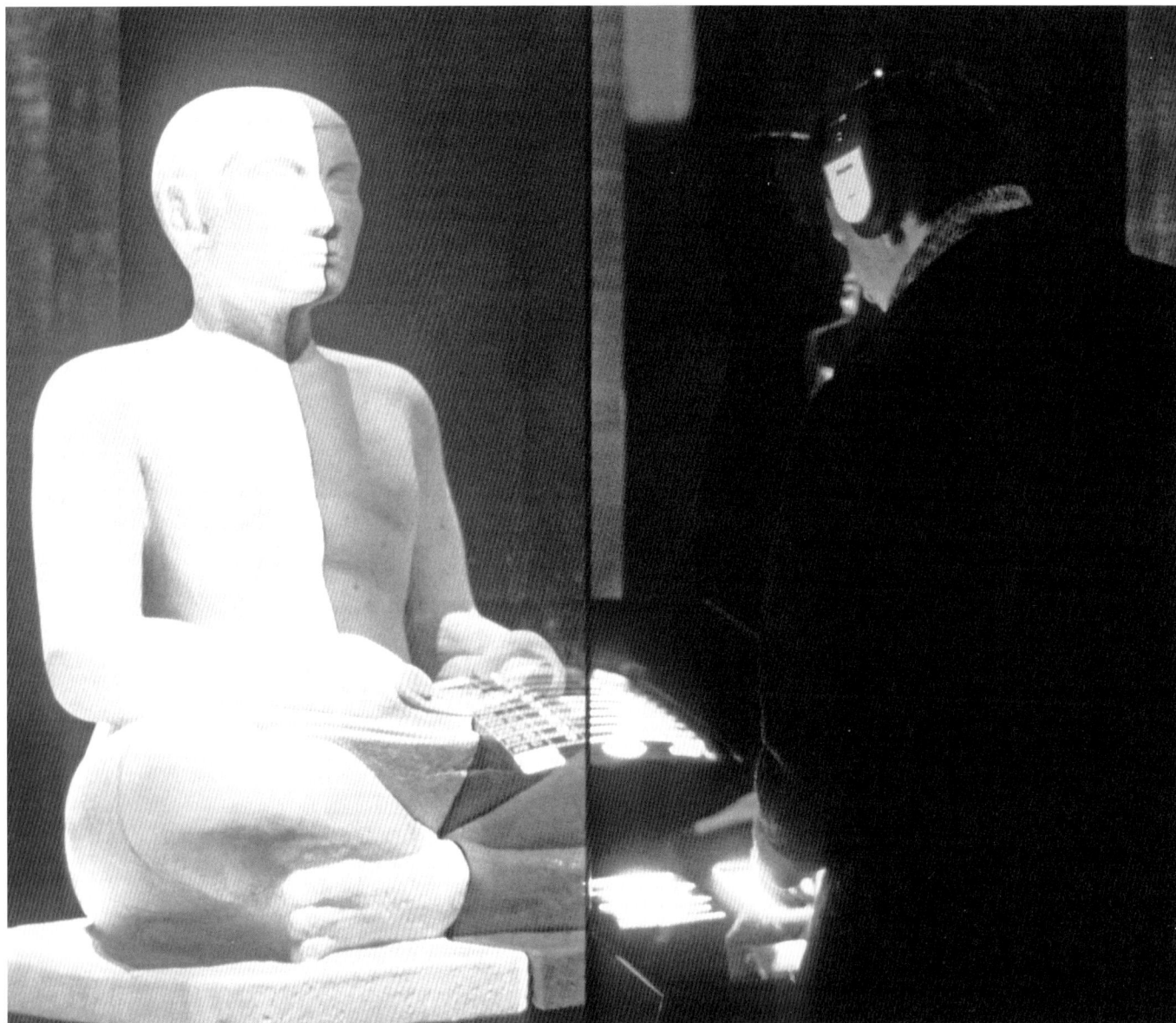

3.5

Dreh- und Angelpunkt dieser Szenografie waren die Besucher. Les Immatériaux sollte »anhand von Materialität und Immaterialität auch die Frage
nach der Identität hervorheben: die Frage nach dem, was wir sind und was
die Objekte sind, die uns umgeben.« Dass »die Frage nach der Identität«
keine einfachen Antworten dulden würde, war ebenso philosophisches
Programm wie didaktische und gestalterische Grundlage: Les Immatériaux
sollte Fragen stellen, die »für den Besucher der Veranstaltung bis zum
Ausgang und noch darüber hinaus« offen blieben.

Mit durchaus enervierender Konsequenz enthielt Lyotard den Besuchern
Eindeutigkeiten vor – das Repertoire reichte vom Kopfhörerprogramm,
das jeder Station komplexe Texte aus Philosophie und Literatur hinzufügte,
über die nicht beschilderten Exponate, deren enge Verflechtung mit
szenografischen Elementen sie bisweilen schwer identifizierbar machte,
bis hin zur Labyrinthstruktur des Gesamtraums, die jeden Versuch,
alle Stationen der Ausstellung systematisch aufzusuchen, vereitelte. ›3.4

Die Spannung zwischen Fragen und Antworten, zwischen Verwirrung und
Erkenntnis, zwischen Objekt und Text oder, wenn man so will, zwischen
Immateriell-Ephemerem und Materiell-Manifestem zog sich durch die
gesamte Ausstellung und ist tief in Lyotards Denken verwurzelt. Seiner
Suche nach dem, was noch nicht zur Darstellbarkeit gefunden hat, nach
dem noch nicht kategorisierten Einzelfall und nach dem begrifflich nicht
fassbaren Ereignis vor jeder Zuschreibung und Durchdringung bot die
Ausstellung das ideale Medium: »Wenn man glaubt, Denken als Selektion
aus ›gegebenen‹ Daten [...] beschreiben zu können, dann verschweigt man
die Wahrheit: die Daten sind nicht ›gegeben‹, sondern können ›gegeben
sein‹, und die Selektion vollzieht sich nicht als ein Wählen. Wie Schreiben
und Malen ist Denken eigentlich nichts anderes als das Kommen-Lassen
dessen, was gegeben sein kann«, schreibt Lyotard 1986 in dem Text
»Ob man ohne Körper denken kann«. Dieses »Kommen-Lassen« ist für ihn
der Ausgangspunkt eines jeglichen wahrhaftigen Philosophierens:
»Gerade dieser Zustand, in dem man nicht mehr weiß, wo man ist, macht
den Ausgangspunkt eines jeden Denkens aus.«

Mit dieser Haltung legt Lyotard seinen Anspruch als eines weit fortgeschrit-
tenen »Meisters seines Faches« offen, dessen intellektueller Horizont die
Komplexität seiner Themen überhaupt erst ermöglicht. Er offenbart aber
auch, dass er bei Les Immatériaux einen wichtigen Aspekt dieser Meister-
schaftsdidaktik übersehen hat: den Dialog, der es dem Meister ermöglicht,

The visitors themselves were the key element and cornerstone of this scenography. Les Immatériaux was supposed to »raise the question of identity
on the basis of materiality and immateriality: the question of what we are
and what the objects that surround us are.« The fact that »the question of
identity« would not be satisfied with elementary responses formed just as
much a philosophical program as it did didactic and creative foundations:
Les Immatériaux was to pose questions that remained unanswered for the
exhibition's visitors »even when you got to the museum exit or beyond.«

It was with irritating resolve that Lyotard withheld any form of clarity from
his visitors – the repertoire spanning from audio programs, which accompanied each station with complex philosophical and literary texts; to exhibits
that weren't labelled, which were closely interwoven with scenographic
elements making them rather difficult to identify at times; to the Labyrinth-
like structure of the entire space, thwarting any attempt to visit the stations
in any kind of logical, systematic sequence. ›3.4

This tension between questions and answers, between confusion and understanding, between object and text, or if you like, between the immaterially-
ephemeral and the materially-manifest remained omnipresent throughout
the entire exhibition and is deeply rooted in Lyotard's philosophical thought.
Before any ascription or pervasion, the exhibition provided him with the ideal
means to conduct his search for that which was yet to find a congruous form
of representation, for the anomaly yet to be categorized and, for the occurrence yet to be grasped in conceptual terms: »When one thinks that they
can describe thought as a selection made from ›disclosed‹ data [...], then
one is denying the truth: data is not ›disclosed‹ but can ›be disclosed‹, and
this selection is not realized by way of choosing. Like writing and painting,
thought is nothing other than summoning that which can be disclosed,«
wrote Lyotard in the 1986 text »Can Thought Go on without a Body?« For
Lyotard, this summoning is the point of departure for any kind of true philosophizing: »It is precisely this state, whereby one no longer knows where
one is, that constitutes the point of departure for each and every thought.

Taking such a stance, Lyotard reveals his claim to be a highly advanced
»master of his field« whose intellectual horizon was what had made the
complexity of his chosen subject a possibility in the first place. But he also
reveals that in the case of Les Immatéraux he had overseen one important
aspect of these didactics of mastery: the dialogue that allows the master
to adapt through interaction with his students and that reassures the

sich auf den Schüler einzustellen und der dem Schüler die Möglichkeit zur Rückversicherung und einen gewissen Schutz, vor allzu großer Komplexität, gibt. Indem Lyotard die Besucher von Les Immatériaux zwar mit der größtmöglichen Komplexität konfrontierte, ihnen aber die mediale Form des Gesprächs verweigerte (und durch die Kopfhörer selbst die Gespräche untereinander »verunmöglichte«), machte er Les Immatériaux zu einem ebenso hermetischen Werk wie ein philosophisches Buch.

Misst man also die Ausstellung an den Zielen, die Lyotard formulierte, kann man sagen, dass sie in einer Hinsicht gelungen war: »Philosopher par exposition [...]«, in Bezug auf einen anderen Aspekt jedoch, den Lyotard im selben Atemzug nannte, scheiterte: »[...] en direction du public«.

students and offers them a certain protection against being overwhelmed by such complexity. While Lyotard may have confronted Les Immatériaux's visitors with the greatest complexity possible under the conditions, he at the same time withheld the medium of this »conversation« from them (and with the headphones themselves, rendered any conservations amongst the visitors impossible, too), such that he turned Les Immatériaux into a work that was just a hermetic as a philosophic book.

Thus if one were to assess the exhibition using Lyotard's own words, one could in one sense say that it was a success: »Philosopher par exposition [...]«, however regarding other aspects, as Lyotard uttered in the very same breath, it was a failure: »[...] en direction du public«.

>>> author p.213

Redaktionelle Anmerkung: ähnlich erschienen im ARTnet-Magazin. Die Zitate in diesem Beitrag stammen allesamt aus dem Buch: Wunderlich, Antonia: Der Philosoph im Museum. Die Ausstellung »Les Immatériaux« von Jean-François Lyotard. Bielefeld 2008.

Editorial note: a similar version was published in ARTnet-Magazin. The citation in this article come from the publication: Wunderlich, Antonia: Der Philosoph im Museum. Die Ausstellung »Les Immatériaux« von Jean-François Lyotard. Bielefeld 2008.

Elisabeth Schweeger

Ein enzyklopädischer Streifzug durch die Menschheitsgeschichte

Elisabeth Schweeger organisierte und leitete in den 1980er und 1990er Jahren das Ausstellungsreferat der Akademie der bildenden Künste Wien und kuratierte zahlreiche Ausstellungen. Anlässlich der 300-Jahr-Feier arbeitete sie mit Peter Greenaway zusammen. Es entstand eine Ausstellung zur Frage: Was wird von der Welt und uns übrig bleiben, wenn sie untergeht?

Greenaway wollte diese Frage beantworten und griff eine Idee der NASA auf: Ein Katalog mit 100 wichtigen Errungenschaften der Menschheit sollte in einer Raumkapsel ins All geschickt werden. Dieser sollte unsere Welt erklären und als Erinnerung nie verloren gehen. Dafür wählte er die 100 für ihn wichtigsten Dinge aus und zeigte sie auf seine besondere Art nach dem Prinzip der Serie und Wiederholungen. Präsentiert wurden Puppen, Küsse, Hintern, Liebespaare, Waffen, Schweine, Panzertiere, Rüstungen, lebende und tote Skulpturen, aber auch Wasser, Blei, Öl, Regen und Licht. Jedes der Objekte wurde 100 Mal gezeigt.

Die Ausstellung erstreckte sich über drei Orte: Akademie der bildenden Künste, Semper Depot und Hofburg. Sie erzählte Geschichten aus unserer Welt – mit alltäglichen und zum Teil skurrilen Objekten, auf eine eigene Art und Weise, abgründig und trotzdem voller Witz. Über zivilisatorische Errungenschaften und deren Aberwitz und Verirrungen. Aber auch darüber, wie der Mensch als eigentlich unfertiges und zerbrechliches Wesen versucht, die Natur permanent zu überlisten oder zu kopieren: Parallele Aufstellungen, zum Beispiel von 100 Panzertieren neben 100 Rüstungen aus früheren Kriegszeiten, zeigten dies anschaulich.

Die Ausstellung war ein Erfolg: 60.000 Menschen besuchten sie in nur fünf Wochen. Peter Greenaway, nun nicht mehr nur als Filmemacher bekannt, sondern auch als Künstler, ermöglichte mit seinen Installationen ganz neue Blicke auf die Welt. Nach dem Erfolg in Wien wurde die Ausstellung dann noch gemeinsam mit den Salzburger Festspielen und dem Marstall/Bayerischen Staatsschauspiel als eine performative Installation in Salzburg und München gezeigt.

An encyclopedic survey of human history

Elisabeth Schweeger organized and chaired the exhibition committee for the Academy of Fine Arts Vienna in the 1980s and 1990s, curating numerous exhibitions. On occasion of the 300th-anniversary celebrations, she joined forces with Peter Greenaway. The result was an exhibition addressing the question: What will remain of the world and indeed us humans, when it all comes to an end?

Greenaway wanted to provide an answer to this question and adopted one of NASA's ideas to do so: A catalog featuring the top 100 of humanity's most significant accomplishments was to be placed in a space capsule and fired up into space. This was intended as an explanation of our world and a memento that would never be lost. To do so, he chose what he con-sidered the 100 most important things and displayed them in his own special way according to the principle of seriality and repetition. He presented dolls, kisses, bottoms, lovers, guns, pigs, armadillos, armor, living and dead sculptures as well as water, lead, oil, rain and light. Each item was exhibited 100 times over.

The exhibition ranged over three locations: Akademie der bildenden Künste, Semper Depot and Hofburg. The exhibition told stories of our own world – with both everyday and, at times, bizarre objects in a very unique way, ins-crutable and yet full of wit. But even more than that, it showed how humans as beings that are in fact themselves incomplete and fragile are constantly trying to permanently outwit or replicate nature: Parallel installations, for example 100 armadillos alongside 100 pieces of armor from past wars, provided a vivid depiction of this notion.

The exhibition was indeed a success; pulling 60,000 visitors in just five weeks. Peter Greenaway, who is no longer in his capacity as a filmmaker alone but also as an artist, opened up entirely new perceptive of own world with his installations. Following its success in Vienna, the exhibition was then shown together with the Salzburg Festival and the Marstall/Bayerisches Staatsschauspiel as a performative installation in both Salzburg and Munich.

>>> author p.213

Anmerkung der Herausgeber:
Nach einem Gespräch mit Elisabeth Schweeger
Note of the editors:
Conversation with Elisabeth Schweeger

185

3.2

3.3

3.4

3.5

3.7

3.8

3.9

3.10

3.11

3.12–3.15 © Peter Greenaway
Photo: Manu Luksch

3.12

3.13

3.14

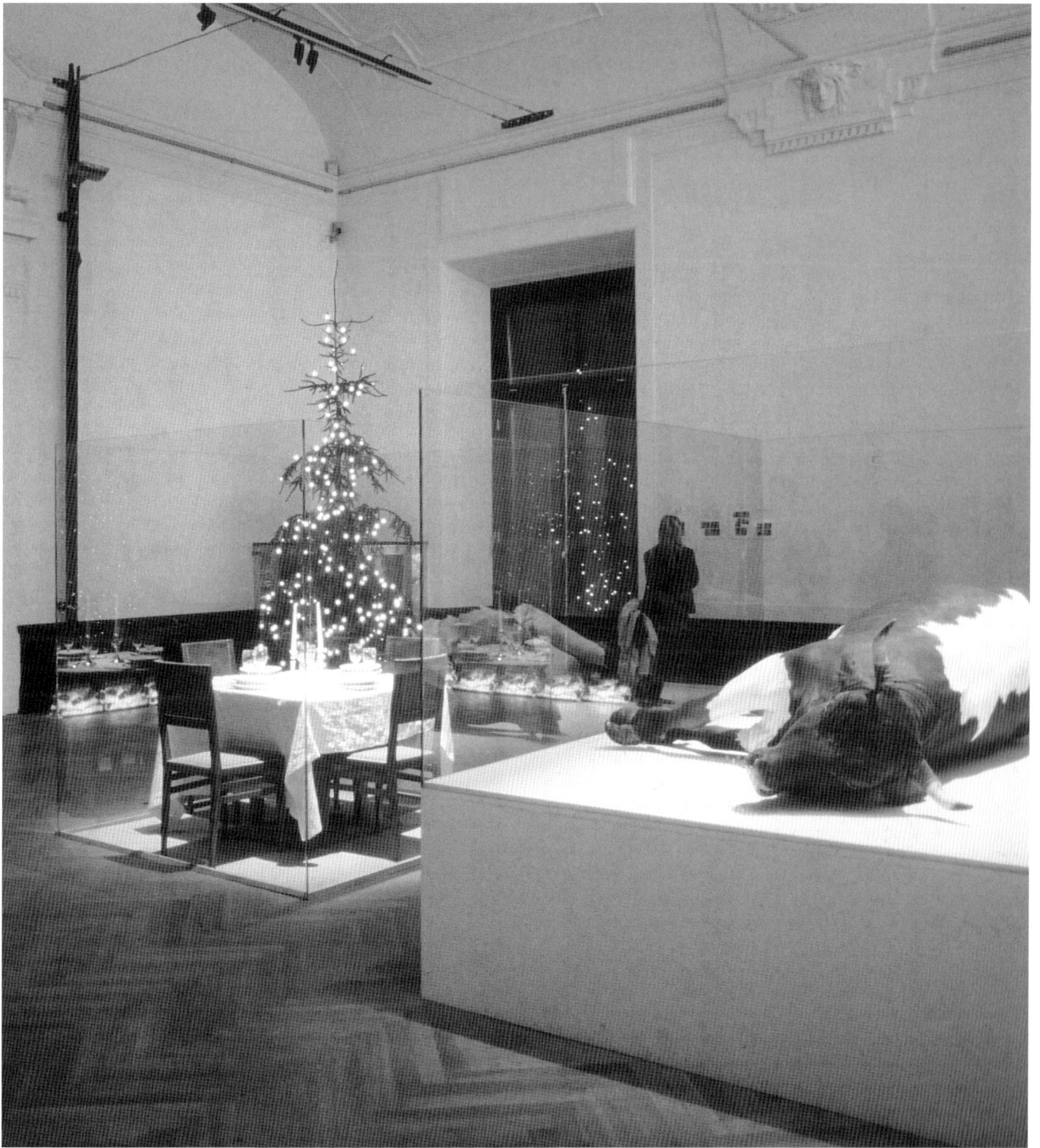

Ralph Appelbaum
Holocaust Museum von RAA

Ziel dieser Dauerausstellung ist es, den Holocaust zu bezeugen, die Art und Weise der Verbrechen zu belegen und die Beweise dafür zu zeigen. Dieser Auftrag stellte eine unglaublich große und vielseitige Aufgabe dar: Wie vermittelt man ein Ereignis mit solch entsetzlichem Inhalt, seine epochenprägenden Auswirkungen und die damit verbundene komplizierte Geschichte auf einer persönlichen Ebene? Ebenso anspruchsvoll gestaltete sich die zusätzliche Herausforderung, dies so auszuführen, dass Besucher unterschiedlicher Herkunft die Ausstellung mit einem neuen Verständnis und dem Entschluss, eine Wiederholung dieser Ereignisse nicht zuzulassen, verlassen würden.

Die Anfänge des USHMM (United States Holocaust Memorial Museum) gehen auf die Überzeugung einiger Überlebender zurück, dass alle Amerikaner auf eine anschauliche Weise und öffentlich von den Ereignissen erfahren sollten. Am 27. September 1979 legte die Holocaust-Kommission des Präsidenten, unter dem Vorsitz von Elie Wiesel, dem damaligen Präsidenten Jimmy Carter die Empfehlung vor, ein »lebendiges Denkmal« zu errichten. Die Legislative beauftragte im Jahr darauf die Regierung, für das Museum ein an die National Mall angrenzendes Grundstück zur Verfügung zu stellen; die Gelder für seinen Bau dagegen sollten aus privater Quelle kommen. Nachdem die entsprechenden Gelder mühevoll aufgebracht worden waren, wurde RAA (Ralph Appelbaum Associates) im Jahr 1988 beauftragt, mit dem fünfjährigen interpretativen Designprozess zu beginnen.

Unter der Aufsicht von Jeshajahu Weinberg und der wissenschaftlichen Leitung von Michael Berenbaum kooperierte RAA intensiv mit dem Ausstellungsdirektor Martin Smith. Eine der bedeutendsten Innovationen des Teams war es, eine »narrative« Ausstellung zu entwerfen – statt eine übliche, von der Sammlung oder der Aufteilung in Disziplinen bestimmte. Dadurch, dass der Holocaust als eine Geschichte mit distinktiven Handlungspunkten und einem erschütternden Verlauf konzipiert wurde, erhoffte man sich, dass die Besucher sich selbst aufgrund von emotionaler Identifikation mitten in diese Geschichte hineinprojizieren würden. Die knapp 11.000 m² große Ausstellung wurde als ein gelenktes emotionales Erlebnis entworfen, das, wie ein Theaterstück, in drei »Akte« unterteilt war: »Das Nazi-Regime 1933–1939«, »Die ›Endlösung‹ 1940–1945« und »Das letzte Kapitel«.

Holocaust Museum by RAA

The purpose of the permanent exhibition is to bear witness to the Holocaust, to give testimony about the nature of the crime, and to present the evidence. This mandate presented an immense and multifaceted challenge: how to communicate, on a personal level, an event with horrifying content, an epoch-making scope, and a complicated storyline. As demanding was the additional challenge of doing so in a way that ensures that visitors from diverse backgrounds depart with renewed mortal clarity, and determination against its recurrence.

The origins of USHMM (United States Holocaust Memorial Museum) lie with the conviction among key survivors, fermenting for some time, that all Americans should learn about the event in some tangible and public way. On September 27, 1979, the President's Commission on the Holocaust, chaired by Elie Wiesel, submitted to President Jimmy Carter a recommendation to establish a »living memorial.« Legislation the following year authorized the federal government to provide land adjacent to the National Mall for the Museum, whereas the funds for its construction had to come from private sources. After a vigorous fundraising period, RAA (Ralph Appelbaum Associates) was commissioned to begin a five-year interpretive design process in 1988.

Under the directorship of Jeshajahu Weinberg and the research leadership of Michael Berenbaum, RAA was paired with exhibitions director Martin Smith to engage in an intensive period of collaboration. One of the team's major innovations was to create a narrative exhibition rather than one driven by the collection or compartmentalized by discipline, as was standard at the time. By conceiving the Holocaust as a storyline with distinct plot points and a harrowing trajectory, it was hoped that visitors would project themselves into its midst, triggering emotional identification. The 36,000-square-foot exhibition was conceived as a controlled emotional experience theatrically organized into three »acts«: »Nazi Assault 1933–1939«; »The ›Final Solution‹ 1940–1945«; and »Last Chapter.«

Three decades ago, this kind of approach was new territory for museums. An interpretive principle developed early on: unflinching honesty was to be conveyed within an environment that acknowledged the visitor's need to pause and reflect as well as confront and comprehend. The designers felt a responsibility, to the scholarship and to the audience's intelligence,

3.1

Vor drei Jahrzehnten war diese Herangehensweise noch Neuland für die Museen. Eines der interpretativen Prinzipien, das sich schon früh entwickelte, war die unerschrockene Ehrlichkeit, die in einer Umgebung vermittelt werden sollte, welche die Bedürfnisse des Besuchers nach Pausen, Reflexion, Konfrontation und Begreifen berücksichtigte. Da es eine Verantwortung gegenüber der Veranstaltung, den wissenschaftlichen Erkenntnissen, aber auch der Intelligenz des Publikums gab, sollten die Inhalte weder abgeschwächt noch vereinfacht oder in anderer Weise beeinträchtigt werden. Mit den ersten Schritten in die Ausstellung sollten die Besucher den Rundgang als geschichtliches und emotionales Zurückverfolgen der Spuren in der Geschichte sehen. Sie sollten ein Teil der Ausstellung werden und die Ausstellung sollte ein Teil von ihnen werden.

Das oberste Stockwerk – der »erste Akt« – deckt den Aufstieg des Nationalsozialismus, die jüdischen und globalen Reaktionen darauf, die Schrecken der Kristallnacht sowie den Einmarsch nach Polen ab und deutet an, was darauf folgen wird: Durch die Stimme eines amerikanischen Soldaten, die man im Aufzug hören kann und die den Anstoß zum aktiven Miterleben des Besuchers gibt (»Du kannst es dir nicht vorstellen. Solche Dinge passieren nicht.«) und durch die eröffnende Fotografie von amerikanischen Soldaten in Ohrdruf im Jahr 1945 wird der Ausgangspunkt für die Beobachtungen der amerikanischen Besucher festgelegt.

not to dilute, simplify, or compromise content. The intention was that visitors understand their walkthrough as an historical and emotional retracing of the story. They would become part of it, and it, in turn, would become part of them.

The top floor – the first act – covers the rise of Nazism, the Jewish and global responses to it, the terror of Kristallnacht, and the invasion of Poland, and gives visitors a sense of what is to come – through the American soldier's voice heard in the elevator, which activates the visitor experience (»You can't imagine it. Things like that don't happen«), and the opening photographic scene of US army troops at Ohrdruf in 1945, an observational vantage point for American visitors is established. This perspective facilitates the objective of a major Holocaust museum outside Europe: to activate the consciences of potential bystanders. As the persecution escalates along this floor, the path becomes increasingly constricted and off-kilter, contributing to an uneasy sense of a darkly aberrant world.

The second act moves into the world of ghettoes and camps that were part of the »Final Solution.« The comparatively complete materials and finishes of the top level give way on this middle floor to a more degraded, spare, and bleak finish: the concrete floor is raw, ceiling tiles are missing, and base building elements are visible. The feeling is makeshift and crude, evoking a scene where human beings could be »processed« in a utilitarian, industrialized manner.

3.2

Diese Perspektive erklärt auch den Wert eines der wichtigsten Holocaust-Museen außerhalb Europas: Wie appelliert man an das Gewissen von potenziellen, unbeteiligten Zuschauern? Mit der schlimmer werdenden Verfolgung auf diesem Stockwerk wird der Weg immer enger und gerät aus dem Gleichgewicht, was zu der unangenehmen Wahrnehmung dieser Welt als dunkel und abnorm beiträgt.

Der »zweite Akt« führt in die Welt der Ghettos und KZs, die Teil der »Endlösung« waren. Die vergleichsweise unversehrten Materialien und Oberflächen im obersten Stockwerk weichen im mittleren Stockwerk vom Zerfall geprägten, spärlichen und trostlosen Oberflächen: unverputzter Betonboden, fehlende Dachplatten und sichtbares Gebäudefundament. In dieser provisorischen und kalten Atmosphäre wird die Vorstellung hervorgerufen, in welch gebrauchsorientierter, industrialisierter Weise die Menschen damals »verarbeitet« wurden.

A powerful moment that interrupts the flow between the floors is the Tower of Faces. Crossing a bridge over a three-story shaft between the first and second acts, visitors are surrounded by 1,500 photographic portraits of people who once lived in the village of Eishishok. Nearly all its inhabitants were murdered by a mobile killing unit in two days. The effect of the massed images is simultaneously monumental and intimate; it acts as both historical memorial and personal shrine.

The third act relates the Holocaust's stories of survival, rescue, and righteousness. The atmosphere shifts through the use of bright white panels, which carry stories of courage. Visitors come to associate with the righteous, pushing back against the weight of tragic events that has accumulated thus far. The result, hopefully, is some degree of transformation by the time of arrival at the Testimony Theater and Hall of Remembrance.

Ein eindrucksvolles Moment, das den Durchlauf dieser beiden Stockwerke unterbricht, ist der »Turm der Gesichter«. › 3.3 Bei der Überschreitung einer Brücke über einen drei Stockwerke tiefen Schacht zwischen dem »ersten« und dem »zweiten Akt« sind die Besucher umgeben von 1.500 Fotografien von Menschen, die einst in dem Dorf Eishishok lebten. Fast all seine Einwohner wurden innerhalb von zwei Tagen von einer mobilen, mordenden Einheit umgebracht. Die Wirkung der angehäuften Bilder hat gleichzeitig monumentalen und vertraulichen Charakter und fungiert demnach sowohl als geschichtliches Denkmal als auch als persönlicher Schrein.

Der »dritte Akt« verbindet die Geschichten des Holocaust von den Überlebenden, den Geretteten und den Gerechten. Die Atmosphäre ändert sich durch die Verwendung großer weißer Elemente, die Geschichten von Mut und Tapferkeit wiedergeben. Die Besucher wenden sich dem Rechtschaffenen zu und verdrängen dabei die angesammelte Last der tragischen Szenen, welche sie zu diesem Punkt gebracht hat. Das Ergebnis ist zum Zeitpunkt des Eintreffens im Testimony Theater und in der Hall of Remembrance – hoffentlich – eine Art Veränderung.

Die Designstrategien wurden mit Rücksicht auf die Geschichte entwickelt – nicht in Bezug auf die Designgeschichte oder nach den gängigen Standards von Museumsausstellungen. Der Architekt James Ingo Freed entwarf das Gebäude als einen »Resonator der Erinnerung« und hoffte, mit fließenden Übergängen zwischen Architektur und Ausstellung das Eintauchen in die Materie ermöglichen zu können. Die Designer waren den bloßen strukturellen Motiven sehr zugeneigt. Um die roten Backsteine und den dunkelgrauen Stahl des Gebäudes zu ergänzen, wurde eine minimalistische Materialpalette, bestehend aus Sichtbeton, Glasplatten auf Stahl, schrägen Oberflächen, geneigtem Glas und Metallrahmen, eingesetzt. Grundlegende abstrakte Stilkonzepte – Kontrast, Proportion, Skalierung – kehren in der Ausstellung in einem modularen Muster wieder.

Die Gegenstände wurden mit einer aufgeladenen, fast schon allegorischen Absicht ausgewählt und ausgestellt. Diese erscheinen typischerweise nicht hinter Glas, sondern in Käfigen oder auf Freiflächen. Die Uniformen der Opfer aus den Konzentrationslagern – die ersten authentischen Ausstellungsstücke, die die Besucher zu sehen bekommen – schockieren aufgrund ihrer zutiefst aufwühlenden Eigenschaften. › 3.4 Nicht ihre Anwesenheit ist emotional manipulierend, sondern im Gegenteil, ihre reale, unveränderte Beschaffenheit.

3.3

Design strategies were developed in dialogue with the story – not with the history of design, nor with the conventions governing museum presentation. Architect James Ingo Freed conceived the building as »a resonator of memory,« and hoped that by erasing the seams between architecture and exhibits a sense of immersion could be created. The designers felt an affinity with his stark structural motifs. Complementing the red brick and dark grey steel of the building, we deployed a minimal materials palette of exposed concrete, slabs of glass on steel, inclined surfaces, tilted glass, and metal frames. Basic abstract concepts of style – contrast, proportion, scale – recur throughout the exhibition in a modular matrix.

Artifacts were sought and displayed with a loaded, almost allegorical purpose. These typically appear not behind glass but suspended in cages or in open areas. The concentration camp victim uniforms – the first authentic objects visitors see – shock due to their visceral qualities. › 3.4 Their presence is not emotionally manipulative, but the opposite: the embodiment of the literal and unmediated textures of reality.

Ein harmloser Gegenstand wie ein Teesieb kann gleichermaßen wirksam sein. Es bietet einen Hoffnungsschimmer angesichts der immer weiter fortschreitenden Entmenschlichung. Sie begann damit, dass den Menschen das Recht auf ihre Stimme in der Politik genommen wurde, dann ihr Beruf, die Schule, das Telefon, die ärztliche Versorgung, dann, nachdem auch das eigene Heimatdorf betroffen war, der Name, die Hygiene, und alles was bleibt, ist das Teesieb. Die Herausforderung des Gestalters ist es, auf dessen Doppeldeutigkeit hinzuweisen: Ist es lediglich ein Utensil oder ein unvergesslicher Drehpunkt für all das, was zuvor aufgegeben wurde? Auf ähnliche Weise wurde von den Nazis produziertes Filmmaterial nicht einfach nur dazu eingesetzt, um ein Ereignis in der Geschichte darzustellen, sondern um die Besucher daran zu erinnern, dass die Erscheinung und Struktur dieser Welt sich gar nicht so sehr von unserer unterscheidet: Es war ein modernes Verbrechen, das in unserem Zeitalter der Massenkommunikation stattgefunden hat. In beiden Fällen vermittelt das Medium einen großen Teil dieser Botschaft.

Bei einigen großen, fundamentalen Objekten wie dem polnischen Güterwagen, dem dänischen Fischerboot, den Kasernen aus Auschwitz und den

A humble artifact, such as a tea strainer, can be similarly potent. It offers a sign of hope in the face of steadily escalating dehumanization that began with giving up the right to have a voice in politics, then a profession, then a school, then a telephone, then a doctor's care, until – after steps involving one's hometown, one's name, one's hygiene – all that is left is the tea strainer. The challenge for the designer is to allude to this double meaning: Is it a utensil, merely? Or a haunting pivot point for all that was given up before it? Similarly, Nazi-produced film footage was used not simply to illustrate a historical point but to remind visitors that the appearance and texture of that world is not so distant from ours: this was a modern crime that took place in our age of mass communications. In both instances, the medium carries much of the message.

Several large anchoring objects, such as the Polish boxcar, Danish fishing boat, and Auschwitz barracks and prisoners' bunks, forgo barriers of any kind; visitors can touch these and create an intimate sensory memory of the experience. Where glass is necessary, sheets are supported minimally and seemingly precariously, enhancing a sense of the fragility of their world. Lighting is also used to dramatic effect. The journey appears to be carved

3.4

3.5

3.6

Schlafkojen der Gefangenen wurde auf jegliche Absperrung verzichtet. Wo Glas nötig war, wurden die Scheiben minimal und sichtbar unsicher befestigt, um das Gespür für die Zerbrechlichkeit dieser Welt zu verstärken. Auch die Beleuchtung wird so eingesetzt, dass sich ein dramatischer Effekt ergibt. Der Weg scheint aus dem Dunkeln herausgearbeitet worden zu sein; das Licht wird ebenso sehr dazu eingesetzt, um die Aufmerksamkeit der Besucher auf den nächsten episodischen Punkt zu lenken und Schatten zu erzeugen, wie es dazu verwendet wird, Texte oder Objekte hervorzuheben.

Die öffentliche Reaktion auf das Museum war immens. Während die Besucherzahlen – ca. zwei Millionen Besucher pro Jahr – erfreulich ausfallen, ist dennoch die Qualität der Erlebnisse jedes Einzelnen von höchster Wichtigkeit. Die Ausstellung ist dazu gedacht, Konversationen zu entfachen, die ohne diese Erlebnisse nicht stattfinden würden. Die Absicht war, die Umgebung so zusammenhängend mit ihrem Inhalt zu gestalten, dass die Erinnerung des Besuchers an das Erlebte einen starken Appell an das Gewissen auslöst.

Die Dauerausstellung hat die Aufmerksamkeit der Fachkollegen von RAA auf sich gezogen. Sie wurde weithin als Wendepunkt in der Museologie anerkannt; ihr Erfolg löste die breite Übernahme von der aus dem Theater entnommenen narrativen Herangehensweise aus, die immer wieder neue Möglichkeiten und Herausforderungen bietet. Die Dauerausstellung sorgt – seit 18 Jahren weitestgehend unverändert – immer noch für bleibende Erinnerungen und ist weiterhin von Relevanz im Vergleich zu den sich wandelnden Arbeiten des Museum's Committee of Conscience und schulischen sowie öffentlichen Aufklärungsprogrammen. Die Beständigkeit der Ausstellung lässt erahnen, dass wir besonders vom Anblick der alltäglichen Erlebnisse der Menschen betroffen sind, die über geografische Distanzen und Generationen hinweg nachhallen.

out of darkness; light is used as much to draw visitors into the next episodic moment and to create shadows as it is to illuminate text or objects.

The public response to the Museum has been immense. While attendance figures – which number around 2 million visitors per year – are gratifying, the quality of each individual's experience is of utmost value. The exhibition sparks conversations that otherwise might not take place without this experience. The intention was to make the environment so cohesive with its subject that the visitor's memory of his or her experience forms a powerful call to conscience.

The permanent exhibition has been recognized by RAA's industry peers. It has been widely acknowledged as representing a turning point in museology; its success has triggered the extensive adoption of a theatrically driven narrative approach that continues to offer opportunities and challenges. The permanent exhibition has continued, largely unchanged over 18 years, to inspire strong memories and remain relevant in parallel with the changing work of the Museum's Committee on Conscience and educational and public programs. The enduring nature of the exhibition suggests that it resonates with aspects of a common human experience across geography and generations.

>>> author p.214

Renate Flagmeier
Unbeständige Ausstellung der Bestände des Werkbund-Archivs

Die »Unbeständige Ausstellung der Bestände des Werkbund-Archivs« war ein langfristiges Projekt zu einer ersten Ausstellung der eigenen Sammlung, das in mehreren Phasen von 1994 bis 1998 realisiert wurde. Die im Laufe von zwei Jahrzehnten – eher als Schleifspur thematischer Ausstellungsprojekte – angesammelten Gegenstände und Dokumente des Museums wurden gesichtet, die Sammlungstätigkeit und die Ausstellungsarbeit wurden in einen neuen Zusammenhang gebracht. Damit sollte eine deutlichere Identität als Museum gewonnen werden – ohne die offene, unkonventionelle Sammlungsstruktur aufzugeben.

Deshalb der schillernde Titel: »Eine unbeständige Bestände-Ausstellung«. Ein Changieren zwischen dem scheinbar Gesicherten, Geordneten, Eindeutigen des Bestandes und der Veränderlichkeit, der Offenheit, dem Mehrdeutigen, das im Umgang mit diesem Bestand lag. Im Rahmen der »Unbeständigen« sollte – wie durch ein Kaleidoskop – eine sich stetig verändernde Sicht auf die Sammlung gewonnen und dem Besucher ermöglicht werden. Deshalb bestand die Ausstellung aus einzeln komponierten, austauschbaren Räumen, die sich jeweils auf einen Sammlungsbereich des Werkbund-Archivs bezogen.

Der zentrale inhaltliche Aspekt der institutionellen Selbstreflexion, der museologische Blick auf die museale Sammlungsarbeit, zeigte sich u. a. in durchgängigen, spezifischen Gestaltungselementen: Die ausgestellten Dinge waren gestapelt, aufgereiht, angesammelt, gruppiert, zugeordnet, inventarisiert, katalogisiert.

Da die Räume für eine dauerhafte Präsentation der gesamten Sammlung nicht vorhanden waren, galt es neben den wechselnden Einzelinstallationen einen Raum zu schaffen, in dem sich der Betrachter ein Bild von der Sammlung des damaligen Werkbund-Archivs machen konnte. Diesem Ziel entsprach die resümierende, dauerhafte Eingangsinstallation in der »Unbeständigen Ausstellung« im damaligen Ausstellungsentree, einem längeren, relativ breiten Flur. Im Kontext dieses Raumbildes war die Museumssammlung fotografisch präsent – in der Art eines Stilllebens. Nicht die Dinge selbst, sondern Bilder der im Museum stillgestellten Dinge wurden gezeigt – eine Einstimmung und Sensibilisierung für das, was mit den Dingen im Museum geschieht, die Reduzierung des Objekts auf seine Zeichenfunktion. ›3.1

Impermanent exhibition of the Werkbund Archive collection

The »Unbeständige Ausstellung der Bestände des Werkbund-Archivs« was a long-running project to exhibit the Deutscher Werkbund's own collection first time and was realized over a number of phases between 1994 and 1998. Objects and documents belonging to the museum, collected over two decades (more as remnants of their activities over the years than for thematic exhibition projects), were examined, the two rather separate activities – collecting and exhibiting – were brought together in an interesting new context. The intention was to lend the Werkbund Archive a more distinct identity as a museum without relinquishing the collection's open, unconventional structure.

Hence the rather hesitant title: »Eine unbeständige Bestände-Ausstellung« (An variable holdings exhibition); indicating an oscillation between the seemingly secured, ordered, categorical nature of the Archive's inventory and the changeability, indeterminateness, ambiguousness that was implicated in their handling of the collection. The »Unbeständige Ausstellung« aimed to provide and present the visitor with a constantly alternating perspective of the collection, as though looking through a kaleidoscope. This was the motivation behind the decision to shape the exhibition using individually conceived, interchangeable rooms, each referencing one area of the Werkbund Archive collection.

As regards the exhibition's content, the central aspect of institutional self-reflection, the museum's own perspective on its collecting activities, manifests itself, inter alia, in the consistent, and highly specific design elements used: The exhibits were namely stacked, lined up, amassed, grouped, ordered, inventoried and cataloged.

Since there was not enough space available for a permanent presentation of the entire collection, the task was to create a room besides the alternating solo installations, where the visitor would be able to gain an impression of the Werkbund Archive's collection at that time. The permanent, overview installation was positioned in, what was at the time, the entrance to the »Unbeständige Ausstellung«, a long, relatively wide hallway. The museum's collection was given a presence within this »stereograph« in the form of photographs – like a still life. The objects themselves were not put on display but rather images of the objects held in the museum – an attunement and sensitization to what happens to such objects in a museum context, the reduction of the object to a symbol. ›3.1

Es wurde ein den räumlichen Proportionen im Ausstellungsentree angepasstes großes Regal gebaut, in das die verschiedenen Sammlungsbereiche nacheinander eingeräumt und dann fotografiert werden konnten. ›3.2 Diese Fotografien wurden dann auf Stoff gedruckt und zu einer räumlichen Struktur zusammengefügt, die an eine Galerie oder Passage erinnerte. Entstanden war ein Gang mit 17 »Regalen«, die verschiedene Sammlungskomplexe vorstellten, ohne Anspruch auf Vollständigkeit zu erheben. Das Regal als Motiv bedeutete die adäquate bildliche Umsetzung des Depot- und Sammlungsgedankens. Es handelte sich um einen virtuellen Sammlungsraum, eine Art »Traumhaus«: kein festes Gehäuse, sondern ein zeltartiger, transitorischer Raum, der eine zugleich offene und geschlossene Struktur hatte und zugleich einen real begehbaren und einen symbolischen Ort bildete.

Anhand der fotografierten Regale konnte man etwas über die Art des Sammelns, d.h. die Sammlungsfelder des Museums, erfahren: werkbundspezifische Sammlungskomplexe wie die Werkbundmarken bzw. die Produkte von Werkbundkünstlern und -firmen (z.B. Braun), materialorientierte Sammlungen – geordnet etwa nach Kunststoff, Aluminium sowie Materialsurrogaten – stilhistorische Sammlungsbereiche wie Jugendstil, themenorientierte Bereiche wie medienabhängiges Spielzeug unserer Gegenwart, zeithistorisch motivierte Sammlungsfelder wie Alltagskultur der DDR sowie Objekte der Kriegs- und Nachkriegszeit.

Eine assoziative Bezugnahme auf die Tradition der Kunst- und Wunderkammern des 16. und 17. Jahrhunderts, die in der Eingangsinstallation der »Unbeständigen« anklang, erschien für das Werkbund-Archiv naheliegend; die Anknüpfungspunkte waren die offene, noch nicht auf Ausschluss bedachte Systematik der Wunderkammern, das scheinbare Sammelsurium merkwürdiger Dinge und der Anspruch, ein Bild der Welt in der Vielfalt ihrer Erscheinungen zu repräsentieren.

Im Werkbund-Archiv war diese historische Bezugnahme verbunden mit dem Versuch der »Unbeständigen«, Sammeln und Ausstellen neu und anders zusammenzudenken. Das Museum hat stets versucht, Alternativen zu einer mittels Objekten illustrierten, linearen Geschichtserzählung zu entwickeln. Das erklärt die bestehende hohe Affinität zu Walter Benjamin und seinen Denkbildern. Benjamin beschreibt die adäquate Methode, das Verhältnis zur Geschichte zu gestalten: »Die wahre Methode, die Dinge sich gegenwärtig zu machen, ist, sie in unserem Raum (nicht uns in ihrem) vorzustellen. […]

A large shelving unit was built, tailored specifically to the spatial dimensions of the entrance hall; this was then filled with the collection's various sections one after another, each of them photographed once in position. ›3.2 The photographs were then printed onto fabric and collated to create a spatial framework, reminiscent of a gallery or an arcade. The result: a walkway fitted with 17 »shelving units«, presenting different systems within the collection without raising claim to completeness. The shelving as a motif signified an appropriate visualization of the deposit and collection mentality. It was a virtual collection space, a kind of »dream house«: Not a permanent enclosure but a tent-like, transitory space with a structure that was both open and closed at the same time, while also serving as a location that could be physically accessed while simultaneously remaining symbolic in its nature.

These photographed shelves also revealed something about the Archive's way of collecting, that is to say the areas from which the museum had taken the items: collection systems that were highly specific to the Werkbund itself like the Werkbund brands, or rather products made by Werkbund artists and companies (e.g., Braun); material-oriented collections arranged into plastic, aluminum and material substitutes; collection systems relating to specific styles such as Art Nouveau; theme-oriented e.g., the media-dependant toys of today's world; and collection areas inspired by historical themes such as everyday culture in former East Germany, or objects from the War and the post-war period.

An associative reference to the tradition of the cabinet of curiosities prominent in the 16th and 17th centuries, which was echoed in the entrance setting of the »Unbeständige Austellung«, seemed natural to those at the Werkbund Archive; there were several links between two – namely, the open classification seen in the cabinet of curiosities, not yet concerned with disqualification; the apparent hodgepodge of curious objects; and the claim to represent an image of the world in the diversity of phenomena it contains.

In the Werkbund Archive, this historical reference was combined with the exhibition's attempt to consider collecting and exhibiting in their relationship to each other in a new and different light. The museum continually tried to develop alternatives to a linear narrative told using objects, and objects alone. This can be used to explain the great affinity to Walter Benjamin and his thought-images seen here. Benjamin describes methods that can be used to shape our relationship to history: »The true method to bring past things to one's mind is, to imagine them in our space (not us in theirs). […]

Die Dinge, so vorgestellt, dulden keine vermittelnde Konstruktion aus ›großen Zusammenhängen‹.« Entsprechend dieser konzeptionellen Ausrichtung war es schlüssig, dass sich hinter der dauerhaften Eingangsinstallation einzelne wechselnde Rauminstallationen anschlossen.

Das Werkbund-Archiv (heute Werkbundarchiv - Museum der Dinge) hat die Ausstellung als eigenständiges künstlerisches Medium begriffen, d.h. den neutralen Museumsraum weitestgehend aufgegeben und räumliche Bilder entworfen, die den sich bewegenden Besucher berücksichtigen. In diesem Zusammenhang wurde der Einsatz zentral gesteuerter, theatraler Bespielungselemente (Licht, Ton, Bildprojektion) auf einem hohen Niveau erarbeitet, die eine zeitweilige Veränderung und Bewegung in der Ausstellung erzeugten und das Element der Verzeitlichung ins Spiel brachten. In der »Unbeständigen Ausstellung« wurde diese spezifische Ausstellungsästhetik des Museums verfeinert und die theatralen Bespielungselemente sehr bewusst, nur zeitweilig und abwechselnd mit Phasen der vollständigen Stillstellung, eingesetzt.

Zwei dieser »Raumbilder« sollen kurz vorgestellt werden: Das Raumbild »Apparatekultur«, ein Titel, der sich von dem Philosophen Vilem Flusser ableitet, zeigte die unseren Alltag bestimmenden, zahlreichen mechanischen, elektrischen und elektronischen Gerätschaften, die sich in der Museumssammlung befanden. In insgesamt 16 Hochregalen (Alu-Lagerregale bis zur ca. 5 m hohen Decke) waren die Dinge nüchtern nach Funktionsgruppen geordnet, d.h. jeweils in einem Regal die Fernseher, die Radios, die Küchenmaschinen und Mixer, die Schreib- und Rechenmaschinen, die Staubsauger, die Telefone usw. Die einzelnen Regale waren zu jeweils vier quadratischen Blöcken zusammengestellt und diese standen mit gleichem Abstand zueinander auf einem etwa quadratischen Raumfeld, dezentriert in einem großen, dunklen und mit schwarzem Boden ausgelegten Raum (ca. 300 m²). Diese Konstellation vermittelte das Bild einer Maschinerie, eines Gesamtapparats. ›3.3

Um die inhaltliche Dimension von Technik im Lebensalltag zu vermitteln, wurde der Raum mit dem theatralen Element einer Klang- und Lichtinstallation zeitweilig »bespielt«, d.h. die Phasen der ruhigen Betrachtungsmöglichkeit bei neutraler Beleuchtung wurden in einem festgelegten Rhythmus unterbrochen. Es veränderte sich das Licht und, dramaturgisch damit verknüpft, hörte man eine Folge technischer Geräusche und Klänge.

Things, when imagined in such a way, do not tolerate any kind of communicative construction made up of ›the bigger picture‹.« In keeping with this conceptual focus, having a number of individual spaces displaying alternating installations adjoining the permanent installation in the entrance, was a logical move.

The Werkbund Archive (today Werkbundarchiv - Museum der Dinge) conceived the exhibition as an independent artistic medium, in other words the neutrality of the museum setting was abandoned entirely in favor of creating spatial images that incorporate the moving visitor. To this end, centrally controlled, theatrical staging elements (light, sound, and image projection) were employed in a highly sophisticated way, creating temporary changes and movements within the exhibition and bringing the element of time into play. The »Unbeständige Ausstellung« provided scope to refine this exhibition aesthetic specific to the museum, whereby these theatrical staging elements were only ever applied deliberately and in intermittent and alternating cadence, interspersed with periods of complete still.

Here is a short introduction to two of these »stereographs«: The »Apparatekultur« (device culture) stereograph, a title derived from the words of philosopher Vilem Flusser, presented numerous mechanical, electrical and electronic devices found within the museum's collection that have a determinative effect on our everyday lives. In a total of 16 tall shelving units (aluminum storage shelving reaching up to the ceiling, approx. 5m tall) the objects were soberly arranged according to their function, such that televisions, radios, kitchen appliances and mixers, typing machines and calculators, vacuum cleaners, telephones etc. were each arranged in one of the shelving units. The individual units were combined into groups of four creating a square shape and then positioned in an almost square area at an equal distance from one another, off-center in a large, dark room (approx. 300 m²) with black flooring. This constellation was intended to portray the image of a machine, a complete device. ›3.3

In order to convey the content-related dimension of technology in everyday life, the space was temporarily »set« with a striking theatrical element, a sound and light installation, which interrupted those phases enabling a quiet moment of contemplation in neutral lighting in a pre-determined rhythm. The lighting suddenly changed, and combined to achieve dramatic effect, the visitor was confronted with a series of mechanic noises and tones.

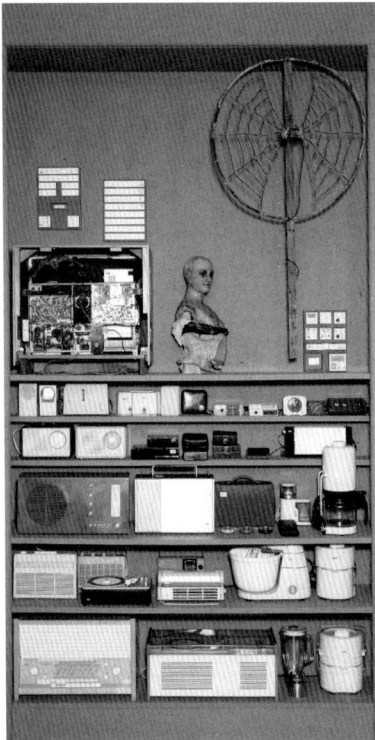

3.2

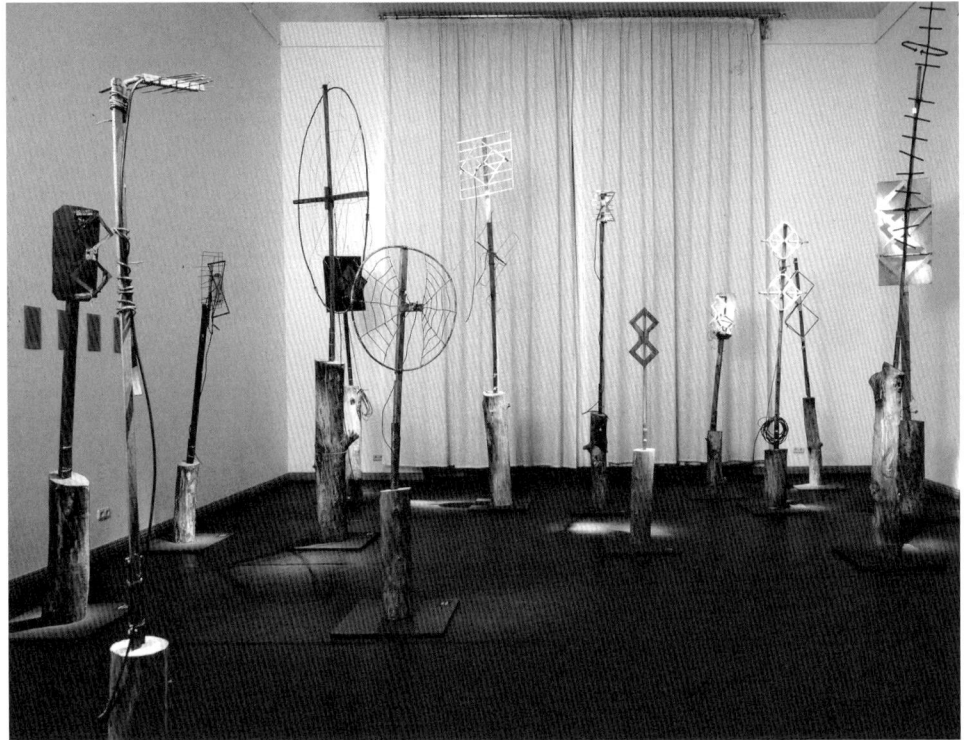

3.3

Ein Teil der ausgestellten Geräte wurde nicht nur virtuell, d.h. über ein entsprechendes Geräusch »angeschaltet«, sondern auch real in Funktion gesetzt.

Der grundlegende, alltägliche Aspekt technischer Kultur sollte mit dieser Installation in Erinnerung gerufen werden: Die Apparate versprechen, den Menschen zu bedienen, und fordern das Bedientwerden. Da die Verzahnung von Mensch und Technik auf einer immateriellen Ebene funktioniert, z.B. durch appellative Ton- und Lichtsignale der Maschinen, auf die jeder mit seiner Wahrnehmung eingestellt ist, war die Ton- und Lichtinstallation das adäquate Mittel zur Steigerung der Gesamtwirkung des Ausstellungs-raums.

Durch die zeitweilige künstliche Belebung der musealisierten Objekte konnte der grundsätzliche Aspekt ihrer musealen Stillstellung, das Her-ausreißen aus ihrem ursprünglichen Kontext, sinnlich erfahrbar gemacht werden.

Eine zweite Rauminstallation aus der zweiten Phase des Projekts (1996) zeigte Fundstücke aus verlassenen Sowjet-Kasernen rund um Berlin, sämt-lich Selbstbau-Objekte, insbesondere Antennen, die vom Werkbund-Archiv gefunden und in seine Sammlung aufgenommen wurden. Aus Blechresten, Metallstangen, Plastikstücken, Lattenfragmenten, Draht, Schnur und Kabel von den russischen Soldaten konstruiert und zum Rundfunk- und Fernseh-empfang benutzt, waren sie beim Abzug der Armee in den 1990er Jahren als Müll zurückgelassen worden. ›3.4

Im Kontext der ehemaligen Kasernen und auch im Alltagsleben Russlands bzw. der GUS-Staaten waren diese Objekte von größter Banalität – Notprodukte. Natürlich repräsentierte diese Ansammlung nicht den technischen Standard der Roten Armee, aber trotzdem waren die Fundstücke dem dort herrschen-den Mangel in Bezug auf die individuellen Bedürfnisse der Soldaten und im alltäglichen Kasernenleben geschuldet.

Trotz der Banalität der Objekte und der Armut des Herkunftszusammen-hangs haben die Antennen eine eigenartige, raumfüllende, skulpturale Kraft. Jede Antenne ist trotz ähnlicher Formen und Materialien ein Unikat. Ihre Ausstellung im musealen Kontext rief ein Changieren zwischen der Banalität des Gegenstandes und seiner ästhetischen Ausstrahlung hervor, die durch die Art der Präsentation noch zugespitzt wurde, da jede Antenne einzeln auf einem Baumstamm befestigt war, der als Sockel fungierte. ›3.3

There were a number of the exhibited devices that were not only »turned on« in a virtual sense, by means of the corresponding sound, but were actually activated.

This installation was intended to remind the visitor of the fundamental, every-day aspect of this technical culture: Devices promise to serve humans, and thus require us to operate them. The fact that the links between humans and technology function on an immaterial level (e.g., by means of the machine's appellative sound and light signals, to which we are all well attuned in our perception of these things) made the sound and light installation the best way to intensify the overall effect of the exhibition space.

The temporary artistic vivification of these objects transplanted into a museum setting took the visitor's experience of this fundamental aspect (these objects' captivity in this world, having been wrenched from their original context) beyond the purely visual bespeak several of our senses.

A second installation from the project's second phase (1996) displayed objects found in abandoned Soviet barracks around Berlin, including self-made objects (antennas were discovered in particular abundance) that had been found by the Werkbund and absorbed into their collection. Made by Russian soldiers using scraps of tin, metal rods, pieces of plastic, wooden slats, wire, thread and cable, these antennas were used to receive radio and television communications and had been left behind as trash when the army withdrew in the 1990s. ›3.4

Within the context of the former barracks and even in everyday life in Russia and the CIS nations, these objects were of the greatest banality, a product of necessity. Of course, this assemblage could not be considered representative of the technological standard in the Red Army, but they nonetheless depicted the prevalent shortages soldiers were experiencing in terms of their individual needs, as well as the scarcities that characterized everyday life in the barracks.

Despite the object's banal nature and the poverty of the situation that bore them, the antennas possess a unique, space-filling, sculptural power. They may be similar to one another in their shape and the materials used, but each of these antennas is in fact a one-off. Exhibited in a museum context, they evoked an oscillation between the banality of the object and its aesthetic radiance, which was emphasized even further thanks to the means of pre-sentation used; each antenna was attached to a piece of tree trunk, which took on the role of the museum pedestal. ›3.3

Die Objekte waren als Skulptur lesbar und es gab Besucher, die in der Präsentation eine Kunstinstallation vermuteten. Gleichzeitig war es eine einfache und sinnvolle Präsentationsweise, die sich aus den vorher an Dächern fixierten Antennen ergab. Das Spiel mit dem Ready-made-Effekt war bewusste Setzung, das Museum als ästhetisierendes System wurde so in diesem Raumbild verdeutlicht, entsprechend der konzeptionellen Basis des Gesamtprojekts »Unbeständige Ausstellung«.

Ein im Ausstellungsraum fixierter literarischer Text charakterisierte den Fundort der ausgestellten Objekte und jede Antenne hatte eine eigene sachliche Objektbeschriftung. Eine ausführlichere Darstellung des ursprünglichen Kontextes hätte die Festlegung auf eine Lesart bedeutet und die Antennen auf die Illustration des Mangellebens in den Kasernen reduziert. Stattdessen ergaben sich Widersprüche, Spannungen und Irritationen, den Antennen wurde ihre starke ästhetische Ausstrahlung gelassen und gleichzeitig der bei Objekten aus fremden Kontexten naheliegende und durchaus heikle ästhetische Zugang erkennbar gemacht.

Die einzeln präsentierten Antennen als Gegenpol zu dem danebenliegenden Raum zur »Apparatekultur« warfen noch eine andere inhaltliche Konstellation auf – die zwischen seriellem Massenprodukt und dem auch technischen, aber individuell erzeugten und archaisch anmutenden Einzelobjekt.

These objects could be seen as a sculptural work and there were even visitors who, upon consideration of the presentation, presumed that this was in fact an art installation. At the same time, the particular means of presentation that had been prescribed by the antennas themselves, having previously been mounted upon rooftops, was both simple and logical. This playful use of the self-made effect was a deliberate move, thus emphasizing the museum within this spatial image as an aestheticizing system, and corresponding to the conceptual basis of the entire »Unbeständige Ausstellung« project.

A literary text displayed in the exhibition room provided an indication of where they had been found, while each antenna was complete with its own informative description. An in-depth portrait of the original context on the other hand would have required them to specify a particular interpretation and would have therefore reduced the antennas to an illustration of a life of deprivation in the barracks. Instead, this produced contradictions, tensions, irritations; the strong aesthetic aura of the antennas was left untouched; and the extremely delicate aesthetic perspective, particularly obvious in objects taken from foreign contexts, was made plain to see.

As the antithesis of the adjacent »device culture« room, the individually antennas exhibited threw open yet another constellation in terms of content – between the mass-produced article and the equally technical but uniquely created and seemingly archaic one-offs.

>>> author p.214

Ausstellungskatalog
Exhibition catalogue
Flagmeier, Renate: ohne Titel. Sichern unter... Unbeständige Ausstellung der Bestände des Werkbund-Archivs. Berlin 1995.

index
annang

Publikationen
Publications

A

Altshuler, Bruce: **Salon to Biennial. Exibitions that made art history, Volume1: 1863-1959.** London 2008.

Archithese. Kunstmuseen in den USA. 5|2007 (37. Jahrgang). Sulgen Oktober 2007.

Archithese. Präsentieren – Inszenieren, Ausstellungsarchitektur. 3|1996 (26. Jahrgang). Sulgen Mai/Juni 1996.

Assmann, Aleida: **Erinnerungsräume: Formen und Wandlungen des kulturellen Gedächtnisses.** München 2011.

B

Bauhaus-Archiv (Ed.): **Herbert Bayer: Kunst und Design in Amerika 1938-1985.** Berlin 1986.

Bätschmann, Oskar: **Ausstellungskünstler. Kult und Karriere in modernen Kunstsystemen.** Köln 1997.

Beier, Rosmarie; Roth, Martin (Eds.): **Der gläserne Mensch – Eine Sensation. Zur Kulturgeschichte eines Ausstellungsobjekts.** Baustein 3 des Deutschen Historischen Museums. Stuttgart 1990.

Beier, Rosmarie: **Prometheus. Menschen. Bilder. Visionen. Eine Schau durch die Jahrhunderte.** Berlin 1998.

Berlinische Galerie (Ed.): **Stationen der Moderne. Die bedeutenden Kunstausstellungen des 20. Jahrhunderts in Deutschland.** Berlin 1988.

Bezzola, Tobia; Kurzmeyer, Roman (Eds.): **Harald Szeemann – with by through because towards despite: Catalogue of all Exhibitions 1957-2005.** Wien 2007.

C

Carboni, Erberto: **Exhibitions and Displays.** Italien 1957.

Coop Himmelblau (Ed.): **Architektur ist jetzt. Projekte, (Un)Bauten, Aktionen, Statements, Zeichnungen, Texte. 1968-1983.** Stuttgart 1983.

Corbusier, Le; Conrads, Ulrich: **Bauwelt Fundamente, Band 2. 1922 Ausblick auf eine Architektur.** Berlin 1969.

D

Dernie, David: **Ausstellungsgestaltung. Konzept und Technik.** Ludwigsburg 2006.

Desmoulins, Christine: **Scenographies d'architectes. 115 Expositions européennes mises en place par des architectes.** Paris 2006.

Dorner, Alexander: **Überwindung der »Kunst«.** Hannover 1959.

E

Eames, Charles; Eames, Ray: **Die Welt von Charles und Ray Eames.** Berlin 1997.

Elliott, Bridget; Purdy, Anthony: **Peter Greenaway. Architecture and Allegory.** Chichester 1997.

F

Fliedl, Gottfried; Rath, Gabriele; Wörz, Oskar (Eds.): **Der Berg im Zimmer: Zur Genese, Gestaltung und Kritik einer innovativen kulturhistorischen Ausstellung.** Bielefeld 2010.

Fleck, Robert: **Die Biennale von Venedig. Eine Geschichte des 20. Jahrhunderts.** Hamburg 2009.

Fleckner, Uwe: **Angriff auf die Avantgarde. Kunst und Kunstpolitik im Nationalsozialismus.** Berlin 2007.

Franck, Klaus: **Ausstellungen. Exhibitions.** Stuttgart 1961.

G

Garn, Andrew (Ed.): **Weltausstellungen 1933-2005: Architektur Design Graphik.** München 2008.

Georgsdorf, Heiner (Ed.): **Arnold Bode - Schriften und Gespräche.** Berlin 2007.

Götz, Matthias; Haldner, Bruno (Eds.): **Aroma, Aroma. Versuch über den Geruch. Museum für Gestaltung Basel.** Basel, Muttenz 1995.

Greenaway, Peter: **100 Objekte zeigen die Welt. 100 Objects to represent the World.** Wien 1992.

Greenberg, Reesa; Ferguson, Bruce W.; Nairne, Sandy (Eds.): **Thinking About Exhibitions.** London, New York 1996.

H

Hareiter, Angela; Ortner, Laurids; Gsoellpointner, Helmuth (Eds.): **Design ist Unsichtbar.** Wien 1981.

Hinz, Berthold: **Die Malerei im deutschen Faschismus: Kunst und Konterrevolution.** München 1984.

Hoh-Slodczyk, Christine (Ed.): **Carlo Scarpa und das Museum.** Berlin 1987.

Huber, Hans Dieter; Locher, Hubert; Schulte, Katrin (Eds.): **Kunst des Ausstellens. Beiträge Statements Diskussionen.** Ostfildern-Ruit 2002.

J

Jacob, George: **Museum Design: The Future.** Charleston 2009.

K

Kandeler-Fritsch, Martina; Kramer, Thomas (Eds.): **Get off of my cloud: Texte 1968-2005 / CoopHimmelb(l)au. Wolf D. Prix.** Ostfildern-Ruit 2005.

Kimpel, Harald; Stengel, Karin (Eds.): **Dokumenta 1955: Erste Internationale Kunstausstellung – eine fotografische Rekonstruktion.** Bremen 1995.

Kimpel, Harald: **Documenta - die Überschau. Fünf Jahrzehnte Weltkunstausstellung in Stichwörtern.** Köln 2002.

Kimpel, Harald: **Documenta. Mythos und Wirklichkeit.** Köln 1997.

Kirsch, Karin: **Die Weißenhofsiedlung: Werkbund-Ausstellung »Die Wohnung« – Stuttgart 1927.** Stuttgart 1987.

Klüser, Bernd; Hegewisch, Katharina (Eds.): **Die Kunst der Ausstellung. Eine Dokumentation dreißig exemplarischer Kunstausstellungen dieses Jahrhunderts.** Frankfurt am Main, Leipzig 1991.

E (continued column)

Borsdorf, Ulrich; Brüggemeier, Franz-Josef; Korff, Gottfried et al. (Eds.): **Feuer & Flamme. Eindrücke einer Ausstellung im Gasometer Oberhausen 1994/95.** Essen 1995.

Brenner, Hildegard: **Die Kunstpolitik des Nationalsozialismus. Rowohlts deutsche Enzyklopädie 167/168.** Hamburg 1963.

Burkhardt, François (Ed.): **Domus Dossier. Esporre. La messinscena dell' effimero/ Exhibiting. How to stage the ephemeral.** 5|1997. Rozzano/Milano 1997.

Koenig, Gloria: **Eames.** Köln, London et al. 2005.

Kölnischer Kunstverein (Ed.): **Le Musée Sentimental de Cologne. Entwurf zu einem Lexikon von Reliquien und Relikten aus zwei Jahrtausenden.** Köln 1979.

König, Kaspar (Ed.): **Von hier aus – Zwei Monate neue deutsche Kunst in Düsseldorf.** Köln 1984.

Koolhaas, Rem; Boeri, Stefano; Sanford, Kwinter et al.: **Mutations.** Barcelona 2001.

Korff, Gottfried; Rürup, Reinhard (Eds.): **Berlin, Berlin. Die Ausstellung zur Geschichte der Stadt.** Berlin 1987.

Korff, Gottfried: **Museumsdinge: deponieren - exponieren.** 2. Auflage. Wien, Köln et al. 2006.

L

Lissitzky-Küppers, Sophie (Ed.): **El Lissitzky. Maler, Architekt, Typograf, Fotograf. Erinnerungen, Briefe, Schriften.** Berlin, Wien et al. 1980.

Lohse, Richard Paul: **Neue Ausstellungsgestaltung. Nouvelles conceptions de l'exposition. New Design in Exhibitions.** Erlenbach-Zürich 1953.

M

Masey, Jack; Lloyd Morgan, Conway: **Cold War Confrontations. US Exhibitions and their Role in the Cultural Cold War.** Zürich 2008.

Mattie, Erik: **Weltausstellungen.** Belgien 1998.

McQuaid, Matilda: **Lilly Reich. Designer and Architect.** New York 1996.

Museum Jean Tinguely (Ed.): **Anekdotomania. Daniel Spoerri über Daniel Spoerri.** Ostfildern-Ruit 2001.

N

Neuburg, Hans: Internationale Ausstellungsgestaltung. Conception internationale d'expositions. Conceptions of International Exhibitions. Zürich 1969.

Neuhart, John; Neuhart, Marilyn: Eames Design: The Work of the Office of Charles and Ray Eames. New York 1989.

Nerdinger, Winfried (Ed.): 100 Jahre Deutscher Werkbund 1907–2007. München 2007.

O

O'Doherty, Brian: In der weißen Zelle. Inside the White Cube. Berlin 1996.

Orchhard, Karin (Ed.): Blast. Vortizismus - die erste Avantgarde in England 1914-1918. Berlin 1996.

P

Perloff, Nancy; Reed, Brian (Eds.): Situating El Lissitzky. Vitebsk, Berlin, Moscow. Los Angeles 2003.

Peters, Olaf; Heftrig, Ruth; Schellewald, Barbara (Eds.): Kunstgeschichte im »Dritten Reich«. Theorien, Methoden, Praktiken. Berlin 2008.

Polano, Sergio: Achille Castiglioni: Complete Works. Milano 2001.

Polano, Sergio: Mostrare. L'allestimento in Italia dagli anni Venti agli anni Ottanta. Exhibition design in Italy from the Twenties to the Eighties. Milano 1988.

Pomian, Krzysztof (Ed.): Der Ursprung des Museums. Vom Sammeln. Berlin 1998.

Posener, Julius (Ed.): Vorlesungen zur Geschichte der Neuen Architektur (1750-1933). Aachen 1983.

Pöhlmann, Wolfger (Ed.): Ausstellungen von A-Z. Gestaltung, Technik, Organisation. Berlin 1988.

Pressler, Monika (Ed.): Friedrich Kiesler. Designer. Sitzmöbel der 30er und 40er. Ostfildern-Ruit 2005.

R

Reinhardt, Uwe J.; Teufel, Philipp: Neue Ausstellungsgestaltung 01/New Exhibition Design 01. Ludwigsburg 2007.

Reinhardt, Uwe J.; Teufel, Philipp: Neue Ausstellungsgestaltung 02/New Exhibition Design 02. Ludwigsburg 2010.

Ribalta, Jorge (Ed.): Public Photographic Spaces: Exhibitions of Propaganda, from Pressa to The Family of Man, 1928-55. Barcelona 2009.

Rice, Leland; Newhall, Beaumont: Herbert Bayer: Potographic Works. Los Angeles 1977.

S

Schäfers, Stefanie: Vom Werkbund zum Vierjahresplan. Die Ausstellung »Schaffendes Volk«, Düsseldorf 1937. Kleve 2001.

Schmidt, Johann-Karl (Ed.): Hans Dieter Schaal. Architekturen 1970-1990. Stuttgart 1990.

Schneede, Uwe M.: Die Geschichte der Kunst im 20. Jahrhundert: Von den Avantgarden bis zur Gegenwart. München 2001.

Schramke, Sandra: Kybernetische Szenografie: Charles und Ray Eames. Ausstellungsarchitektur 1959-1965 Bielefeld 2010.

Schriefers, Thomas: Ausstellungsarchitektur: Geschichte, wiederkehrende Themen, Strategien. Bramsche 2004.

Schröder, Vanessa: Geschichte ausstellen - Geschichte verstehen: Wie Besucher im Museum Geschichte und historische Zeit deuten. Bielefeld 2013.

Schulte, Karin: Messedesign Jahrbuch 1999. Trade-Fair Design Annual 1999. Ludwigsburg 1999.

Schwarz, Ulrich; Teufel, Philipp (Eds.): Museografie und Ausstellungsgestaltung. Ludwigsburg 2001.

Schwencke, Olaf (Ed.): Museum - Verklärung oder Aufklärung. Kulturpolitisches Kolloquium zum Selbstverständnis der Museen. Rehburg-Loccum 1986.

Spalding, Julian: The Poetic Museum: Reviving Historic Collections. New York 2002.

Staniszewski, Mary Anne: The Power of Display. A History of Exhibition Installations at the Museum of Modern Art. London 1998.

Stercken, Angela (Ed.): 1926–2004 GeSoLei. Kunst, Sport und Körper. 3 Bilder einer Ausstellung – Rundgänge. Weimar 2004.

T

te Heesen, Anke; Padberg, Susanne (Eds.): Musée Sentimental 1979: Ein Ausstellungskonzept. Ostfildern 2011.

Thiekötter, Angelika: Kristallisationen, Splitterungen. Bruno Tauts Glashaus. Basel 1993.

Thomas, Elizabeth (Ed.): Matrix/Berkeley: A Chaniging Exhibition of Contemporary Art. Berkeley 2009.

W

Wackerbarth, Horst (Ed.): Kunst und Medien. Materialien zur Documenta 6. Kassel 1977.

Weissweiler, Lilli: Futuristen auf Europa-Tournee. Zur Vorgeschichte, Konzeption und Rezeption der Ausstellungen futuristischer Malerei (1911-1913). Bielefeld 2009.

Werner, Frank R. (Ed.): Hans Dieter Schaal. In-Between. Ausstellungsarchitektur. Stuttgart, London 1999.

Wunderlich, Antonia: Der Philosoph im Museum. Die Ausstellung »Les Immatériaux« von Jean-François Lyotard. Bielefeld 2008.

Württembergisches Landesmuseum (Ed.): 13 Dinge: Form, Funktion, Bedeutung. Katalog zur gleichnamigen. Ausstellung im Museum für Volkskultur in Württemberg. Stuttgart 1992.

Württembergisches Landesmuseum (Ed.): Die Zeit der Staufer. Katalog der Ausstellung Stuttgart 1977. Band 1-5. Stuttgart 1977.

Z

Zim, Larry; Lerner, Mel; Rolfes, Herbert (Eds.): The World of Tomorrow: The 1939 New York World's Fair. New York 1988.

Zuschlag, Christoph (Ed.): Entartete Kunst. Ausstellungsstrategien im Nazi-Deutschland. Worms 1995.

Herausgeber

Editors

>>> Anna Müller, Frauke Möhlmann

Beide Diplom-Kommunikationsdesignerinnen, Abschluss im Sommer 2008 an der Fachhochschule Düsseldorf mit dem Thema »1900–2000 The History of Exhibition Design»; 2008–2010/11 Master-Studiengang am edi – Exhibition Design Institute in Düsseldorf, Forschungsthema: »Neue Ausstellungsgestaltung 1900–2000«; Mitarbeit »New Exhibition Design 01« und »New Exhibition Design 02« und Herausgeberinnen »New Exhibition Design 1900–2000«.

Both communication designers graduated in summer 2008 from the Düsseldorf University of Applied Sciences with a dissertation on »1900–2000 The History of Exhibition Design«; 2008–2010/11 Master's course at edi – Exhibition Design Institute in Düsseldorf, research topic: »New Exhibition Design 1900–2000«; assistance with »New Exhibition Design 02« and editors of »New Exhibition Design 1900–2000«.

>>> Uwe J. Reinhardt

Studium der Empirischen Kulturwissenschaft, Politikwissenschaft, Germanistik und des Designs in Tübingen, Stuttgart und Rom, mit den Schwerpunkten Gestaltung, Grafikdesign und Kommunikation von Kulturprojekten; seit 2005 Professor für Text/Verbale Kommunikation im Fachbereich Design an der FH Düsseldorf und Leiter des edi – Exhibition Design Institute, Schwerpunkte: Text und Drehbuch, Redaktion und Konzeption, Ausstellungsgestaltung und Szenografie, Bücher und Kataloge.

Studied Empirical Culture, Politics, German Language and Literature and Design in Tübingen, Stuttgart and Rome, majoring in Design, Graphic Design and Communication of Cultural Projects; since 2005 Professor of Text/Verbal Communication in the Department of Design at the Düsseldorf University of Applied Sciences and head of edi – Exhibition Design Institute, main interests: Text and screenplays, editing and concepts, exhibition design and scenography, books and catalogs.

>>> Philipp Teufel

Studium der Visuellen Kommunikation an der HfG Schwäbisch Gmünd; seit 1985 zahlreiche Museums- und Ausstellungsprojekte; seit 1994 Professor für Kommunikationsdesign im Fachbereich Design an der FH Düsseldorf mit den Schwerpunkten Ausstellung und medienspezifische Visualisierung, Koleiter des edi – Exhibition Design Institute; kuratiert, konzipiert und gestaltet Ausstellungen und Museen sowie Leit- und Orientierungssysteme.

Studied Visual Communication at the Academy of Design (HfG) in Schwäbisch Gmünd; since 1985 numerous museum and exhibition projects; since 1994 Professor of Communications Design in the Department of Design at Düsseldorf University of Applied Sciences specializing in exhibitions and media-specific visualization, joint head of edi – Exhibition Design Institute; curates, conceives, and designs exhibitions and museums, as well as guidance and orientation systems.

>>> Kai-Uwe Hemken

Professor für Kunstwissenschaft (20. Jahrhundert) an der Kunsthochschule Kassel; Studium der Kunstgeschichte, Philosophie und Literaturwissenschaft in Marburg und München; 1989 Magister Artium; 1993 Promotion über El Lissitzky; 2004 Habilitation zur Gedächtnis-Kunst der Gegenwart seit 1960 (Gerhard Richter, Jochen Gerz, Hanne Darboven); kuratorische Arbeit z. B. am Sprengel Museum Hannover und Van Abbemuseum Eindhoven; zahlreiche Buchpublikationen zur modernen Kunst.

Professor of Art (20th century) at Kassel Academy of Art; Studied History of Art, Philosophy, and Literature in Marburg and Munich; 1989 Magister Artium; 1993 doctorate on El Lissitzky; 2004 habilitation on Contemporary Commemorative Art since 1960 (Gerhard Richter, Jochen Gerz, Hanne Darboven); curatorial work e.g., at the Sprengel Museum in Hanover and Van Abbemuseum Eindhoven; has published widely on modern art.

Autoren

Authors

>>> Eva Citzler

2006–2009 Studium der Betriebswirtschaftslehre und der Anglistik an der Universität Duisburg-Essen; 2009 Abschlussarbeit über Preisbildungsprozesse im Kunstmarkt; 2009–2011 Master-Studium der Kunstwissenschaft an der Kunsthochschule Kassel; 2011 Abschlussarbeit über den Skandal als gesellschaftliches Phänomen in der Kunst der Gegenwart.

2006–2009 Studied Business Administration and English Language and Literature at the University of Duisburg-Essen; 2009 degree thesis on pricing processes in the art market; 2009–2011 Master's in Art at Kassel Academy of Art; 2011 degree dissertation on scandal as a social phenomenon in contemporary art.

>> 014 Die Wohnung p.100

>>> Ines Katenhusen

Wissenschaftliche Mitarbeiterin an der Philosophischen Fakultät der Leibniz Universität Hannover; 1997 Promotion, lehrt seitdem zu Aspekten der Kultur-, Kunst- und Sozialgeschichte im 19. und 20. Jahrhundert an der Leibniz Universität Hannover, der Hochschule für Bildende Künste Braunschweig, der Universität Siegen sowie, im Rahmen von Kurzdozenturen, an verschiedenen anderen europäischen Hochschulen; Buchprojekte z. B. über den deutsch-amerikanischen Kunsthistoriker und Museumsdirektor Alexander Dorner.

Research associate in the Faculty of Philosophy at Leibniz University in Hanover; 1997 awarded a doctorate, since when she has been lecturing on aspects of 19th and 20th century cultural, art, and social history at Leibniz University in Hanover, Braunschweig University of Art, Siegen University, and as a visiting lecturer at various other European universities; book projects, for example, on German-American art historian and museum director Alexander Dorner.

>> 016 Der Raum der Abstrakten p.104

>>> Simon Großpietsch

Kunstwissenschaftler mit Schwerpunkt Kunst des 20./21. Jahrhunderts und documenta; Studium der Kunstwissenschaften, Philosophie und Germanistik in Kassel; 2013 Magister Artium; kuratorische Tätigkeiten u. a. B 3 - 2005 und b4. 2009 in Kassel; 2010/11 studentischer Mitarbeiter im Projektbüro der dOCUMENTA (13); 2004/05 Praktikant und freier Mitarbeiter im documenta Archiv Kassel; zahlreiche Katalogbeiträge und Künstlerrezensionen.

Scientist of fine arts with focus on the 20th and 21st century art and documenta; He studied fine arts, philosophy and German philology in Kassel, Magister artium 2013; curatorial activities including salary scale B 3 - 2005 and b4. 2009 in Kassel; 2010–11 student assistant in the dOCUMENTA (13) project office; 2004–05 intern and freelance member of staff in the documenta archive in Kassel; numerous articles in catalogs and artists' reviews.

>> 048 documenta p.140

>>> Janina Poesch

Zusammen mit Sabine Marinescu Herausgeberin der Zeitschrift PLOT – Inszenierungen im Raum; bis 2000 Ausbildung zur Bauzeichnerin; anschließend Studium der Architektur an der Universität Stuttgart (2000–2006), Thema der Diplomarbeit: »Architekturvermittlung in Ausstellungen«; 2006–2008 Volontariat bei der Zeitschrift AIT; 2008 Gründung von PLOT – Internationale Plattform für Inszenierungen im Raum sowie freiberufliche Tätigkeit als Architektur-Journalistin.

Together with Sabine Marinescu editor of the magazine PLOT – Creative Spaces; until 2000 apprentice draftswoman; then studied Architecture at the University of Stuttgart (2000–2006), degree thesis topic: »The Presentation of Architecture in Exhibitions«; 2006–2008 training at the magazine AIT; 2008 founding of PLOT – International Platform for Creative Spaces, as well as freelance work as an architecture journalist.

>> 050 Le poème électronique p.148

>>> Jürgen Münch

Diplom-Sozialarbeiter und Medienpädagoge; Mitarbeiter und Vorstands-mitglied der Hugo Kükelhaus Gesellschaft e.V. in Soest; hauptberuflich in der Kinder- und Jugendarbeit tätig.

Graduate social worker and teacher of media studies; member of the staff and Board of Hugo Kükelhaus Gesellschaft e.V. in Soest; main field of activity children's and youth work.

>> 059 Erfahrungsfeld zur Entfaltung der Sinne p.160

>>> Anke te Heesen

Wissenschaftshistorikerin und Kuratorin; Studium der Kulturpädagogik an der Universität Hildesheim (1985–1991); Promotion 1995; Forschungs-und Lehrtätigkeit an verschiedenen Universitäten im In- und Ausland, sowie Ausstellungen in verschiedenen Museen; seit 2011 Lehrstuhl für Wissenschaftsgeschichte mit dem Schwerpunkt der Bildung und Organisation des Wissens im 19. und 20. Jahrhundert an der Humboldt-Universität zu Berlin.

Specialist in the history of knowledge and curator; studied Cultural Education at the University of Hildesheim (1985–1991); awarded a doctorate in 1995; research and teaching posts at various universities in and outside Germany, as well as exhibitions in various museums; since 2011 Chair of the History of Knowledge focusing on the compilation and organization of knowledge in the 19th and 20th centuries at the Humboldt University Berlin.

>> 068 Musée Sentimental de Cologne p.168

>>> Antonia Wunderlich

Studium der Kunstgeschichte, Philosophie und Vergleichenden Religions-wissenschaften in Köln und Bonn (1994–1999); Promotion 2006 in Witten-Herdecke: »Der Philosoph im Museum. Die Ausstellung ›Les Immatériaux‹ von Jean-François Lyotard«; wissenschaftliche Mitarbeiterin am Institut für Kunst und Kunsttheorie der Humanwissenschaftlichen Fakultät und am Kunsthistorischen Institut, beide Universität zu Köln; Wissenschaftscoach und Trainerin im Bereich Hochschuldidaktik an verschiedenen Hochschulen.

Studied History of Art, Philosophy and Comparative Religion in Cologne and Bonn (1994–1999); awarded a doctorate in 2006 in Witten-Herdecke: »The Philosopher and the Museum. The Exhibition ›Les Immatériaux‹ by Jean-François Lyotard«; research assistant at the Institute of Art and Theory of Art at the Humanities Faculty and at the Institute of art History, both at the University of Cologne; academic coach and trainer for University Didactics at various universities.

>> 075 Les Immatériaux p.176

>>> Elisabeth Schweeger

Studium der Vergleichenden Literaturwissenschaft, Romanistik, Germanistik und Philosophie in Wien, Innsbruck und an der Sorbonne, Paris; 1979 Promotion zum Doktor der Philosophie; Ausstellungskuratorin u. a. für Ars Electronica, documenta, OK Linz, Museumsquartier Wien; Kommissärin der 49. Biennale Venedig/Österreichischer Pavillon; 2001–2009 Intendantin Schauspiel Frankfurt; 2009–2014 Intendantin KunstFestSpiele Herrenhausen; ab September 2014 Geschäftsführerin/Künstlerische Leiterin der Akademie der Darstellenden Kunst/Baden-Württemberg.

Studied Comparative Literature, Romance Languages and Literature, German Language and Literature, and Philosophy in Vienna, Innsbruck and at the Sorbonne, Paris; awarded a doctorate in Philosophy in 1979; exhibition curator among other things for Ars Electronica, documenta, OK Linz, Museumsquartier Vienna; Commissioner for the Austrian pavilion at the 49th Venice Biennale; Artistic Director of Schauspiel Frankfurt; 2009–2014 Artistic Director of KunstFestSpiele Herrenhausen; from September 2014 Managing and Artistic Director of the Academy of Dramatic Art, Baden-Württemberg.

>> 081 100 Objects to represent the World p.184

>>> Ralph Appelbaum

Unter seiner Leitung hat das Studio weltweit über 300 Ausstellungen und Museen realisiert, die vielfach ausgezeichnet worden sind, unter anderem mit dem National Design Award und dem United States Presidential Award for Design Excellence. Das Interesse der Designteams aus über 200 Gestaltern – mit Büros in New York, London, Berlin, Moskau und Peking – liegt in der Schaffung erzählerisch inspirierter Besuchererlebnisse in der Sozial- und Kulturgeschichte, der Naturkunde, sowie den Naturwissenschaften, mit einem besonderen Augenmerk auf Unternehmensgeschichte und biografische Inhalte. Als außerordentlicher Professor am Pratt Institute und an der New York University ist Appelbaum häufig als Vortragender bei internationalen Konferenzen zu Gast.

The practice, under his direction, has built more than 300 exhibitions and museums worldwide, which have been awarded honors such as the National Design Award, and the United States Presidential Award for Design Excellence. With a design team of more than 200 – based in New York, London, Berlin, Moscow, and Beijing –the practice pursues narratively driven visitor experiences in social and cultural history, natural history, and the sciences, and specializes in corporate history and biographical content. An adjunct professor at both Pratt Institute and New York University, he is a frequent speaker at international conferences.

>> 082 United States Holocaust Memorial Museum p.192

>>> Renate Flagmeier

Leitende Kuratorin Werkbundarchiv – Museum der Dinge Berlin; Studium der Kunstwissenschaft und Romanischen Literaturen in Berlin und Paris; Kuratorin zahlreicher Ausstellungen, u. a.: »ohne Titel. Sichern unter... (1995–1998)«, »ware schönheit – eine zeitreise« *(1999)*, »Kampf der Dinge – Eine Ausstellung im 100. Jahr des Deutschen Werkbunds« *(2007)*.

Head Curator at Werkbundarchiv – Museum der Dinge in Berlin; studied Art and Romance Languages in Berlin and Paris; curator of numerous exhibitions, including: »ohne Titel. Sichern unter... (1995–1998)«, »ware schönheit – eine zeitreise« (1999), »Kampf der Dinge – Eine Ausstellung im 100. Jahr des Deutschen Werkbunds« (2007).

>> 086 ohne Titel. Sichern unter … p.198

214

Dank
Thanks to

Ein besonderer Dank an Kai-Uwe Hemken für zahlreiche Beiträge, Exkurse in die Geschichte und seine Hilfe bei der Recherche. Danke für Tipps, Denkanstöße und die jahrelange Unterstützung an Uwe J. Reinhardt, Philipp Teufel und das edi – Exhibition Design Institute. Ein großer Dank an alle Autoren, die Rezensionen und wertvolles Hintergrundwissen beigesteuert haben. Danke an Kerstin Neumann-Teufel, Paul Wenert und Jan-Christian Warnecke für Beratung und Unterstützung. Ein ganz spezieller Dank an alle, die uns privat unterstützt und motiviert haben und den langen Weg mit uns gegangen sind.

Verlag und Herausgeber danken allen beteiligten Designern und Kuratoren, Gestaltungsbüros, Museen, Institutionen und Unternehmen, Archiven und Privatpersonen für die zur Verfügung gestellten Bilder und Materialien.

Particular thanks go to Kai-Uwe Hemken for his numerous articles, elaborations on history and his help with the research. Many thanks to Uwe J. Reinhardt, Philipp Teufel and the edi – the Exhibition Design Institute – for the tips, food for thought and the many years of support. A big thank you to all the authors, who provided reviews and valuable background knowledge. Many thanks to Kerstin Neumann-Teufel, Paul Wenert and Jan-Christian Warnecke for the advice and support and a very special thank you to all those, who supported and motivated us privately and travelled this long road with us.

The editors and publisher would like to thank all the designers and curators involved, design agencies, museums, institutions and companies, archives and private individuals for the images and materials supplied.

Impressum
Imprint

Herausgegeben von
Edited by
Anna Müller
Frauke Möhlmann

In Zusammenarbeit mit
In cooperation with
Uwe J. Reinhardt
Philipp Teufel
Kai-Uwe Hemken
edi – Exhibition Design Institute
Fachhochschule Düsseldorf
www.fh-duesseldorf.de/edi

Konzeptionelle Mitarbeit
Content support
Uwe J. Reinhardt
Philipp Teufel

Übersetzung
Translation
Jeremy Gaines

Redaktion
Editing
Petra Kiedaisch
Anika Piano
Cornelia Reinhardt
Anja Schrade

Redaktionsassistenz
Editorial assistance
Nuriet Dolo
Frank Frey
Christine Pfirrmann
Björn Stratmann

Gestaltung
Design
Anna Müller
Frauke Möhlmann

Druckvorstufe
Pre-print services
Corinna Rieber, Marbach

Papier
Paper
Claro Bulk, 150g Vol.1, 05

Printed in Europe

Coverfoto
Cover photo
© Bauhaus-Archiv Berlin /
6751/20 / Berliner Bild-Bericht
VG Bild-Kunst, Bonn 2014

Fotos
Photos
Wir haben uns bemüht, sämtliche
Rechteinhaber ausfindig zu
machen. Sollte es uns in Einzel-
fällen nicht gelungen sein, die
Rechteinhaber zu benachrichtigen,
so bitten wir diese, sich bei der
av edition GmbH zu melden.
*We have taken great pains to locate
all copyright holders. Should we
have been unsuccessful in individual cases, we kindly ask the rights
holders to get into contact with
av edition GmbH.*

av edition GmbH
Senefelderstr. 109
D-70176 Stuttgart
Phone +49 (0)711 220 22 79-0
Fax +49 (0)711 220 22 79-15
www.avedition.com
ISBN 978-3-89986-145-7